Hands-On Activities   With Scripture Values

LEVEL F

TEACHER GUIDEBOOK

ISBN #1-58938-151-3

Published by The Concerned Group, Inc.
700 East Granite • PO Box 1000 • Siloam Springs, AR 72761

Authors	**Dave & Rozann Seela**
Publisher	**Russ L. Potter, II**
Senior Editor	**Bill Morelan**
Project Coordinator	**Rocki Vanatta**
Creative Director	**Daniel Potter**
Proofreader	**Renee Decker**
Step Illustrations	**Steven Butler**
Character Illustrations	**Josh Ray**
Colorists	**Josh & Aimee Ray**

Printed on recycled paper in the United States

For more information about **A Reason For®** curricula,
write to the address above, call, or visit our website.

www.areasonfor.com
800.447.4332

TABLE OF CONTENTS

Overview

How To Use This Guidebook

Weekly Lessons

Assessment

"A sound grounding in science strengthens many of the skills that people use every day, like solving problems creatively, thinking critically, working cooperatively in teams, using technology effectively, and valuing life-long learning."*

*National Science Education Standards, 1999 Washington, D.C.: National Academy Press. (p. ix)

A NEW PARADIGM

A Reason For® Science was designed for children, the handiwork of an infinite God — young minds created with an unlimited capacity to think, to learn, and to discover!

Because of this emphasis on children and how they learn, **A Reason For® Science** is based on a different paradigm from the traditional textbook approach. Why? In an effort to address standards and accountability, many of today's science textbooks seem to get learning backwards. They focus primarily on building a knowledge base, assuming students will later attach meaning to memorized facts. The problem is that few elementary students master information presented this way because they simply never become engaged with the material.

By contrast, **A Reason For® Science** is based on the premise that learning science is an *active* process. It's "something children do, not something done to them."[2]

According to the **National Science Education Standards**, ". . . active science learning means shifting emphasis away from teachers presenting information and covering science topics. The perceived need to include all the topics and information . . . is in direct conflict with the central goal of having students learn scientific knowledge with understanding."[3]

To paraphrase William Butler Yeats, "Teaching is not filling a pail. It's lighting a fire!"

INQUIRY-BASED LEARNING

A Reason For® Science is designed to teach basic Life, Earth, and Physical Science concepts through fun, hands-on activities. Its focus is to make learning both fun and meaningful.

But hands-on activities by themselves are not enough. To truly master a concept, students must have "minds-on" experiences as well! This means actively engaging the material through a variety of activities such as group discussion, problem solving, and journaling. It also requires thought-provoking questions that help develop higher-level cognitive skills. The weekly format of **A Reason For® Science** is designed to reflect this inquiry-based model.

According to the **National Science Education Standards**, "Inquiry is central to science learning. When engaging in inquiry, students describe objects and events, ask questions, construct explanations, test those explanations against current scientific knowledge, and communicate their ideas to others . . . In this way, students actively develop their understanding of science by combining scientific knowledge with reasoning and thinking skills."[4]

Since different students achieve understanding in different ways and to different degrees, the flexible format of **A Reason For® Science** also encourages multiple learning styles and allows for individual differences. Activities challenge students to develop their own unique skills, and encourage them to come up with creative solutions.

NATIONAL STANDARDS

National standards referred to in **A Reason For® Science** come from the **National Science Education Standards**[1]. More specifically, they reflect the "K-4 Science Content Standards" (p.121 - 142) and "5-8 Science Content Standards" (p. 143 - 172).

The Teacher Guidebook includes a list of content standards that relate to each individual lesson. References are based on the NSES alphabetic format, plus a numeric code to indicate the bulleted sub-topic. For example, **C1** in a fourth grade lesson would indicate Content Standard **C** and sub-topic **1**. (A detailed description of this content standard can be found on pages 127 - 229 of the **Standards**.)

As noted above, lower grade and upper grade standards are found in different sections of the book. A **C1** reference for a third grade lesson, for example, would be found on page 127 (characteristics of organisms). By contrast, a **C1** reference for a seventh grade lesson would be found on page 155 ("structure and function in living systems").

METHODOLOGY

Master teachers know that a science curriculum is much more than information in a textbook. It has to do with the way content is organized and presented in the classroom. It is driven by underlying principles, and by attitudes and beliefs about how learning occurs. It is expressed in the practices and procedures used in its implementation.

In other words, textbooks don't teach science — *teachers* do!

That's why it's important for you to understand how this curriculum is designed to be used, and how you can enhance the learning process in your classroom.

Concepts, Not Content

The needs of children in elementary school are very different from high school students, especially when it comes to science education. The presentation of the Periodic Table provides a good example. High school students may find it useful to memorize each element, its atomic weight, and its position on a chart. By contrast, elementary school students must first understand the concept of such a table. What is it? How is it used? Why is it arranged this way? Has it always looked like this? How (and why) has it changed over time? Such an approach leads to a foundational understanding of a concept, rather than a body of memorized "facts" that may change over time.*

As Nobel prize winner, Dr. Richard Feynman, once said, "You can know the name of a bird in all the languages of the world, but when you're finished, you'll know absolutely nothing whatever about the bird . . . (that's) the difference between knowing the name of something and knowing something!"

---

* For example, less than 30 years ago many students were still being taught the "fact" that matter only has three states (solid, l Alfven won the Nobel prize for identifying a fourth state of matter (plasma). There are many such examples in education — includ themselves, which are being replaced in many colleges by a new 3D computer model that offers new insights into relationships bet

Multi-Sensory Learning

In addition to focusing on concepts instead of just content, **A Reason For® Science** uses a multi-sensory approach to learning that supports multiple learning styles.

Visual events include watching teacher demonstrations, studying diagrams and illustrations, and reading summaries. **Auditory** events include participating in group discussions with team members, listening to teacher directions and explanations, and hearing the unique sounds associated with the activities. **Kinesthetic** events include tactile interaction with activity materials, hands-on experimentation, and taking notes, writing answers, and drawing diagrams in individual Student Worktexts.

Omitting any of these components can significantly weaken the learning process, especially for children with specific learning disabilities.

Student-Driven, Teacher-Directed

As long-time educators, the authors of this series recognize that many elementary teachers don't consider themselves "science people." Therefore, this series avoids unnecessary technical jargon, and deals with complex interactions in simple, easy-to-understand language that's reinforced with concrete, hands-on activities.

The Teacher Guidebook is designed to give you the confidence that you need to teach science effectively. In addition to the usual answer keys and explanations, it includes several sections just for teachers.

"Additional Comments" offers tips and techniques for making each lesson run smoothly. "Teacher to Teacher" provides expanded science explanations to increase your understanding. "Extended Teaching" presents a variety of extension ideas for those who wish to go further.

During the first year, we strongly recommend that you try every activity a day or two in advance. Although most activities are relatively simple, this added practice will give you a better feel for any potential problems that might arise.

Most of all, remember that one of the primary goals of this series is to make science FUN for the participants. And that includes you, too!

COMPONENTS

The following are some of the key components in this series:

Letter to Parents

Positive communication between home and school is essential for optimum success with any curriculum. The "Letter to the Parents" (page 3, Student Worktext) provides a great way to introduce **A Reason For® Science** to parents. It covers the lesson format, safety issues, connections with national standards, and the integration of Scripture. Along with the opening sections of this Guidebook, the parent letter provides information you need to answer common questions about the series.

Student Research Teams

A Reason For® Science was created to model the way scientific study works in the adult world. Students are divided into "research teams" to work through activities cooperatively. Ideally, each research team should be composed of three to five students. (Fewer students per team makes monitoring more difficult; more students per team minimizes participation opportunities.) The best groupings combine students with different "gifts" (skills or abilities), complimentary personalities, etc. — the same kinds of combinations that make effective teams in the corporate or industrial world.

In addition, **A Reason For® Science** encourages collaboration between the different teams, again modeling the interactions found in the scientific community.

Individual Student Worktexts

Although students collaborate on activities and thought questions, the Student Worktexts provide opportunities for individual reaction and response. The importance of allowing students to write their own response to questions, keep their own notes, and journal about their individual experiences cannot be underestimated. (While collaboration is essential in the scientific community, no true scientist would neglect to keep his/her own personal notes and records!)

Individual Student Worktexts also provide teachers with an objective way to monitor student participation and learning throughout the school year.

Materials Kits

Quality materials are an integral part of any "hands-on" curriculum. **A Reason For® Science** offers complete, easy-to-use materials kits for every grade level. With some minor exceptions*, kits contain all the materials and supplies needed by one research team for an entire school year. Materials for each team come packaged in an attractive, durable storage container. You can choose to restock consumable portions of the kit from local materials, or purchase the convenient refill pack.

Personal Science Glossary

A glossary is a common component in many science textbooks, yet students rarely use traditional glossaries except when assigned to "look up" a word by the teacher. Since words and terms used in elementary science are not highly technical, this activity is better served by referring students to a standard dictionary.

A more effective approach to helping students learn science words at this level is to encourage them to develop and maintain a **personal science glossary**. This can be a plain spiral-bound notebook with one page (front and back) dedicated to each letter of the alphabet. Throughout the school year, students continually add new words and definitions — not only from their own reading and research, but from the findings of their team members as well. (For your convenience, a black-line master for a glossary cover is included in Appendix A.)

---

* To help minimize expenses, kits do not include common classroom supplies (pencils, paper, etc.) and a few large items (soft drink cans, etc.) that are easily obtained by the teacher. Kit and non-kit materials needed for each lesson are clearly marked in this

SAFETY ISSUES

When using hands-on science activities, teachers must be constantly aware of the potential for safety problems. Even the simplest activities using the most basic materials can be dangerous when used incorrectly. **Proper monitoring and supervision is required at all times!**

Although the publisher and authors have made every reasonable effort to ensure that all science activities in **A Reason For® Science** are safe when conducted as instructed, neither the publisher nor the authors assume any responsibility for damage or injury resulting from implementation.

It is the responsibility of the school to review available science safety resources and to develop science safety training for their teachers and students, as well as posting safety rules in every classroom.

An excellent source of science safety information is the Council of State Science Supervisors at: http://csss.enc.org/safety. The CSSS website offers a FREE, downloadable safety guide, "Science and Safety, Making the Connection." This booklet was created with support from the American Chemical Society, the Eisenhower National Clearinghouse for Mathematics and Science Education, the National Aeronautics and Space Administration, and the National Institutes of Health.

To support appropriate safety instruction, every **A Reason For® Science** Student Worktext includes a special section on safety. In addition to the safety precautions above, it is strongly recommended that every teacher verify all students clearly understand this information *before* beginning any science activities.

ASSESSMENT METHODS

Authentic assessment is an important part of any quality curriculum. **A Reason For® Science** offers a duel approach to assessment. First, participation, understanding, and higher-level thinking skills and can be assessed by periodically collecting and reading students' responses to the essay-style questions in the Student Worktext.

Second, this Teacher Guidebook provides black-line masters for a "weekly quiz" (see page 163). These quizzes offer a more traditional assessment based on fact acquisition. Questions are similar to the type that students might face on any standardized test.

In addition, you can use both these methods to create a customized quarterly or yearly assessment tool. Simply select a combination of true/false and multiple choice questions from the quizzes and essay-style questions from the Student Worktext.

SCRIPTURE CONNECTION

Integrating faith and learning is an essential part of a quality religious education. A unique component of **A Reason For® Science** is the incorporation of Scripture Object Lessons into every unit. As students discover basic science principles, they are encouraged to explore various spiritual connections through specific Scripture verses.

Since some school systems may prefer one Scripture translation to another, Scriptures are referenced by chapter and verse only, rather than direct quotations in the text.

CREATIONISM

Many people (including many notable scientists) believe that God created the universe and all the processes both physical and biological that resulted in our solar system and life on Earth.

However, advocates of "creation science" hold a variety of viewpoints. Some believe that Earth is relatively young, perhaps only 6,000 years old. Others believe that Earth may have existed for millions of years, but that various organisms (especially humans) could only be the result of divine intervention since they demonstrate "intelligent design."

Within the creation science community, there are dozens of variations on these themes, even within the specific denominational groups. Instead of promoting a specific view, the authors of this series have chosen to focus on the concept that "God created the Heavens and the Earth," and leave the specifics up to the individual school. Creationism is a faith-based issue.* As such, schools are strongly urged to have a clear position on this topic, and an understanding of how that belief is to be conveyed to their students.

For that matter, so is the theory of evolution.

[1] *National Science Education Standards*, 1999 Washington, D.C.: National Academy Press. (p. ix)
[2] *Ibid.* (p. 2)
[3] *Ibid.* (p. 20)
[4] *Ibid.* (p. 2)

This Teacher Guidebook . . .

is based on a simple, easy-to-understand format. Lessons throughout the series follow the same pattern, so once you're familiar with the format for one lesson, you can find information quickly for any other lesson. The samples on the following pages explain the purpose of each section.

Category
All lessons are divided into one of three primary categories — Life Science, Earth Science, or Physical Science. Physical Science is further divided into two parts — Forces or Energy/Matter.

Focus
"Focus" states the topic of the lesson.

Objective
"Objective" describes the purpose of the lesson.

National Standards
"National Standards" refers to content standards found in the **National Science Education Standards**. (For details on standards, see page 6.)

Materials Needed:
"Materials Needed" is a comprehensive list of materials used in the lesson. **Bold-faced** words indicate items provided in the Materials Kit.

Safety Concerns:
"Safety Concerns" provides details about potential safety hazards. (For more on Safety, see page 9.)

Sample lesson page shown:

NAME _____

SEARCHING SPROUTS

LESSON 1

FOCUS Germination

OBJECTIVE To explore the process of growth in plants

OVERVIEW We know that animals behave in different ways depending on their surroundings. But do plants behave in different ways, too? In this activity, we'll explore some things that might have an impact on how plants behave.

Category
Life Science

Focus
Germination

Objective
To explore growth in plants

National Standards [1]
A1, A2, B1, B2, B3, C1, C2, C3, E3, F2, F3, F4, G1

Materials Needed [2]
petri dishes (3)
pipette
seeds (assorted)
water
paper towels
tape
scissors

Safety Concerns
4. Sharp Objects
Remind students to be careful using scissors.

[1] See page xx for a description of standards source and code.

[2] Bold-face type indicates items included in Materials Kit.

Additional Comments
Seeds provided for this activity are common American grain crops: oats, corn, wheat, and soybeans. If students wish to repeat this activity, have them try seeds like alfalfa, radish, sunflower, or pumpkin. Be sure to clean petri dishes thoroughly after each use to sterilize.

Overview
Read the overview aloud to your students. The goal is to create an atmosphere of curiosity and inquiry.

Here's a great way to introduce this activity: Seat two students at the front of the class. Ask them both to point straight down. Praise their accuracy. Now blindfold them. Repeat your request to point down. Praise their ability again, remove their blindfolds, and have them return to their seats. Ask the class, "Do you think animals might have this same ability?" Follow this by asking, "What about fish?" Then ask, "What about living things with no brains, like plants? Do they have this ability, too?" Many students respond "no" to this last question, setting the stage to explore the answer.

LIFE **15**

Additional Comments:
"Additional Comments" offers tips and techniques for making each lesson run more smoothly.

Overview:
The "Overview" provides lesson summaries, thoughts on introducing the lesson, ideas for dealing with materials, and other valuable lesson-specific tips.

What To Do

"What to Do" expands on the Steps found in the Student Workbook. It outlines potential problems, offers alternative procedures, and explains ways to enhance the lesson.

WHAT TO DO

Monitor student research teams as they complete each step.

Step 2
Grouping instructions are purposely ambiguous to allow several options. Depending on class size and materials available, 1) have each research team create their own set of three, 2) have each team create only one dish, then combine dishes to create groupings, 3) create a unique combination to meet your specific classroom needs. Regardless of the total number of dishes, at least one dish must lie flat, one must be on edge with seeds up, and one must be on edge with seeds down. These three environments are necessary for the primary comparisons.

Step 4
Emphasize the instruction, "*Don't change their position in any way!*" If dishes are moved, the results will be invalid.

Teacher to Teacher

Another name for the energy stored in seeds is endosperm. Humans and animals use plant endosperm as a food source, too. For instance, flour is ground-up wheat endosperm!

Be sure students realize the two phases of a plant's life cycle that are involved: sprouting and growing. The sprouting process only requires warmth and water. A seed soaks up moisture, swells, splits, and a new plant emerges. But light is needed for the next stage. Light stimulates the new plant into producing the chemical chlorophyll (the green in plants). Without chlorophyll, plants have no way to make food once they've used up the energy in the endosperm. The process of using chlorophyll to direct more food is called photosynthesis.

Teacher To Teacher

"Teacher to Teacher" offers expanded science explanations designed to increase teacher understanding.

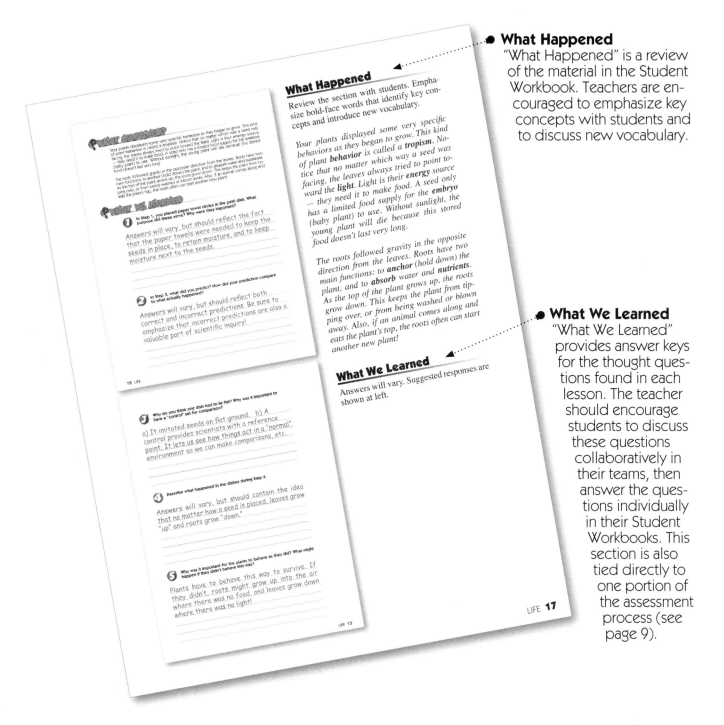

What Happened
Review the section with students. Emphasize bold-face words that identify key concepts and introduce new vocabulary.

Your plants displayed some very specific behaviors as they began to grow. This kind of plant **behavior** is called a **tropism**. Notice that no matter which way a seed was facing, the leaves always tried to point toward the **light**. Light is their **energy** source — they need it to make food. A seed only has a limited food supply for the **embryo** (baby plant) to use. Without sunlight, the young plant will die because this stored food doesn't last very long.

The roots followed gravity in the opposite direction from the leaves. Roots have two main functions: to **anchor** (hold down) the plant, and to **absorb** water and **nutrients**. As the top of the plant grows up, the roots grow down. This keeps the plant from tipping over, or from being washed or blown away. Also, if an animal comes along and eats the plant's top, the roots often can start another new plant!

What We Learned
Answers will vary. Suggested responses are shown at left.

What Happened
"What Happened" is a review of the material in the Student Workbook. Teachers are encouraged to emphasize key concepts with students and to discuss new vocabulary.

What We Learned
"What We Learned" provides answer keys for the thought questions found in each lesson. The teacher should encourage students to discuss these questions collaboratively in their teams, then answer the questions individually in their Student Workbooks. This section is also tied directly to one portion of the assessment process (see page 9).

Conclusion
The "Conclusion" is a summary of the key concepts presented in the lesson.

Food for Thought
"Food for Thought" suggests ways to enhance the Scripture Object Lesson. This section provides an important tool for integrating faith and learning.

Journal
"Journal" suggests ways to expand journaling opportunities related to the lesson. The teacher should encourage the students not only to take notes and keep records, but also to make sketches, draw diagrams, and create charts and lists as needed.

Conclusion
Read this section aloud to the class to summarize the concepts learned in this activity.

Food for Thought
Read the Scripture verse aloud to the class. Discuss why it's important to listen to parents, teachers, and other adults in authority. Point out the phrase, ". . . always face in the right direction." Ask your students, "What does this mean? How can we be sure we're doing this?"

Journal
If time permits, have a general class discussion about notes and drawings various students added to their journal pages. Discuss correct and incorrect predictions, and remind students that this "trial and error" process is part of the scientific process.

Extended Teaching

1. Have students repeat this activity using different seeds. Share and compare results.

2. Seeds provided for this activity are common American grain crops. Research other American grain crops (rice, barley, etc.), as well as common crops in other countries.

3. Have students make lists of seeds that humans use for food. Discuss how and where these crops are grown.

4. Take a field trip to a grocery store. Have students list any product that is made of seeds (popcorn, rice), and products that are derived from seeds (flour, cornmeal).

5. Have students split peanuts in half and look for the peanut embryo (the little knot on one end). The rest of the seed is the endosperm.

Extended Teaching
"Extended Teaching" presents a variety of extension ideas for those who wish to go further.

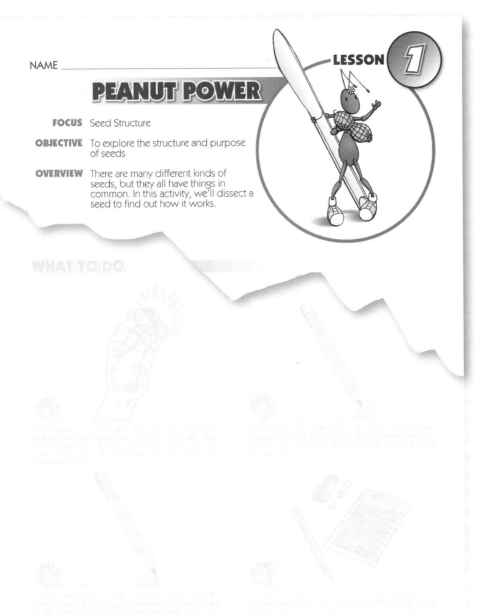

NAME _____

PEANUT POWER

FOCUS Seed Structure

OBJECTIVE To explore the structure and purpose of seeds

OVERVIEW There are many different kinds of seeds, but they all have things in common. In this activity, we'll dissect a seed to find out how it works.

Category
Life Science

Focus
Seed Structure

Objective
To explore the structure and purpose of seeds

National Standards [1]
A1, A2, B1, B2, B3, C1, C3, D1, E3, F1, F4, G1

Materials Needed [2]
peanut (in shell)

Safety Concerns
3. Skin Contact
Some people have a serious allergy to peanuts. Such students should participate as observers only!

Additional Comments

While some people are allergic to peanuts, the opposite problem will be much more common. Many students love to *eat* peanuts. Monitor closely to make sure materials aren't consumed.

Overview

Read the overview aloud to your students. The goal is to create an atmosphere of curiosity and inquiry.

[1] *See page 6 for a description of standards source and code.*

[2] *Bold-face type indicates items included in Materials Kit.*

WHAT TO DO

Monitor student research teams as they complete each step.

LESSON 1

PEANUT POWER

FOCUS Seed Structure

OBJECTIVE To explore the structure and purpose of seeds

OVERVIEW There are many different kinds of seeds, but they all have things in common. In this activity, we'll dissect a seed to find out how it works.

WHAT TO DO

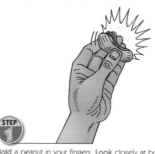

STEP 1

Hold a peanut in your fingers. **Look** closely at both ends and **describe** any differences. **Observe** the shell, especially its shape and texture. Now gently **crack** the shell. **Open** it lengthwise along the seams. **Record** (and **draw**) your observations.

STEP 2

Carefully **lift out** one seed (the nut). **Observe** the thin red covering. **Remove** the covering if it hasn't already fallen off. **Examine** the seed closely and **make notes** about its shape and texture.

STEP 3

Use your thumbnail to carefully **split** the seed lengthwise along its seam. **Find** the bump between the halves (usually on one end). **Predict** what this might be. **Examine** this part closely, then **draw** the seed in your journal.

STEP 4

Discard the remains of your peanut project as directed by your teacher. Now **review** each step in this activity. **Share** and **compare** observations with your research team.

LIFE **11**

Teacher to Teacher

Scientists call the stored food inside a seed "endosperm." Wheat is a good example. Grinding wheat produces flour — essentially finely-ground endosperm. The embryo in the wheat seed is called "germ." Whole grain flour contains endosperm, germ, and even seed coatings. White flour is "degerminated," meaning the embryo (and seed covering) is removed. Unfortunately, this process also removes most vitamins and nutrients. When some of these are added back, the flour is referred to as "enriched."

WHAT HAPPENED?

Seeds are the foundation for the next generation of plants. Locked inside every seed is an embryo (baby plant) covered by a protective **seed coat**, plus food for the embryo as it starts to grow. This growth process (**germination**) begins when the correct amount of **moisture** and heat becomes available.

First, the seed absorbs water. As the seed swells, it splits the seed coat so that the embryo can grow out. Then the roots begin to grow down in a **behavior** called geotropism. "Tropos" means "turn" and "geo" means "Earth," so geotropism indicates a turning toward Earth. At the same time, the seed's top grows upward in a behavior called **phototropism**. "Photo" means "light," so phototropism indicates turning toward **light energy**. The roots keep digging deeper, and the leaves keep pushing upward — and you have a new peanut plant!

WHAT WE LEARNED

1 What is the purpose of a peanut's shell? Based on your observations, why do you think the peanut's shell is well suited for this purpose?

a) to protect the seed

b) answers will vary, but should include the idea that it is hard, tough, strong, etc.

2 Describe the shape, color, and texture of the seed you removed in Step 2. What is the purpose of the red skin covering?

a) answers will vary — oval, tan, smooth, slick, oily, etc.

b) another layer of protection

3 What was the small, curved "bump" you found in Step 3? Describe the section of the seed in detail.

a) embryo or baby plant

b) answers will vary — curled, curved, hard, pointy, etc.

4 What is the purpose of the material surrounding the bump? How does this help the new plant?

a) nourishment for the emerging plant

b) provides food until it can make its own

5 What are the plant behaviors that make roots grow down and leaves grow up? Why are they important to a plant's survival?

a) geotropism and phototropism

b) roots need to reach the soil for nourishment; leaves need to face the sun for photosynthesis

What Happened

Review the section with students. Emphasize bold-face words that identify key concepts and introduce new vocabulary.

Seeds are the foundation for the next generation of **plants**. *Locked inside every seed is an* **embryo** *(baby plant) covered by a protective* **seed coat***, plus* **food** *for the embryo as it starts to grow. This growth process (***germination***) begins when the correct amount of* **moisture** *and* **heat** *becomes available.*

First, the seed absorbs **water***. As the seed swells, it splits the seed coat so that the embryo can grow out. Then the* **roots** *begin to grow down in a* **behavior** *called* **geotropism***. "Tropos" means "turn" and "geo" means "Earth," so geotropism indicates a turning toward Earth. At the same time, the seed's top grows upward in a behavior called* **phototropism***. "Photo" means "light," so phototropism indicates turning toward* **light energy***. The roots keep digging deeper, and the leaves keep pushing upward — and you have a new peanut plant!*

What We Learned

Answers will vary. Suggested responses are shown at left.

Conclusion

Read this section aloud to the class to summarize the concepts learned in this activity.

Food for Thought

Read the Scripture aloud to the class. Talk about the blessings God surrounds us with. Discuss ways we can show our thankfulness to God.

Journal

If time permits, have a general class discussion about students' journal entries. Share and compare observations. Be sure to emphasize that "trial and error" is a valuable part of scientific inquiry!

CONCLUSION

Seeds contain an embryo and food to start its growth. Seeds not only create new plants, but are also an important food source for people and animals.

FOOD FOR THOUGHT

Genesis 8:22 Seeds are a vital part of the life cycle on Earth. Seeds grow into plants, plants grow and are harvested for food, and more seeds are planted to continue the cycle. God has promised that this cycle will continue as long as the Earth remains.

Yet even though God maintains this great cycle of life to provide for our needs, we often take natural things (like food cycles, sunrise, and rain) for granted. Be sure to take time this week to thank God for these wonderful blessings!

JOURNAL   My Science Notes

14 LIFE

Extended Teaching

1. Common crop seeds are rice, wheat, corn, and soybeans. Have students research where these crops are grown worldwide. Have each team make a map showing primary cultivation areas for one crop.

2. Have students make a bulletin board showing similarities and differences between various seeds. Focus on size, shape, color, hardness of seed coat, etc.

3. Remind students that many plants have seeds inside tasty fruit. The fruit is eaten and the seeds are spread around. Challenge each team to research at least one example, then depict their findings on a poster.

4. Using the Internet, have students research seed sizes. Have each team document the largest seed they can find. Repeat this process looking for the smallest seed. Share and compare results with the class.

5. Have students research George Washington Carver. Write stories, make bulletin boards, and create posters to celebrate the achievements of this revered scientist. Discuss his amazing work with peanuts.

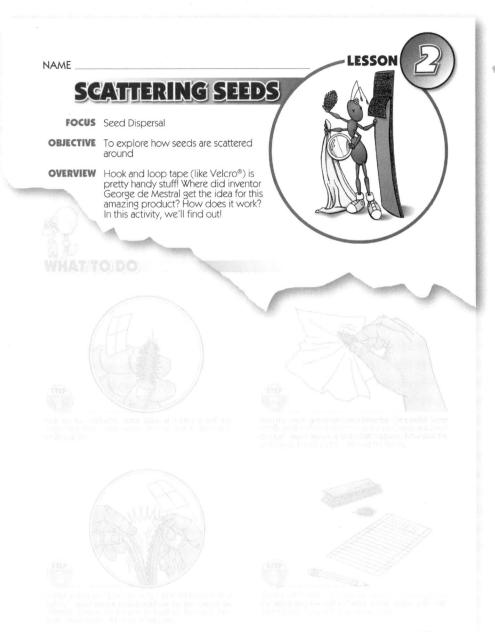

SCATTERING SEEDS

FOCUS Seed Dispersal

OBJECTIVE To explore how seeds are scattered around

OVERVIEW Hook and loop tape (like Velcro®) is pretty handy stuff! Where did inventor George de Mestral get the idea for this amazing product? How does it work? In this activity, we'll find out!

WHAT TO DO

Category
Life Science

Focus
Seed Dispersal

Objective
To explore how seeds are scattered around

National Standards
A1, A2, B1, B2, B3, C1, C3, D1, E3, F1, F4, G1

Materials Needed
cocklebur seed
magnifying lens
cloth
velcro

Safety Concerns

4. Sharp Objects
Remind students to be careful with the sharp points on the cocklebur.

4. Other
Make sure that students avoid the temptation to eat the seeds.

Additional Comments

There's a tendency for horseplay with these seeds. Monitor students closely to make sure no one gets stuck. To avoid accidental propagation of a pesky weed, be sure to collect *all* the seeds when the activity is over. These seeds should last for years if you keep them dry.

Overview

Read the overview aloud to your students. The goal is to create an atmosphere of curiosity and inquiry.

WHAT TO DO

Monitor student research teams as they complete each step.

NAME

SCATTERING SEEDS

LESSON 2

FOCUS Seed Dispersal

OBJECTIVE To explore how seeds are scattered around

OVERVIEW Hook and loop tape (like Velcro®) is pretty handy stuff! Where did inventor George de Mestral get the idea for this amazing product? How does it work? In this activity, we'll find out!

WHAT TO DO

STEP 1

Pick up the cocklebur seed. **Look** at it closely with the magnifying lens. **Make notes** in your journal describing what you see.

STEP 2

Feel the hooks gently with your fingertip. (Be careful! Some hooks are like thorns!) Gently **rub** the seed against a piece of cloth. **Make notes** about what happens. Now **pull** the seed away from the cloth. **Record** the results.

STEP 3

Using the magnifying lens, **look** closely at the two pieces of Velcro®. **Make notes** describing how the two pieces are different. Now **push** the pieces together, then **pull** them apart. **Make notes** about what happens.

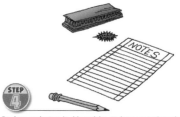

STEP 4

Review each step in this activity. **Make notes** about how the seeds and the Velcro® were similar. **Share** and compare observations with your research team.

LIFE **15**

Teacher to Teacher

Engineers and inventors (like George de Mestral) are very clever at copying ideas from living things. For instance, large building and bridge frames have many similarities to animal skeletons. Another example comes from aviation. Birds' wings are essentially hollow with light-weight bones connecting the sides to give them strength. Most aircraft wings are based on a similar concept. And, of course, the velcro used in this activity is just one more example.

WHAT HAPPENED?

Plants must produce lots of seeds because many end up in locations where they can't grow. Not only that, but if all of a plant's seeds landed in the same spot, there wouldn't be enough water, sun, or soil to go around.

God gave many plants unique ways to scatter (**disperse**) their seeds. Some seeds are light and blow away on the wind. Some float on the water, drifting great distances down rivers and streams. Some are **hitchhikers**, using little hooks to hitch rides on passing animals. Inventor George de Mestral wondered how such seeds attached themselves to his dog. He looked closer, and as a result he eventually developed a man-made version to create a quick, handy fastener!

WHAT WE LEARNED

 1 Describe what you discovered in your examination of the cocklebur in Step 1.

Answers will vary, but should include a description of the "hooks".

2 Describe the interaction between the cocklebur and the cloth in Step 2. Why did this happen?

a) they tried to stick together

b) the hooks in the cocklebur caught the loops in the cloth

3 Describe the difference between the two strips of Velcro®. Which strip is similar to a cocklebur? Which strip is similar to the cloth?

a) one had hooks, one had loops

b) cocklebur: the piece with the hooks; cloth: the piece with the loops

4 Compare the interaction between the cocklebur and cloth in Step 2 with the interaction between the strips of Velcro in Step 3. How were they similar? How were they different?

a) similar: they both stuck together, etc.

b) different: cocklebur natural; velcro man-made; velcro stuck tighter; etc.

5 What advantage do the hooks give a cocklebur plant? Why do plants want to scatter their seeds as far away as possible?

a) it can hitch a ride on passing animals

b) to avoid overcrowding

What Happened

Review the section with students. Emphasize bold-face words that identify key concepts and introduce new vocabulary.

Plants must produce lots of *seeds* because many end up in locations where they can't grow. Not only that, but if all of a plant's seeds landed in the same spot, there wouldn't be enough *water*, *sun*, or *soil* to go around.

God gave many plants unique ways to scatter (disperse) their seeds. Some seeds are light and blow away in the wind. Some float on the water, drifting great distances down rivers and streams. Some are hitchhikers, using little hooks to hitch rides on passing animals. Inventor, George de Mestral, wondered how such seeds attached themselves to his dog. He looked closer, and as a result he eventually developed a man-made version to create a quick, handy fastener!

What We Learned

Answers will vary. Suggested responses are shown at left.

Conclusion

Read this section aloud to the class to summarize the concepts learned in this activity.

Food for Thought

Read the Scripture aloud to the class. Talk about different kinds of friends. Discuss ways to be a good friend, and how this relates to our relationship with God.

Journal

If time permits, have a general class discussion about students' journal entries. Share and compare observations. Be sure to emphasize that "trial and error" is a valuable part of scientific inquiry!

CONCLUSION

Plants scatter their seeds in a variety of ways. The dispersal of seeds avoids overcrowding, and helps insure the survival of plants.

FOOD FOR THOUGHT

Proverbs 18:24 Cockleburs and similar seeds can really stick to you, even if you're bouncing around or the road gets really rough! Once they're attached, you can be sure they'll always try to stay right there with you.

This Scripture reminds us there are two kinds of friends — someone who pretends to be friendly, and someone who sticks close to you no matter what happens. Remember, God is your greatest friend! Wherever life may take you, he can always be there by your side. As long as you trust him, God will never abandon you. Who would you rather spend more time with — a pretend friend, or a real friend?

JOURNAL My Science Notes

Extended Teaching

1. Challenge teams to find various tools, structures, and devices that reflect designs found in nature. Have them choose one such item, then present their findings to the class.

2. Share books like David McCauley's *How Things Work*, and websites like *howstuffworks.com* with your class. These are full of fascinating inventions and how they work!

3. Some seeds don't sprout for years! Discuss this with students, then have them research several examples. Find out what conditions are necessary for these kinds of seeds to sprout. (Some even require a fire!)

4. Challenge teams to make "form and function" lists. (Example: leaves are flat so they are exposed to more light.) Have each group make a poster depicting at least one example of form and function in nature.

5. Make a "seed dispersal collection" for future classes to use. Label each jar, describing the plant that produced the seeds, who collected them, when the seeds were found, and where they were collected.

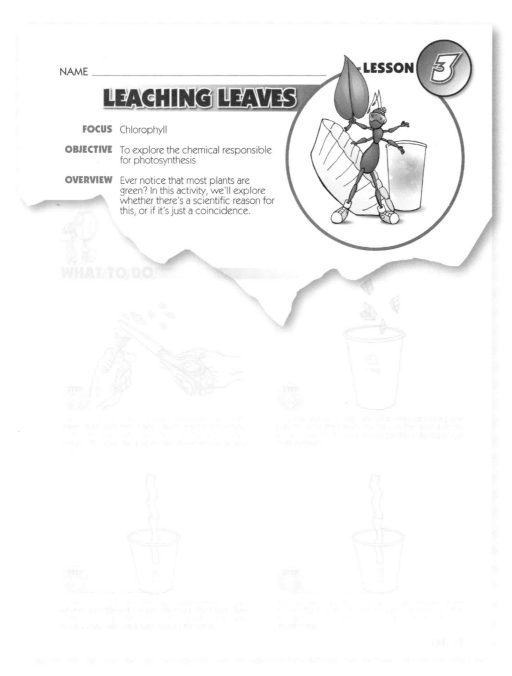

NAME _____

LEACHING LEAVES

FOCUS Chlorophyll

OBJECTIVE To explore the chemical responsible for photosynthesis

OVERVIEW Ever notice that most plants are green? In this activity, we'll explore whether there's a scientific reason for this, or if it's just a coincidence.

LESSON 3

WHAT TO DO

Category
Life Science

Focus
Chlorophyll

Objective
To explore the chemical responsible for photo-synthesis

National Standards
A1, A2, B1, B2, B3, C1, C3, D1, E3, F1, F4, G1

Materials Needed
paper cup
coffee filter
leaves
scissors
fingernail polish
  remover

Safety Concerns

1. Goggles/Gloves
Always protect eyes when working with chemicals. Gloves provide additional protection.

2. Burn Hazard
Fingernail polish is flammable. Use appropriate precautions.

3. Vapor
Use proper ventilation. Avoid breathing fumes from fingernail polish.

3. Skin Contact
Be certain leaves collected are from safe, non-toxic plants.

4. Sharp Objects
Remind students to exercise caution when using scissors.

Additional Comments

There are several safety precautions listed. Make certain you understand this activity thoroughly before beginning, or do it as a demonstration only. To avoid problems with toxic plants, you may wish to collect leaves for students before the school day begins. If so, schedule this activity early in the day to avoid leaves drying out, or keep the leaves moist in a container.

Overview

Read the overview aloud to your students. The goal is to create an atmosphere of curiosity and inquiry.

WHAT TO DO

Monitor student research teams as they complete each step.

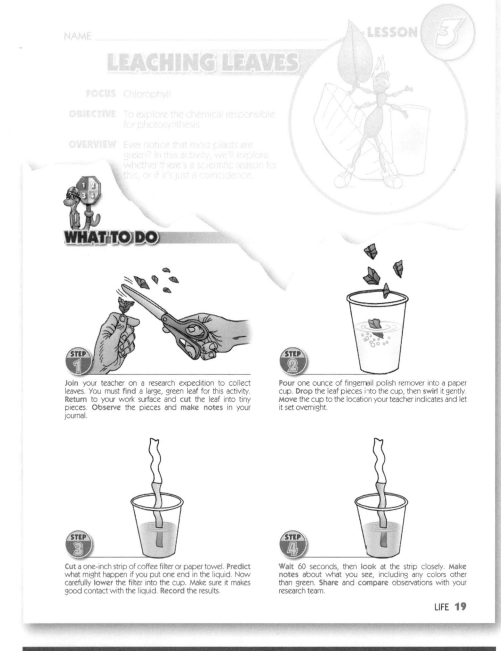

WHAT TO DO

NAME _____

LESSON 3

LEACHING LEAVES

FOCUS Chlorophyll

OBJECTIVE To explore the chemical responsible for photosynthesis

OVERVIEW Ever notice that most plants are green? In this activity, we'll explore whether there's a scientific reason for this, or if it's just a coincidence.

STEP 1
Join your teacher on a research expedition to collect leaves. You must find a large, green leaf for this activity. Return to your work surface and cut the leaf into tiny pieces. Observe the pieces and make notes in your journal.

STEP 2
Pour one ounce of fingernail polish remover into a paper cup. Drop the leaf pieces into the cup, then swirl it gently. Move the cup to the location your teacher indicates and let it set overnight.

STEP 3
Cut a one-inch strip of coffee filter or paper towel. Predict what might happen if you put one end in the liquid. Now carefully lower the filter into the cup. Make sure it makes good contact with the liquid. Record the results.

STEP 4
Wait 60 seconds, then look at the strip closely. Make notes about what you see, including any colors other than green. Share and compare observations with your research team.

LIFE **19**

Teacher to Teacher

Chromatography (the filter strip process) is an important procedure in chemistry, with useful applications in industry, forensics, and research. The fantastic colors found in plants and flowers are caused by pigments. What you see as color is the light not absorbed by the pigment. The two types of chlorophyll absorb light in the yellow and orange bands, so you see shades of green. The carotenoids absorb light in the blue and purple colors, so you see red, yellow, or orange.

WHAT HAPPENED?

The fingernail polish remover **dissolved** an important plant chemical (**chlorophyll**) that was then **absorbed** by the filter paper. The presence of chlorophyll causes the green color in **plants**. Plants need chlorophyll for a vital **chemical reaction** called **photosynthesis**. Photosynthesis combines **carbon dioxide** from the air with water, creating **food** for the plant and releasing **oxygen**. Human survival depends on the food and oxygen plants produce!

The chemicals that produce colors in living things are called **pigments**. If you saw colors other than green on your filter strip, other pigments were present. As the fingernail polish remover was absorbed, large pigment particles were trapped near the bottom of the paper, while smaller pigment particles moved further up the strip.

WHAT WE LEARNED

1 Compare the appearance of the leaves in Step 1 with Step 3. What color change happened to the leaves after soaking? What color change occurred in the solution?

a) they faded after soaking

b) it turned from clear to green

2 What did you predict in Step 3? How did your prediction reflect what actually happened?

a) answers will vary, but should reflect logical comparisons

3 What is the name of the chemical that makes plants green? Why is this chemical important to plants?

a) chlorophyll

b) plants need chlorophyll for photosynthesis

4 What is the name of the chemical reaction that takes place in plants? What two products does this produce? Why is this important for human survival?

a) photosynthesis

b) food, oxygen

c) answers should reflect the fact that we need food and oxygen to live

5 Notice the colors on your filter paper. Which color has the largest pigment particles? Which has the smallest? How do you know this?

a) largest: dark yellows

b) smallest: light greens

c) answers should reflect the fact that smaller, lighter particles wick higher up the filter strip

What Happened

Review the section with students. Emphasize bold-face words that identify key concepts and introduce new vocabulary.

*The fingernail polish remover **dissolved** an important plant chemical (**chlorophyll**) that was then **absorbed** by the filter paper. The presence of chlorophyll causes the green color in **plants**. Plants need chlorophyll for a vital **chemical reaction** called **photosynthesis**. Photosynthesis combines **carbon dioxide** from the air with **water**, creating **food** for the plant and releasing **oxygen**. Human survival depends on the food and oxygen plants produce!*

*The chemicals that produce colors in living things are called **pigments**. If you saw colors other than green on your filter strip, other pigments were present. As the fingernail polish remover was absorbed, large pigment particles were trapped near the bottom of the paper, while smaller pigment particles moved further up the strip.*

What We Learned

Answers will vary. Suggested responses are shown at left.

Conclusion

Read this section aloud to the class to summarize the concepts learned in this activity.

Food for Thought

Read the Scripture aloud to the class. Talk about inward beauty versus outward beauty. Discuss ways we can cultivate a beautiful spirit.

Journal

If time permits, have a general class discussion about students' journal entries. Share and compare observations. Be sure to emphasize that "trial and error" is a valuable part of scientific inquiry!

CONCLUSION

The chemical chlorophyll causes the green color in plants. Plants need chlorophyll for the photosynthesis process that creates food and releases oxygen. These plant traits are essential for human survival.

FOOD FOR THOUGHT

1 Peter 3:3, 4 Many plants seem to be just one color — green! But in this activity, we discovered pigments that weren't visible on the outside of the plant. These beautiful colors became visible when we took the extra effort to find them.

This Scripture reminds us that it's what's inside that makes someone beautiful. Just as the leaves contained hidden pigments, so there are often precious things hidden inside people's hearts. Instead of focusing on mere outward beauty (clothes, hair, etc.), we should learn to look for a beautiful spirit in others. By keeping close to God, we can learn to cultivate that kind of inward beauty ourselves!

JOURNAL My Science Notes

Extended Teaching

1. Have students research how crime labs use chromatography for solving crimes. Challenge each team to create a poster depicting their findings.

2. Invite a chemist to visit your classroom. Discuss the extraction process. Find out what chemicals can be separated by extractions.

3. Have students research the history of pigment usage. Create a bulletin board showing what pigments from animals or plants were used by ancient peoples for dyes, body paint, and even makeup.

4. Take a field trip to a medical lab. Ask a medical technician to demonstrate some lab tests that use chromatography or similar processes.

5. If you have an advanced class, try separating pigments from various flowers using acetone, alcohol, or similar solvents. (Different solvents will extract different materials.) Remember to use all safety precautions.

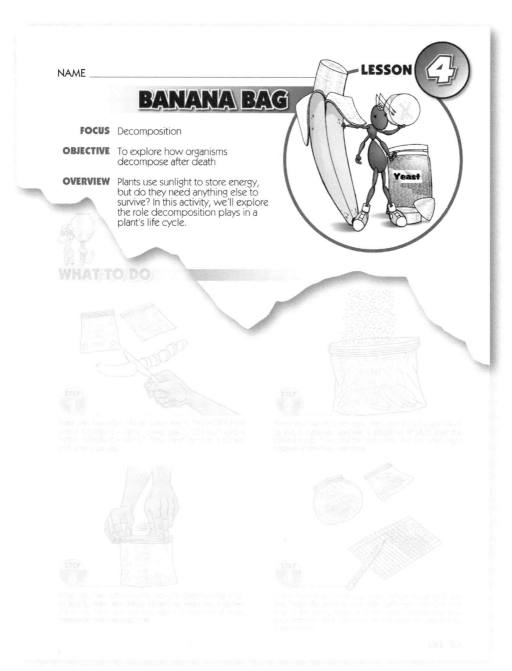

NAME _____

BANANA BAG

FOCUS Decomposition

OBJECTIVE To explore how organisms decompose after death

OVERVIEW Plants use sunlight to store energy, but do they need anything else to survive? In this activity, we'll explore the role decomposition plays in a plant's life cycle.

WHAT TO DO

STEP 1

STEP 2

STEP 3

STEP 4

LIFE

Category

Life Science

Focus

Decomposition

Objective

To explore how organisms decompose after death

National Standards

A1, A2, B1, B2, B3, C1, C3, D1, E3, F1, F4, G1

Materials Needed

yeast - 1 pkg.
plastic bags - 2
  (sealable)
spoon
knife
banana - sliced
sticky labels - 2

Safety Concerns

3. Hygiene
Don't allow students to eat banana slices. Have them wash hands thoroughly when done.

4. Sharp Objects
Remind students to exercise caution when using the knife

4. Slipping
Keep banana peels off the floor.

4. Other
See the special disposal suggestions at left.

Additional Comments

Since bananas are easy to slice, plastic knives are a good alternative. Room temperature has an impact on how quickly decomposition takes place. Use your judgment on how many days the activity should continue. After completion, place all banana bags in a heavy trash bag, and place this directly in the dumpster. (This will keep from exposing the students to mold and avoid a big mess for the custodian.)

Overview

Read the overview aloud to your students. The goal is to create an atmosphere of curiosity and inquiry.

WHAT TO DO

Monitor student research teams as they complete each step.

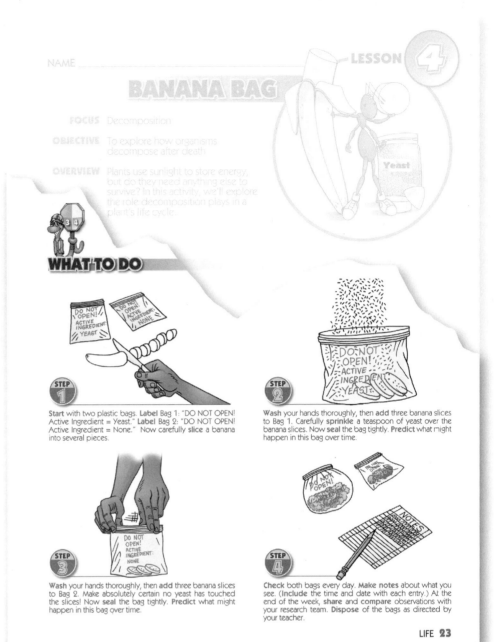

NAME

BANANA BAG

LESSON 4

FOCUS Decomposition

OBJECTIVE To explore how organisms decompose after death

OVERVIEW Plants use sunlight to store energy, but do they need anything else to survive? In this activity, we'll explore the role decomposition plays in a plant's life cycle.

WHAT TO DO

STEP 1
Start with two plastic bags. **Label** Bag 1: "DO NOT OPEN! Active Ingredient = Yeast." **Label** Bag 2: "DO NOT OPEN! Active Ingredient = None." Now carefully **slice** a banana into several pieces.

STEP 2
Wash your hands thoroughly, then **add** three banana slices to Bag 1. Carefully **sprinkle** a teaspoon of yeast over the banana slices. Now **seal** the bag tightly. **Predict** what might happen in this bag over time.

STEP 3
Wash your hands thoroughly, then **add** three banana slices to Bag 2. Make absolutely certain no yeast has touched the slices! Now **seal** the bag tightly. **Predict** what might happen in this bag over time.

STEP 4
Check both bags every day. **Make notes** about what you see. (Include the time and date with each entry.) At the end of the week, **share** and **compare** observations with your research team. **Dispose** of the bags as directed by your teacher.

LIFE **23**

Teacher to Teacher

Plant nutrients are the atoms and molecules essential to their growth and function. Important nutrients include carbon, nitrogen, magnesium, calcium, iron, and phosphorous. Decomposers (bacteria, fungi, and other microbes) are an important part of the nutrient cycle. The nutrient cycle ensures that nutrients don't get "stuck" somewhere. When a plant dies, decomposers in the soil break down plant tissue, freeing up the nutrients which can then be used by other plants growing in the same soil.

What Happened

Review the section with students. Emphasize bold-face words that identify key concepts and introduce new vocabulary.

Scientists call most material produced by living creatures **organic**. *Organic* **matter** *is constantly being attacked by* **bacteria**, **fungi** *(like yeast), and other* **microbes**, *which attempt to break it down through a process called* **decomposition**. *The microbes that cause decomposition are everywhere. That's why it's so important to always wash your hands and the utensils you use!*

As the decomposition process takes place, **nutrients** *(plant foods) are released.* **Plants** *need these nutrients to grow and develop. Decomposition also releases by-products. As the yeast munched on the sugar in the bananas, it gave off* **carbon dioxide gas** *— which caused the bag to swell. Decomposition is very important because it allows plants to* **recycle** *chemicals that dead creatures no longer need, and to provide essential nutrients.*

What We Learned

Answers will vary. Suggested responses are shown at left.

Conclusion

Read this section aloud to the class to summarize the concepts learned in this activity.

Food for Thought

Read the Scripture aloud to the class. Talk about the ongoing work of the Holy Spirit in our lives. Discuss ways we can "feed our souls."

Journal

If time permits, have a general class discussion about students' journal entries. Share and compare observations. Be sure to emphasize that "trial and error" is a valuable part of scientific inquiry!

CONCLUSION

Forces can create the illusion of momentary weightlessness, but gravity and inertia still affect everything on Earth.

FOOD FOR THOUGHT

Job 26:7-14 Everything must obey the law of gravity. In this activity, gravity was exerting a constant pull on every object. No matter where you go in the Universe, gravity is present to some degree, constantly pulling you.

This Scripture reminds us that God is present everywhere. Like gravity, God is constantly pulling everyone closer, seeking to draw them into a relationship with him. Remember, no matter what happens, no matter how frightened or sad or lonely you become, God is always there for you.

JOURNAL My Science Notes

Extended Teaching

1. Have students research composting. Compare similarities and differences in home gardens, municipal "leaf and grass clipping" operations, and huge county landfills. Challenge each team to create a poster depicting one kind of composting.

2. Invite a farmer or commercial gardener to visit your classroom. Discuss ways they supply needed nutrients to plants. Have students write a paragraph about one thing they learned.

3. Set up a compost bin at school using waste from lunches. List and follow all the rules for proper composting. Place the bin in an out-of-the-way spot away from buildings and windows.

4. Have students research food preservation. Challenge teams to list as many methods as they can find. Have students report their findings to the class.

5. Based on what they've learned, have students produce safety posters that deal with food preservation and food safety. (Examples: "Always wash your hands!" "Watch those bacteria!" "There's a fungus among us!", etc.)

NAME _____

SAVING SALT

LESSON **5**

FOCUS Preservatives

OBJECTIVE To explore how preservatives affect decomposition

OVERVIEW Microbes cause food to spoil (decompose) if it's not protected. How can you stop this process without a refrigerator? In this activity, we'll explore one alternative.

WHAT TO DO

Category
Life Science

Focus
Preservatives

Objective
To explore how preservatives affect decomposition

National Standards
A1, A2, B1, B2, B3, C1, C3, D1, E3, F1, F4, G1

Materials Needed
salt
plastic bags - 2 (sealable)
spoon
knife
banana - sliced
sticky labels - 2

Safety Concerns

3. Hygiene
Don't allow students to eat banana slices. Have them wash hands thoroughly when done.

4. Sharp Objects
Remind students to exercise caution when using the knife

4. Other
Use the same disposal procedures as Lesson 4.

Additional Comments

This is the same experiment as Lesson 4, but with a different variable. Again, room temperature has an impact on how quickly decomposition takes place. Use your judgment on how many days the activity should continue.

Overview

Read the overview aloud to your students. The goal is to create an atmosphere of curiosity and inquiry.

WHAT TO DO

Monitor student research teams as they complete each step.

SAVING SALT

LESSON 5

FOCUS Preservatives

OBJECTIVE To explore how preservatives affect decomposition

OVERVIEW Microbes cause food to spoil (decompose) if it's not protected. How can you stop this process without a refrigerator? In this activity, we'll explore one alternative.

WHAT TO DO

STEP 1
Start with two plastic bags. **Label** Bag 1: "DO NOT OPEN! Active Ingredient = Salt." **Label** Bag 2: "DO NOT OPEN! Active Ingredient = None." Now carefully **slice** a banana into several pieces.

STEP 2
Wash your hands thoroughly, then **add** three banana slices to Bag 1. Carefully **sprinkle** two teaspoons of salt over the banana slices. Now **seal** the bag tightly. **Predict** what might happen in this bag over time.

STEP 3
Wash your hands thoroughly, then **add** three banana slices to Bag 2. Make absolutely certain no salt has touched the slices! Now **seal** the bag tightly. **Predict** what might happen in this bag over time.

STEP 4
Check both bags every day. **Make notes** about what you see. (**Include** the time and date with each entry). At the end of the week, **share** and **compare** observations with your research team. **Dispose** of the bags as directed by your teacher.

LIFE **27**

Teacher to Teacher

As we've learned, microbes cause organic material to decompose. These atoms are constantly recycled. For instance, take a carbon atom from an ancient frog. The frog dies and decomposes. A tree recycles the carbon atom into wood. A storm topples the tree into the sea. The tree releases carbon dioxide which is absorbed by an ocean plant. The plant is eaten by a shellfish which uses the carbon atom in its shell. The shellfish dies and becomes part of a limestone ledge. The limestone is quarried and thus the atom from the frog ends up as part of your state capitol building!

What Happened

Review the section with students. Emphasize bold-face words that identify key concepts and introduce new vocabulary.

Plants use nutrients, they grow, they die, they decompose, and they change back into nutrients to start the life cycle over again. While humans are dependent on this cycle for survival, sometimes we prefer to change the pace a bit, allowing us to store food for later use. Preservatives (like salt) slow or stop the decomposition process by interrupting the action of microbes. Salt does this by removing essential water, while other types of preservatives use different means.

Preventing spoilage means more (and cheaper) food for humans. Although God created the Earth to supply an abundance of good things to eat, food supplies do have a limit. Humans compete with everything from microbes to mice for this food. Preservatives are one way to keep food from being wasted, and to keep it available when it's out of season.

What We Learned

Answers will vary. Suggested responses are shown at left.

WHAT HAPPENED?

Plants use nutrients, they grow, they die, they decompose, and they change back into nutrients to start the life cycle over again. While humans are dependent on this cycle for survival, sometimes we prefer to change the pace a bit, allowing us to store food for later use. Preservatives (like salt) slow or stop the decomposition process by interrupting the action of microbes. Salt does this by removing essential water, while other types of preservatives use different means.

Preventing spoilage means more (and cheaper) food for humans. Although God created the Earth to supply an abundance of good things to eat, food supplies do have a limit. Humans compete with everything from microbes to mice for this food. Preservatives are one way to keep food from being wasted, and to keep it available when it's out of season.

WHAT WE LEARNED

1 Why are labels (like those you applied to the bags in Step 1) so important in Science? What might happen without labels?

a) to ensure accurate records

b) they might be switched or mixed up

2 What did you predict in Step 2? What did you predict in Step 3? How did these predictions reflect what actually happened?

Answers will vary, but should reflect logical comparisons.

3 What is the role of a preservative? How does it keep food from spoiling?

a) to slow or stop decomposition

b) it removes something microbes need to thrive (air, water, etc.)

4 Compare the two bags in Step 4. How were they similar? How were they different?

a) similar: same type bag, both had banana slices, etc.

b) different: Bag 1 wasn't decomposing much.

5 Which bag preserved the banana slices the best? Why? How was it different from the other bag?

a) Bag 1

b) salt removed much of the water

c) it contained salt

Conclusion

Read this section aloud to the class to summarize the concepts learned in this activity.

Food for Thought

Read the Scripture aloud to the class. Talk about the need to be refilled with God's love every day. Discuss ways we can share God's love with others.

Journal

If time permits, have a general class discussion about students' journal entries. Share and compare observations. Be sure to emphasize that "trial and error" is a valuable part of scientific inquiry!

CONCLUSION
Although microbes cause all organic matter to decompose, preservatives can help slow or stop this process.

FOOD FOR THOUGHT
Mark 9:50 You've seen that salt can keep food from spoiling. In ancient times, before refrigeration and modern preservatives, salt was even more important. Often salt was the difference between having food and not having food — the difference between life and death!

In this Scripture, Jesus compares his followers to salt. We can truly save lives by sharing God's love with others. But if we're not refilled with God's love each day, we soon become like salt that isn't "salty" anymore. We have nothing left to share. Don't become worthless salt! Take time for God every day.

JOURNAL My Science Notes

Extended Teaching

1. Repeat this activity using similar materials (baking soda, pepper, cumin, flour, etc.). Have students record the results.

2. Bring a food dehydrator to class. Prepare some dehydrated fruit treats for your students. (Be sure to follow all food safety rules.)

3. Ancient peoples, including Native Americans, used many kinds of dehydrated foods. Discuss this with students and have them research the methods used and kinds of food. Encourage them to report their findings to the class.

4. Invite someone who cans food at home to visit your classroom. Ask him/her to bring samples of their work to show. Discuss the process and why it works so well.

5. Invite a food service worker to visit your classroom. Talk about the precautions workers take to avoid contaminating food. After discussion, have students write a paragraph connecting this information to home food preparation.

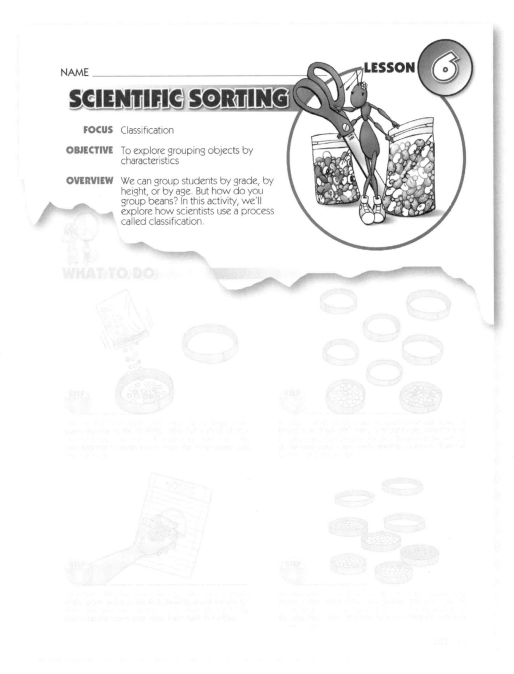

NAME _____

SCIENTIFIC SORTING

FOCUS Classification

OBJECTIVE To explore grouping objects by characteristics

OVERVIEW We can group students by grade, by height, or by age. But how do you group beans? In this activity, we'll explore how scientists use a process called classification.

WHAT TO DO

Category
Life Science

Focus
Classification

Objective
To explore grouping objects by characteristics

National Standards
A1, A2, B1, B2, B3, C1, C3, D1, E3, F1, F4, G1

Materials Needed
"few beans" bag
"many beans" bag
construction paper
scissors
ruler
tape

Safety Concerns

3. Hygiene
Do not allow students to eat beans.

4. Sharp Objects
Remind students to exercise caution when using scissors.

4. Slipping
Spilled beans can pose a slipping hazard.

Additional Comments

The "few beans" bag contains only a few types of beans. The "many beans" bag contains a wider variety of beans. Be sure students put the "few beans" back in their bag after Step 3, or the contents of the two bags could become mixed! If you keep these beans dry and sorted, they can be used year after year.

Overview

Read the overview aloud to your students. The goal is to create an atmosphere of curiosity and inquiry.

WHAT TO DO

Monitor student research teams as they complete each step.

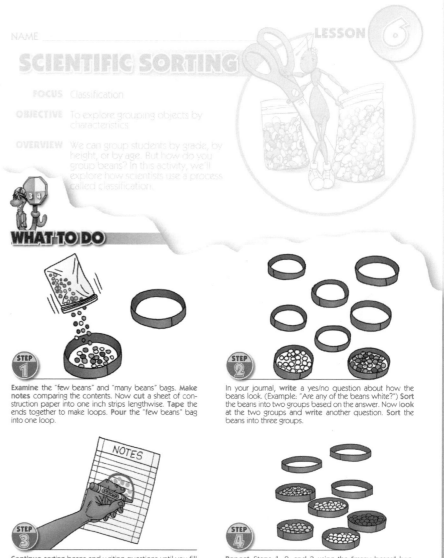

SCIENTIFIC SORTING

FOCUS Classification

OBJECTIVE To explore grouping objects by characteristics

OVERVIEW We can group students by grade, by height, or by age. But how do you group beans? In this activity, we'll explore how scientists use a process called classification.

WHAT TO DO

STEP 1
Examine the "few beans" and "many beans" bags. Make notes comparing the contents. Now cut a sheet of construction paper into one inch strips lengthwise. Tape the ends together to make loops. Pour the "few beans" bag into one loop.

STEP 2
In your journal, write a yes/no question about how the beans look. (Example: "Are any of the beans white?") Sort the beans into two groups based on the answer. Now look at the two groups and write another question. Sort the beans into three groups.

STEP 3
Continue sorting beans and writing questions until you fill all the loops. Make notes and drawings about the groups. When everyone on your team is finished, lift the loops, scoop up the beans, and place them back in the bag.

STEP 4
Repeat Steps 1, 2, and 3 using the "many beans" bag. Make notes about these new groups. Discuss how the "many beans" process was different. Put the beans back in the bag, then share and compare observations with your research team.

LIFE **31**

Teacher to Teacher

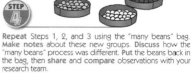

Taxonomy is also used in genetics (the study of genes and DNA sequences). Standard taxonomy is based on an organism's physical appearance (phenotype). Genetic taxonomy is based on the organism's interior structure (genotype).

Using modern technology, genotyping allows scientists to study organisms in greater depth since phenotyping usually only shows the dominant genes, and may miss recessive traits.

WHAT HAPPENED?

Sorting **organisms** based on their characteristics is called **classification** (also known as **taxonomy**). Scientists use classification to name and divide living things into logical groups. This allows scientists from all over the world to know that they're studying and discussing the same kind of creature!

For example, the **scientific name** for humans is *Homo sapiens*. This is a Latin phrase, roughly translated as "thinking man." Scientists always use Latin because it's a "dead" language — it never changes. Since no present-day country speaks it, no new words are being added or old words being given new meanings.

Here's a grammar note: When you're using scientific terms, the entire name is always italicized, but only the first word is capitalized.

WHAT WE LEARNED

1 Compare the two bags from Step 1. How were they similar? How were they different?

a) similar: bags the same, both filled with beans, etc.

b) different: one bag has more kinds of beans

2 What was your first question in step 2? How did it affect your sorting?

a) answers will vary, but should reflect logical sorting rules

3 What were the rest of your sorting questions? How did they affect the sorting process?

a) answers will vary, but should reflect logical sorting rules

4 What is classification based on? What does it allow scientists to do? Why is this important?

a) external characteristics

b) to clearly identify organisms

c) to avoid confusing similar organisms

5 Compare your final groups with other teams' groups. How were their groups similar? How were they different? What could have happened if you'd all used identical questions?

a) answers will vary

b) answers will vary

c) final groups might have been identical

What Happened

Review the section with students. Emphasize bold-face words that identify key concepts and introduce new vocabulary.

Sorting **organisms** *based on their* **characteristics** *is called* **classification** *(also known as* **taxonomy***). Scientists use classification to name and divide living things into logical* **groups***. This allows scientists from all over the world to know that they're studying and discussing the same kind of creature!*

For example, the **scientific name** *for humans is Homo sapiens. This is a Latin phrase, roughly translated as "thinking man." Scientists always use Latin because it's a "dead" language — it never changes. Since no present-day country speaks it, no new words are being added or old words being given new meanings.*

Here's a grammar note: When you're using scientific terms, the entire name is always italicized, but only the first word is capitalized.

What We Learned

Answers will vary. Suggested responses are shown at left.

Conclusion

Read this section aloud to the class to summarize the concepts learned in this activity.

Food for Thought

Read the Scripture aloud to the class. Talk about the question asked in this verse. Discuss why spending more time with God makes the answer easier.

Journal

If time permits, have a general class discussion about students' journal entries. Share and compare observations. Be sure to emphasize that "trial and error" is a valuable part of scientific inquiry!

CONCLUSION

Organisms can be classified into groups based on their characteristics. Scientists use this system to make certain they are observing or discussing the same thing.

FOOD FOR THOUGHT

Luke 14:26 In this activity, you sorted beans into groups based on their characteristics. Once you really understood the question, it was simply a matter of saying "yes" or "no." The correct answer was very clear.

In this Scripture, Jesus asks a very clear question — "Do you love me more than anything else?" If you truly want to be a follower of Jesus, you must first decide on your answer. But just like sorting beans, the more time you spend with God, the easier the correct answer becomes. Why not say "yes" to Jesus, and let God be the master of your life?

JOURNAL My Science Notes

Extended Teaching

1. Have students invent pseudo-scientific names for various beans. For example, a plain red bean might be *Rubius borimus* (red and boring) while a speckled red bean might be *Rubius spectacus* (red and speckled). Remember the order: genus/species.

2. Have students research tropical rain forests. Discuss the bio-diversity there and why it could be very important in the future. Find out why rain forests are being destroyed.

3. Invite a biologist, zoologist, ecologist, or biochemist to visit your classroom. Discuss taxonomy and how it contributes to their work. Have students write a paragraph about one thing they learned.

4. Do a survey of the trees at your school or in your community. Find out how many different species there are. Produce a bulletin board with drawings and leaf tracings depicting your findings.

5. Have students research scientific names on the Internet. Challenge each team to find at least three unusual names and what they mean. Have them report their findings to the class.

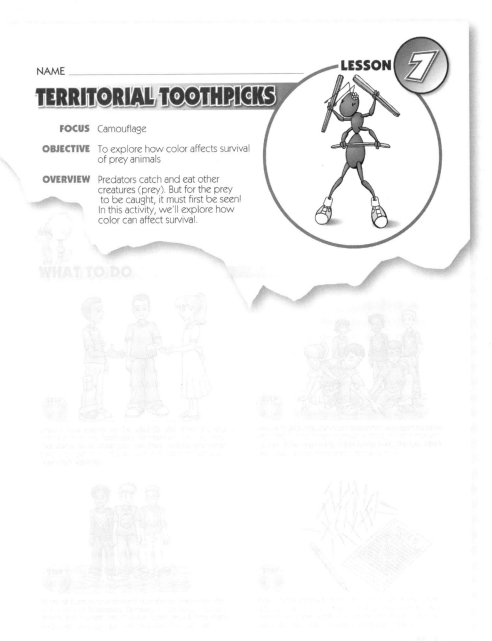

NAME _____

TERRITORIAL TOOTHPICKS

FOCUS Camouflage

OBJECTIVE To explore how color affects survival of prey animals

OVERVIEW Predators catch and eat other creatures (prey). But for the prey to be caught, it must first be seen! In this activity, we'll explore how color can affect survival.

Category
Life Science

Focus
Camouflage

Objective
To explore how color affects survival of prey animals

National Standards
A1, A2, B1, B2, B3, C1, C3, D1, E3, F1, F4, G1

Materials Needed
toothpicks (colored) *
stopwatch
container

Safety Concerns
4. Sharp Object
Remind students to be cautious picking up sharp toothpicks.

Toothpicks can be colored by rolling them in dry tempera paint or by spray painting them.

Additional Comments

Mark off a grassy area (30-foot square) using chalk or a rope on the ground. Scatter colored toothpicks (red, green, yellow, blue, and natural) inside this area. Use the same number of each color, and about 20 toothpicks per student. When class begins, have students line up just outside the "habitat." Allow 20 seconds for each hunt. Caution students: "No running!" "Watch for sharp toothpicks!" and "Don't bump heads!"

Overview

Read the overview aloud to your students. The goal is to create an atmosphere of curiosity and inquiry. As the activity proceeds, focus on the fact that red toothpicks are easy to find, while green and natural ones blend in.

WHAT TO DO

Monitor student research teams as they complete each step.

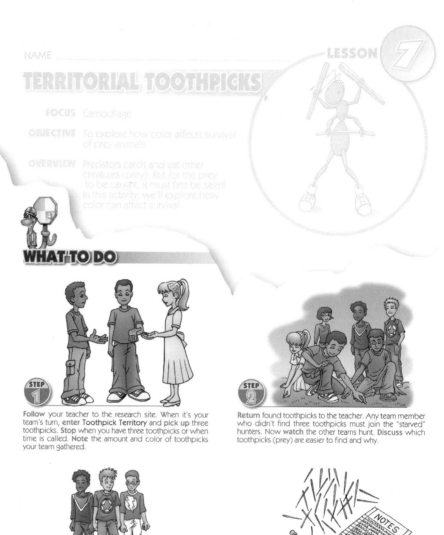

NAME _____

TERRITORIAL TOOTHPICKS

LESSON 7

FOCUS Camouflage

OBJECTIVE To explore how color affects survival of prey animals

OVERVIEW Predators catch and eat other creatures (prey). But for the prey to be caught, it must first be seen! In this activity, we'll explore how color can affect survival.

WHAT TO DO

STEP 1

Follow your teacher to the research site. When it's your team's turn, enter Toothpick Territory and pick up three toothpicks. Stop when you have three toothpicks or when time is called. Note the amount and color of toothpicks your team gathered.

STEP 2

Return found toothpicks to the teacher. Any team member who didn't find three toothpicks must join the "starved" hunters. Now watch the other teams hunt. Discuss which toothpicks (prey) are easier to find and why.

STEP 3

When all hunters have starved, stand shoulder-to-shoulder at the end of Toothpick Territory. Walk slowly forward. Watch for "hidden prey." Make notes about how many and what color toothpicks are found in this final hunt.

STEP 4

Rejoin your research team and review each step in this activity. Make notes about what you discovered. Also, discuss why the safety rules were important. Share and compare observations with other research teams.

LIFE **35**

Teacher to Teacher

In addition to camouflage, some creatures use mimicry to avoid being attacked. For example, the harmless Scarlet Snake resembles the deadly venomous Coral Snake. Some moths have huge "eye spots" on their wings to resemble large birds. Bull Snakes coil up and strike just like a rattlesnake, even though they're not venomous. And members of the Walkingstick family resemble twigs or leaves. These are just a few examples.

WHAT HAPPENED?

Notice that the *easier* a color was to see, the easier it was to "catch" that particular toothpick. On the other hand, the colors that were *harder* to see helped the toothpick stay hidden. It's much the same way in the wild. Animals and insects that blend into their surroundings are a lot less likely to become lunch!

Keep in mind that God created many ways for **animals** to protect themselves, and **color** is only one. Some animals (like rabbits) can run and turn very fast. Others (like porcupines) have special **physical defenses** built in. Still others (like skunks) have less subtle techniques to discourage hungry **predators**. All of these things help maintain the important **balance** between predator and **prey**.

WHAT WE LEARNED

1 Describe the research site (habitat) your teacher created. How did this affect which toothpicks were easiest to find?

a) large, square area on the grass

b) the grass made it harder to see the green toothpicks

2 What color toothpick was found most often? What color toothpick was found least often? Why?

a) red

b) green or natural

c) answers will vary, but should reflect the concept of camouflage

3 Suppose the toothpicks were relocated to a different habitat (like a bright red piece of carpet). How would this affect the results? Why?

a) results would be very different

b) different habitat needs different camouflage

4 Characteristics that lead to survival become more common over time. Why? If these toothpicks had offspring, what color might be more common in the next generation?

a) parents that survive pass traits on to their offspring

b) green or natural

5 Besides color, what are some other ways animals, birds, and insects protect themselves from predators? Do these protection techniques always work? Why or why not?

a) speed, physical defenses (spines, smell), mimicry, etc.

b) no

c) answers will vary, but should include the idea that nothing is fool-proof all the time

What Happened

Review the section with students. Emphasize bold-face words that identify key concepts and introduce new vocabulary.

Notice that the easier a color was to see, the easier it was to "catch" that particular toothpick. On the other hand, the colors that were harder to see helped the toothpick stay hidden. It's much the same way in the wild. Animals and insects that blend into their surroundings are a lot less likely to become lunch!

*Keep in mind that God created many ways for **animals** to protect themselves, and **color** is only one. Some animals (like rabbits) can run and turn very fast. Others (like porcupines) have special **physical defenses** built in. Still others (like skunks) have less subtle techniques to discourage hungry **predators**. All of these things help maintain the important **balance** between predator and **prey**.*

What We Learned

Answers will vary. Suggested responses are shown at left.

Conclusion

Read this section aloud to the class to summarize the concepts learned in this activity.

Food for Thought

Read the Scripture aloud to the class. Talk about the beautiful world and abundant resources God has given us. Discuss ways we can help protect the environment.

Journal

If time permits, have a general class discussion about students' journal entries. Share and compare observations. Be sure to emphasize that "trial and error" is a valuable part of scientific inquiry!

CONCLUSION

The relationship between an animal's color and its habitat impacts its potential survival. Characteristics that lead to survival tend to become more common over time.

FOOD FOR THOUGHT

Genesis 1:24-26 God created this world with a complex ecosystem, where the life of one creature interrelates with the lives of many other creatures. For instance, too many predators and the prey all die. Soon the predators starve. But if there are not enough predators, prey will multiply beyond what an area can support. Soon they eat up all the plants, and the prey begin to starve.

This Scripture talks about the creatures God created in his beautiful new world. The last verse reminds us that we are responsible for taking care of this world. Learn to love and care for it. After all, it's the only world we have!

JOURNAL My Science Notes

38 LIFE

Extended Teaching

1. Have students research the amazing reproductive ability of prey animals. Challenge them to calculate what an area would be like if there were no predators.

2. Invite a representative from the Department of Natural Resources or Fish and Game Department to visit your classroom. Discuss ways they protect wildlife and their habitats, including through hunting.

3. Have students research ways animals protect themselves. Ask each team to create a poster depicting at least one animal they've studied, and how it protects itself.

4. Invite an outdoorsman to visit your classroom. Ask him/her to dress up in camouflage clothing. Have them stand against a blank wall, then move to a wooded or brushy area outdoors. Have students discuss the difference.

5. Make a bulletin board showing examples of mimicry. Discuss how animals use this technique to protect themselves.

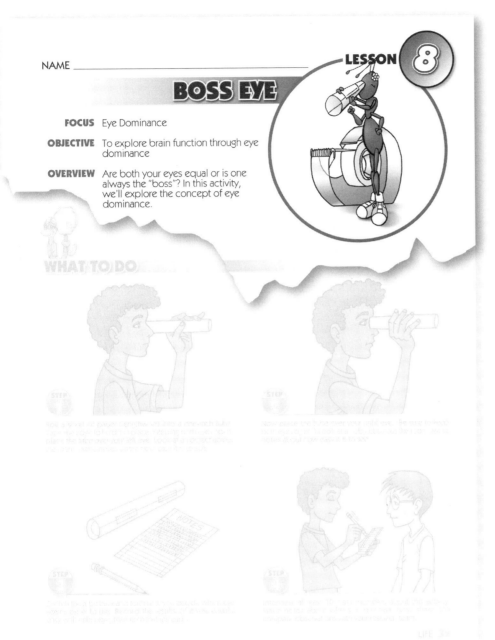

NAME _____

BOSS EYE

FOCUS Eye Dominance

OBJECTIVE To explore brain function through eye dominance

OVERVIEW Are both your eyes equal or is one always the "boss"? In this activity, we'll explore the concept of eye dominance.

WHAT TO DO

Category
Life Science

Focus
Eye Dominance

Objective
To explore brain function through eye dominance

National Standards
A1, A2, B1, B2, B3, C1, C3, D1, E3, F1, F4, G1

Materials Needed
sheet of paper
ruler
tape

Safety Concerns
4. Slipping
Possible tripping hazard. Don't let students walk around while looking through the tube.

Additional Comments

Here's a great way to introduce this activity: Ask students to raise the hand they write with. Point out the fact that this is their dominant (boss) hand. Explain that people have a dominant eye, too, and this activity will help them find it! For added fun, tape a colorful picture high on one wall for the students' focal point.

Overview

Read the overview aloud to your students. The goal is to create an atmosphere of curiosity and inquiry.

WHAT TO DO

Monitor student research teams as they complete each step.

Step 1 & 2

If students have trouble seeing a difference between Step 1 and Step 2, have them move closer to the object and try again. Be sure they're not moving their head between the Steps, but only shifting the tube from eye to eye.

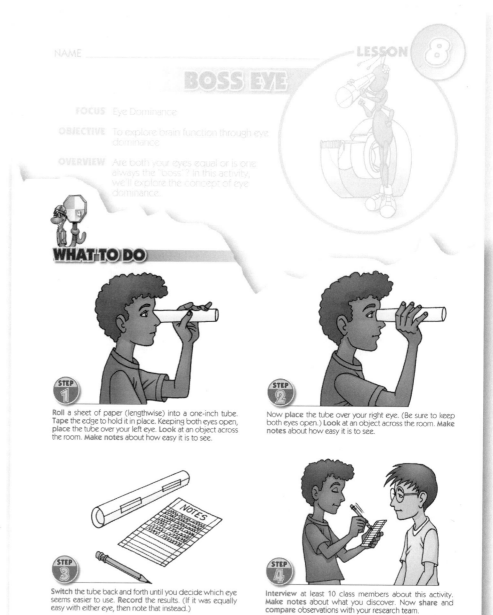

BOSS EYE

FOCUS Eye Dominance

OBJECTIVE To explore brain function through eye dominance

OVERVIEW Are both your eyes equal or is one always the "boss"? In this activity, we'll explore the concept of eye dominance.

WHAT TO DO

STEP 1
Roll a sheet of paper (lengthwise) into a one-inch tube. Tape the edge to hold it in place. Keeping both eyes open, place the tube over your left eye. Look at an object across the room. Make notes about how easy it is to see.

STEP 2
Now place the tube over your right eye. (Be sure to keep both eyes open.) Look at an object across the room. Make notes about how easy it is to see.

STEP 3
Switch the tube back and forth until you decide which eye seems easier to use. Record the results. (If it was equally easy with either eye, then note that instead.)

STEP 4
Interview at least 10 class members about this activity. Make notes about what you discover. Now share and compare observations with your research team.

LIFE **39**

Teacher to Teacher

Each of your eyes has an optic nerve. These nerves cross each other in a spot centered behind your eyes (the optic chiasma). The optic nerves continue on toward the back of your brain, ending in the occipital lobe of the cerebrum. Scientists tell us that this is the spot in your brain where information perceived by the eyes (the image) is processed, resulting in what we call "vision."

Left page (student worksheet)

WHAT HAPPENED?

Your **eyes** help your **brain** to **perceive** the world around you. Each eye reports to a different half (**hemisphere**) of your brain! The left side of your brain reads **images** from your right eye, and the right side reads images from your left eye. Sounds complicated, but your brain figured out how to combine those images correctly when you were still a baby.

Even though both eyes report what they see, one eye is **dominant** — the eye your brain relies on most. Many left-handed people are left eye dominant, and right-handed folks usually prefer their right eye. But as you probably noticed in your classmates' results, everyone doesn't follow this pattern. In fact, one of the authors of this science series is right-handed, but left-eyed. (That's a little awkward for some things, but a great combination for baseball!)

WHAT WE LEARNED

1 Compare Step 1 and Step 2. How were the results similar? How were they different?

a) answers will vary, but almost everyone should find the object easier to see in one step versus the other

2 Which eye did you select in Step 3? How difficult was the selection? What factors influenced your decision?

a) answers will vary

b) answers will vary

c) answers will vary, but should reflect logical decisions

40 LIFE

3 Review your notes from Step 4. How many students were right-eye dominant? How many were left-eye dominant? How many indicated no preference?

Answers will vary, but should be consistant with other students' observations.

4 List the right-eye dominant students. Are any of them left-handed? List the left-eye dominant students. Are any of them right-handed?

Answers will vary. This question is designed to help them discover any cross-dominant students.

5 If the right side of a person's brain was injured in a car accident (but their face was okay), which eye might be affected? Why?

a) the left eye

b) because the right side of the brain reads images from the left eye

LIFE 41

Right page (teacher guide)

What Happened

Review the section with students. Emphasize bold-face words that identify key concepts and introduce new vocabulary.

*Your eyes help your **brain** to **perceive** the world around you. Each eye reports to a different half (**hemisphere**) of your brain! The left side of your brain reads **images** from your right eye, and the right side reads images from your left eye. Sounds complicated, but your brain figured out how to combine those images correctly when you were still a baby.*

*Even though both eyes report what they see, one eye is **dominant** — the eye your brain relies on most. Many left-handed people are left eye dominant, and right-handed folks usually prefer their right eye. But as you probably noticed in your classmates' results, everyone doesn't follow this pattern. In fact, one of the authors of this science series is right-handed, but left-eyed. (That's a little awkward for some things, but a great combination for baseball!)*

What We Learned

Answers will vary. Suggested responses are shown at left.

Conclusion

Read this section aloud to the class to summarize the concepts learned in this activity.

Food for Thought

Read the Scripture aloud to the class. Talk about the importance of letting God control our lives. Discuss ways we can get closer to God.

Journal

If time permits, have a general class discussion about students' journal entries. Share and compare observations. Be sure to emphasize that "trial and error" is a valuable part of scientific inquiry!

CONCLUSION

Even though both eyes report what they see, one eye is dominant. Your right eye works with the left side of your brain, and your left eye works with the right side of your brain.

FOOD FOR THOUGHT

Ephesians 4:14-16 In this activity, you discovered that one of your eyes is dominant. Your body always operates its very best when this eye takes the lead.

This Scripture reminds us that Jesus should always be our leader. Under his direction, the body of the church works together perfectly. Sometimes we forget this, changing our minds about what we believe just because someone has cleverly made a lie sound like the truth. But remember, when Christ is in control of your life, you're always at your very best!

JOURNAL My Science Notes

Extended Teaching

1. Encourage students to read the inspirational book, *Gifted Hands* — the autobiography of one of the world's most gifted brain surgeons. Have teams dialog about what they discover. (Note: An easy reading level, this book is also available in audio form.)

2. Have students research what science tells us about other functions of each brain half (hemisphere). Challenge teams to create a poster depicting at least one function and the spot in the brain that controls it.

3. Have students research differences in dominance (eye, hand, brain hemisphere) between males and females. Have them report their findings to the class, citing their sources of information.

4. Invite a trauma nurse to visit your classroom. Discuss strokes and other brain injuries and how they impact an individual's ability to function. Have students write a paragraph about at least one thing they learned.

5. Using the Internet, have students research the history of epilepsy. How does it affect the brain? How has treatment changed in the past 100 years?

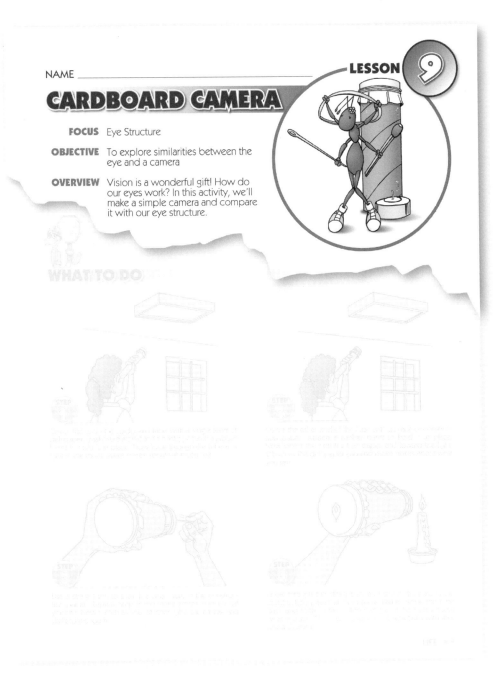

NAME _____

CARDBOARD CAMERA

FOCUS Eye Structure

OBJECTIVE To explore similarities between the eye and a camera

OVERVIEW Vision is a wonderful gift! How do our eyes work? In this activity, we'll make a simple camera and compare it with our eye structure.

WHAT TO DO

Category
Life Science

Focus
Eye Structure

Objective
To explore similarities between the eye and a camera

National Standards
A1, A2, B1, B2, B3, C1, C3, D1, E3, F1, F4, G1

Materials Needed
deli paper
rubber band
straight pin
candle
cardboard tube
construction paper
lighter

Safety Concerns

2. Open Flame
Remind students to exercise caution around open flame (loose clothing, long hair, etc.).

4. Sharp Objects
Remind students to exercise caution with straight pins

4. Eye Damage
Do not allow students to use this device to look at the sun!

Additional Comments

To avoid a tripping hazard, don't let students walk around while using their "camera." This simple device can significantly concentrate light, so DO NOT allow students near windows where they might be tempted to look at the sun!

Overview

Read the overview aloud to your students. The goal is to create an atmosphere of curiosity and inquiry. Focus on the fact that this is a simple camera — a device to focus light and reflect an image.

WHAT TO DO

Monitor student research teams as they complete each step.

Step 3

Depending on your group, you may wish to make the hole for students when they reach Step 3. This will avoid problems with straight pins.

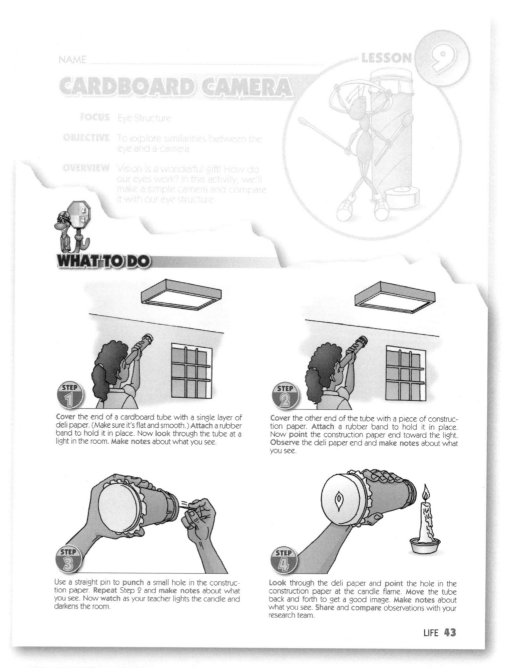

CARDBOARD CAMERA

FOCUS Eye Structure

OBJECTIVE To explore similarities between the eye and a camera

OVERVIEW Vision is a wonderful gift! How do our eyes work? In this activity, we'll make a simple camera and compare it with our eye structure.

WHAT TO DO

STEP 1
Cover the end of a cardboard tube with a single layer of deli paper. (Make sure it's flat and smooth.) Attach a rubber band to hold it in place. Now look through the tube at a light in the room. Make notes about what you see.

STEP 2
Cover the other end of the tube with a piece of construction paper. Attach a rubber band to hold it in place. Now point the construction paper end toward the light. Observe the deli paper end and make notes about what you see.

STEP 3
Use a straight pin to punch a small hole in the construction paper. Repeat Step 2 and make notes about what you see. Now watch as your teacher lights the candle and darkens the room.

STEP 4
Look through the deli paper and point the hole in the construction paper at the candle flame. Move the tube back and forth to get a good image. Make notes about what you see. Share and compare observations with your research team.

LIFE **43**

Teacher to Teacher

Vision is actually a series of complex actions. It begins with light energy hitting light-sensitive cells on the retina called rods and cones. Cones function best in bright light and help us see colors. Rods work best in low light conditions. Rods and cones collect information (the image) which is then passed through the optic nerves to the back of the brain. There it is processed to create vision.

WHAT HAPPENED?

The purpose of a lens (including the one in your eye) is to focus available light. Common applications include telescopes, cameras, binoculars, and microscopes. Some devices contain a complex series of lenses, like a set of funnels and gates. These funnels and gates help control the size and direction of an image.

In a camera, the lens focuses the light on film (or a digital device) which records and stores the image. In your eye, the lens focuses light onto the retina, a surface used for much the same purpose.

Glasses and contacts simply provide an additional lens that is used to assist the eye's lens when needed.

 WHAT WE LEARNED

1 Describe what you observed in Step 1. What did you see through the deli paper. Compare this with what you observed in Step 2.

a) answers will vary

b) nothing except light

c) nothing at all, it was dark

2 Describe what you observed in Step 3. How was this similar to Step 1? How was it different?

a) a spot of light

b) both showed light

c) light was much more concentrated (focused) in Step 3

 Describe what you observed in Step 4. How was this similar to Step 3? How was it different?

a) a flickering image of the flame

b) both were focused light

c) there was an image

 Name the two primary parts of the eye modeled in this activity, and describe the purpose of each.

a) lens and retina

b) lens: to focus available light; retina: to collect the image

5 What is the purpose of any lens (including the eye's lens)? Name three common devices that use lenses, and describe their purpose.

a) to focus light

b) answers will vary, but should include items like microscopes, telescopes, cameras, etc.

What Happened

Review the section with students. Emphasize bold-face words that identify key concepts and introduce new vocabulary.

*The purpose of a **lens** (including the one in your **eye**) is to **focus** available **light**. Common applications include telescopes, cameras, binoculars, and microscopes. Some devices contain a complex series of lenses, like a set of funnels and gates. These funnels and gates help control the size and direction of an image.*

*In a camera, the lens focuses the light on film (or a digital device) which records and stores the **image**. In your eye, the lens focuses light onto the **retina**, a surface used for much the same purpose.*

Glasses and contacts simply provide an additional lens that is used to assist the eye's lens when needed.

What We Learned

Answers will vary. Suggested responses are shown at left.

Conclusion

Read this section aloud to the class to summarize the concepts learned in this activity.

Food for Thought

Read the Scripture aloud to the class. Talk about the importance of keeping focused on God. Discuss ways we can maintain that focus.

Journal

If time permits, have a general class discussion about students' journal entries. Share and compare observations. Be sure to emphasize that "trial and error" is a valuable part of scientific inquiry!

CONCLUSION

The purpose of any lens is to focus light. In the eye, the lens focuses light on the retina. The retina then sends the image to the brain for interpretation.

FOOD FOR THOUGHT

John 8:12 In your Cardboard Camera, the deli paper screen was completely dark until light was focused on it. But when the light came into focus, suddenly there was a clear image!

This Scripture reminds us that Jesus is the light of the world. When our eyes are focused on Jesus, everything begins to become clear. Just like the Cardboard Camera, it's easy to lose our focus — and we can end up stumbling through the darkness. Remember to stay focused by spending time with God each day!

JOURNAL My Science Notes

Extended Teaching

1. Invite a professional photographer to visit your classroom. Discuss the kinds of lenses they use and why different lenses are required for different situations. Have students write a paragraph about one thing they learned.

2. Not all light is visible. Have students research other types of light (ultraviolet, infrared, etc.) and how they are used in medicine or science. Challenge teams to create a poster depicting their findings.

3. Using the Internet, have students research cameras — from the early primitive ones to the latest digital versions. If you have a collector in your area, ask them to bring some antique cameras for viewing. Have a group discussion about what they've discovered and seen.

4. Have students research color blindness (cone related) and night blindness (rod related). Ask them to write a story telling how their life might change if they had either condition.

5. Invite an optometrist to visit your classroom. Ask them to explain some of the tests they use (visual acuity, refraction, visual field testing, etc.). Have students write a paragraph about one thing they learn.

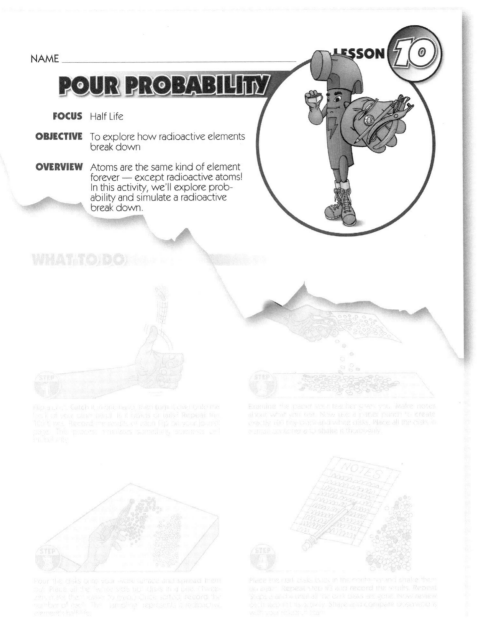

LESSON 10

POUR PROBABILITY

FOCUS Half Life

OBJECTIVE To explore how radioactive elements break down

OVERVIEW Atoms are the same kind of element forever — except radioactive atoms! In this activity, we'll explore probability and simulate a radioactive break down.

Category

Physical Science
Forces

Focus

Half Life

Objective

To explore how radio-active elements break down

National Standards

A1, A2, B1, B2, B3, E1, E2, F3, F4, F5, G1, G2

Materials Needed

penny
paper (black/white)
hole punch
container
tweezers

Safety Concerns

Additional Comments

Lift the lid of the copy machine and make a copy — one side will be black and the other white. Make one of these sheets for each team. If you don't have enough hole punches for this activity, borrow them from other teachers or the office. Be sure to return them the same day!

Overview

Read the overview aloud to your students. The goal is to create an atmosphere of curiosity and inquiry.

WHAT TO DO

Monitor student research teams as they complete each step.

POUR PROBABILITY

FOCUS Half Life

OBJECTIVE To explore how radioactive elements break down.

OVERVIEW Atoms are the same kind of element forever — except radioactive atoms! In this activity, we'll explore probability and simulate a radioactive break down.

WHAT TO DO

STEP 1

Flip a coin. **Catch** it in one hand, then **turn** it over onto the back of your other hand. Is it heads or tails? **Repeat** this 100 times. **Record** the results of each flip on your journal page. This process simulates something scientists call probability.

STEP 2

Examine the paper your teacher gives you. **Make notes** about what you see. Now use a paper punch to **create** exactly 100 tiny black and white disks. **Place** all the disks in a small container and **shake** it thoroughly.

STEP 3

Pour the disks onto your work surface and **spread** them out. **Place** all the "white side up" disks in a pile. (Tweezers make them easier to grab.) Once sorted, **record** the number of each. This "sampling" represents a radioactive element's half-life.

STEP 4

Place the dark disks back in the container and **shake** them up again. **Repeat** step #3 and **record** the results. **Repeat** Steps 3 and 4 until all the cark disks are gone. Now **review** each step in this activity. **Share** and **compare** observations with your research team.

FORCES **49**

Teacher to Teacher

Radioactive materials take huge amounts of time to completely break down. Uranium 235 has a half life of over 700 million years, and some physicists consider this a "short" half life! Combine this with the fact that gamma radiation is deadly to humans, and you can understand scientific concerns about the disposal of nuclear waste.

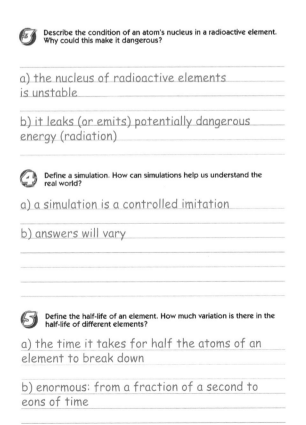

WHAT HAPPENED?

The inside of an atom (nucleus) contains **protons** and **neutrons**. Normally the **nucleus** is incredibly stable, so an **atom** stays the same **element** forever. But some kinds of atoms are **unstable**, constantly breaking down into more **stable** forms, releasing potentially dangerous **energy** in the process. These are **radioactive** atoms.

In this activity, we simulated that breakdown. Each time a white disk fell face up, it represented the **probability** (chance) that one atom of an element would break down. The time it takes for half the atoms of an element to break down is called its **half-life**. In our **simulation** this was probably less than a minute. In the real world, half-lives of elements vary enormously! Some half-lives are measured in tiny fractions of a second, others are measured in eons of time.

WHAT WE LEARNED

1 Compare your coin toss probability from Step 1 with your disk probabilities in the other steps. How were they similar? How were they different?

a) answers will vary

2 Review your results from each shake and toss. How many white disks and how many black disks occurred in each? What does this tell you about probability?

a) answers will vary

b) the "odds" are fairly constant

3 Describe the condition of an atom's nucleus in a radioactive element. Why could this make it dangerous?

a) the nucleus of radioactive elements is unstable

b) it leaks (or emits) potentially dangerous energy (radiation)

4 Define a simulation. How can simulations help us understand the real world?

a) a simulation is a controlled imitation

b) answers will vary

5 Define the half-life of an element. How much variation is there in the half-life of different elements?

a) the time it takes for half the atoms of an element to break down

b) enormous: from a fraction of a second to eons of time

What Happened

Review the section with students. Emphasize bold-face words that identify key concepts and introduce new vocabulary.

*The inside of an atom (nucleus) contains **protons** and **neutrons**. Normally the **nucleus** is incredibly stable, so an **atom** stays the same **element** forever. But some kinds of atoms are **unstable**, constantly breaking down into more **stable** forms, releasing potentially dangerous **energy** in the process. These are **radioactive** atoms.*

*In this activity, we simulated that breakdown. Each time a white disk fell face up, it represented the **probability** (chance) that one atom of an element would break down. The time it takes for half the atoms of an element to break down is called its **half-life**. In our **simulation** this was probably less than a minute. In the real world, half-lives of elements vary enormously! Some half-lives are measured in tiny fractions of a second, others are measured in eons of time.*

What We Learned

Answers will vary. Suggested responses are shown at left.

Conclusion

Read this section aloud to the class to summarize the concepts learned in this activity.

Food for Thought

Read the Scripture aloud to the class. Talk about the power of prayer. Discuss how praying together in a common cause can bring us closer together and closer to God.

Journal

If time permits, have a general class discussion about notes and drawings various students added to their journal pages. Discuss correct and incorrect predictions, and remind students that this "trial and error" process is part of the scientific process.

CONCLUSION

Although most atoms are incredibly stable, radioactive atoms are constantly breaking down, releasing potentially dangerous energy. The time it takes for half an element's atoms to break down is known as the half-life.

FOOD FOR THOUGHT

James 5:16 One radioactive atom breaking down releases some energy. When large numbers of radioactive atoms break down, it releases an enormous amount of force! A nuclear power plant can produce enough electricity for an entire city, and provides a good example of the collective force of tiny, individual changes.

This Scripture tells us that the earnest prayer of just one believer has great power. Imagine what might happen if we all begin to pray together! Prayer links us with the most powerful force in the universe — our creator God. Why not experience the power of prayer today?

JOURNAL My Science Notes

_____

_____

_____

_____

_____

_____

_____

_____

_____

_____

_____

_____

_____

_____

_____

_____

_____

_____

52 FORCES

Extended Teaching

1. Using the Internet, have teams research other forms of radiation (like ultraviolet and infrared). Challenge each team to create a poster describing one form of radiation.

2. Take a field trip to a nuclear power plant. Discuss the advantages and concerns about nuclear power. Have students write a paragraph about one thing they learn.

3. Have teams research fission and fusion. Challenge each team to create a presentation (posters, powerpoint, models, etc.) explaining the differ-ence. Have teams share their presentations with the class.

4. Have teams research Chernobyl and Three Mile Island. How were these nuclear accidents similar? How were they different? Have students write a paper comparing these two situations.

5. Using the Internet, visit the U.S. Atomic Energy Commission's website. Research the history of atomic energy and find out about research currently being done.

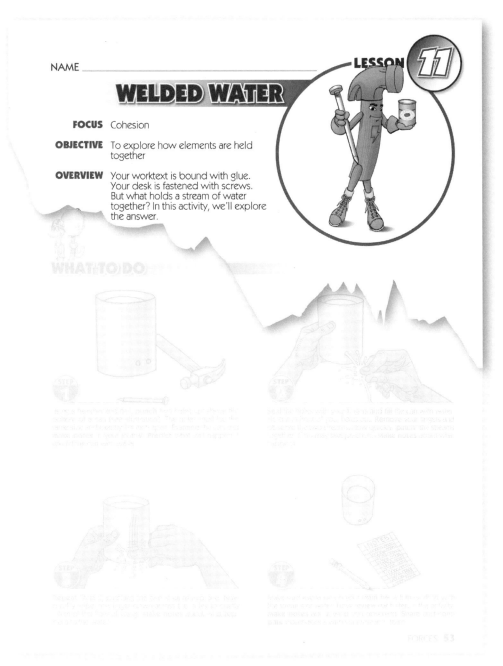

NAME _____

WELDED WATER

FOCUS Cohesion

OBJECTIVE To explore how elements are held together

OVERVIEW Your worktext is bound with glue. Your desk is fastened with screws. But what holds a stream of water together? In this activity, we'll explore the answer.

WHAT TO DO

Category

Physical Science
Forces

Focus

Cohesion

Objective

To explore how elements are held together

National Standards

A1, A2, B1, B2, B3, G1, G2

Materials Needed

nail
hammer
can
water

Safety Concerns

4. Sharp Objects
Remind students to exercise caution with the hammer and nails.

4. Slipping
There is a potential for spills with this activity. Remind students to exercise caution.

Additional Comments

This activity works best in an outdoor setting. To lessen the chance for smashed fingers, you may want to skip Step 1 and prepare the cans in advance. Adjust (bend) the holes with the nail, as needed, to make the streams connect easier.

Overview

Read the overview aloud to your students. The goal is to create an atmosphere of curiosity and inquiry.

WHAT TO DO

Monitor student research teams as they complete each step.

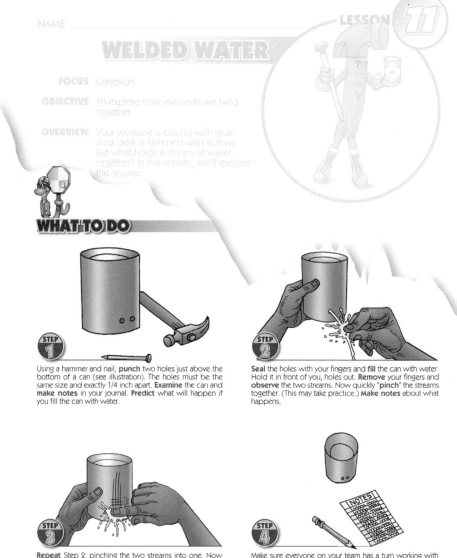

WELDED WATER

FOCUS Cohesion

OBJECTIVE To explore how elements are held together

OVERVIEW Your worktext is bound with glue. Your desk is fastened with screws. But what holds a stream of water together? In this activity, we'll explore the answer.

WHAT TO DO

STEP 1

Using a hammer and nail, **punch** two holes just above the bottom of a can (see illustration). The holes must be the same size and exactly 1/4 inch apart. **Examine** the can and **make notes** in your journal. **Predict** what will happen if you fill the can with water.

STEP 2

Seal the holes with your fingers and **fill** the can with water. Hold it in front of you, holes out. **Remove** your fingers and **observe** the two streams. Now quickly "**pinch**" the streams together. (This may take practice.) **Make notes** about what happens.

STEP 3

Repeat Step 2, pinching the two streams into one. Now quickly **wipe** one finger down across the holes to briefly interrupt the flow of water. **Make notes** about what happens to the water.

STEP 4

Make sure everyone on your team has a turn working with the streams of water. Now **review** each step in this activity. **Make notes** about what you observed. **Share** and **compare** observations with your research team.

FORCES **53**

Teacher to Teacher

This activity demonstrated hydrogen bonding. Other bonds include covalent (equally shared electrons), ionic (unequally shared electrons), and metallic (free flowing electrons). Quartz has strong covalent bonding. Table salt demonstrates an ionic bond. Metallic bonds, found in materials like copper, allow electricity to flow.

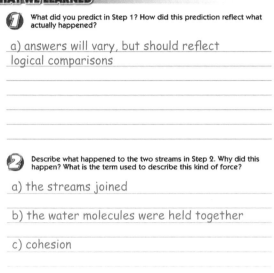

WHAT HAPPENED?

When **molecules** are held together by **mutual attraction**, it's known as **cohesion**. Cohesion causes the molecules to act like tiny magnets, attracting and sticking to each other. When you "welded" the streams of water, you actually just pinched them close enough for cohesion to turn them into one stream. When you wiped your finger across the holes, you broke the cohesion. This resulted in separate streams.

Cohesion is also what allows some insects (like pond skaters and water striders) to walk on water. The water molecules at the surface are attracted to each other and also to the molecules just below them. This forms a kind of "skin" at the surface, a type of cohesion that is known as **surface tension**.

WHAT WE LEARNED

1 What did you predict in Step 1? How did this prediction reflect what actually happened?

a) answers will vary, but should reflect logical comparisons

2 Describe what happened to the two streams in Step 2. Why did this happen? What is the term used to describe this kind of force?

a) the streams joined

b) the water molecules were held together

c) cohesion

3 Describe what happened to the streams in Step 3. What caused this to occur?

a) the streams separated

b) wiping finger down the can brakes cohesion

4 What might have happened if we'd used a liquid with no cohesion? Why?

a) the streams would not have joined

b) the liquid's molecules would not bond together or attract

5 Name another example of cohesion and describe how it works.

a) surface tension

b) answers will vary

What Happened

Review the section with students. Emphasize bold-face words that identify key concepts and introduce new vocabulary.

*When **molecules** are held together by **mutual attraction**, it's known as **cohesion**. Cohesion causes the molecules to act like tiny magnets, attracting and sticking to each other. When you "welded" the streams of water, you actually just pinched them close enough for cohesion to turn them into one stream. When you wiped your finger across the holes, you broke the cohesion. This resulted in separate streams.*

*Cohesion is also what allows some insects (like pond skaters and water striders) to walk on water. The water molecules at the surface are attracted to each other and also to the molecules just below them. This forms a kind of "skin" at the surface, a type of cohesion that is known as **surface tension**.*

What We Learned

Answers will vary. Suggested responses are shown at left.

Conclusion

Read this section aloud to the class to summarize the concepts learned in this activity.

Food for Thought

Read the Scripture aloud to the class. Continue and expand last week's discussion about the power of prayer and the importance of praying together.

Journal

If time permits, have a general class discussion about notes and drawings various students added to their journal pages. Discuss correct and incorrect predictions, and remind students that this "trial and error" process is part of the scientific process.

CONCLUSION

Cohesion is a force that holds elements together through mutual attraction. Cohesion at the top of a body of water is called surface tension.

FOOD FOR THOUGHT

Acts 1:12-14 When the streams of water were rushing from the can, they were each going their own way. Each stream was following its own path, and they definitely weren't working together. But when the streams made contact with each other, their combined power made a much greater impact!

Prayer is a very important part of spiritual health. Having a personal prayer life is very important, but don't overlook the power of praying with others. This Scripture tells us how the early church members joined together in prayer. If one prayer is powerful, imagine the strength of many prayers!

JOURNAL My Science Notes

Extended Teaching

1. Repeat this activity using different hole spacing, different hole sizes, or different size cans. Have teams compare the results with the original activity. How were they similar? How were they different?

2. Invite a chemistry teacher to visit your classroom. Talk about different kinds of bonding. Ask him/her to bring some models or slides. Have students write a paragraph about one thing they learn.

3. Take a field trip to a water garden. Have teams watch for examples of cohesion, taking notes and drawing pictures. Challenge each team to create a presentation about a specific example and share it with the class.

4. Have teams research various types of fountains. Challenge each team to create a poster describing a unique fountain or water feature, and explaining how cohesion plays a role in the design.

5. Have teams research "laminar flow" fountains ("LeapFrog" at Epcot, "Sky Rockets" at Navy Pier, Chicago, etc.). What makes water behave this way? How does cohesion play a role?

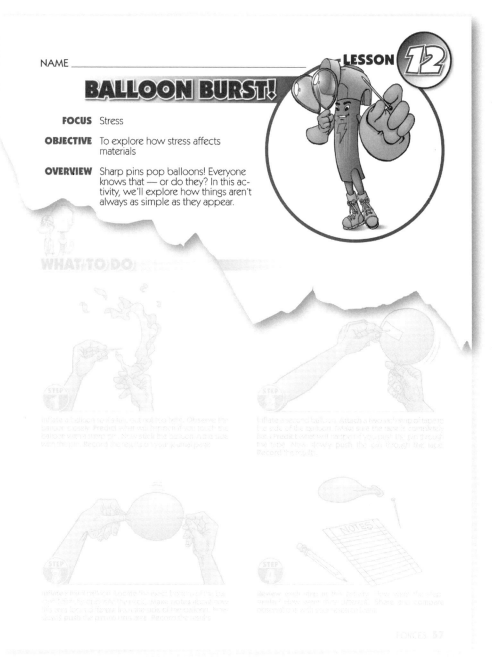

NAME _____

BALLOON BURST!

FOCUS Stress

OBJECTIVE To explore how stress affects materials

OVERVIEW Sharp pins pop balloons! Everyone knows that — or do they? In this activity, we'll explore how things aren't always as simple as they appear.

LESSON 12

Category

Physical Science
Forces

Focus

Stress

Objective

To explore how stress affects materials

National Standards

A1, A2, B1, B2, B3, G1, G2

Materials Needed

balloons - 3
straight pin
tape

Safety Concerns

4. Sharp Objects
Remind students to exercise caution when holding or using straight pins.

4. Other
Watch that the "pop!" of balloons doesn't cause anyone to jump and stumble.

Additional Comments

A great way to begin this activity is to tell students you can poke a pin in a balloon without popping it! Follow this by demonstrating Step 3. Once curiosity is aroused, let students begin the lesson. Keep extra balloons on hand to cover accidental breakage.

Overview

Read the overview aloud to your students. The goal is to create an atmosphere of curiosity and inquiry.

WHAT TO DO

Monitor student research teams as they complete each step.

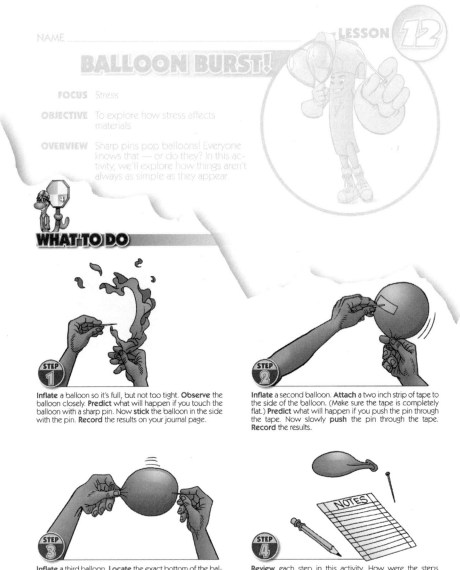

BALLOON BURST!

FOCUS Stress

OBJECTIVE To explore how stress affects materials

OVERVIEW Sharp pins pop balloons! Everyone knows that — or do they? In this activity, we'll explore how things aren't always as simple as they appear.

WHAT TO DO

STEP 1

Inflate a balloon so it's full, but not too tight. **Observe** the balloon closely. **Predict** what will happen if you touch the balloon with a sharp pin. Now stick the balloon in the side with the pin. **Record** the results on your journal page.

STEP 2

Inflate a second balloon. **Attach** a two inch strip of tape to the side of the balloon. (Make sure the tape is completely flat.) **Predict** what will happen if you push the pin through the tape. Now slowly **push** the pin through the tape. **Record** the results.

STEP 3

Inflate a third balloon. **Locate** the exact bottom of the balloon (directly opposite the neck). **Make notes** about how this area looks different from the side of the balloon. Now slowly **push** the pin into this area. **Record** the results.

STEP 4

Review each step in this activity. How were the steps similar? How were they different? **Share** and **compare** observations with your research team.

FORCES **57**

Teacher to Teacher

Balloons are made of latex, a polymer material. Polymers are compounds which have large, long molecules that are generally in the shape of a chain. Polymers (like plastics) are very useful because of their flexibility, strength, and low cost. They also have the ability to resist stress and return to their original shape.

WHAT HAPPENED?

An inflated balloon normally pops when a pin hits it. This is because its tightly stretched latex surface is under a lot of **stress**! (In this case, the stress comes from the **force** of the air you **pushed** into the balloon.) When a pin makes a hole, the stressed latex can't deal with the rapidly rushing air, so it tears and the balloon explodes!

Some **materials** can handle a lot of stress. Others can be modified to increase their ability to handle stress. Sometimes stress areas can be bypassed altogether.

In Step 2, you increased an area's ability to handle stress. By adding the adhesive tape, you gave the latex some backing and support. In Step 3, your bypassed the stressed areas, focusing on a spot where the latex was not as stressed (stretched). When the pin made a hole, the material didn't tear, and the balloon didn't pop!

WHAT WE LEARNED

1 What did you predict in Step 1? How did this prediction reflect what actually happened?

Answers will vary, but should reflect logical comparisons.

2 What did you predict in Step 2? How did this prediction reflect what actually happened?

Answers will vary, but should reflect logical comparisons.

3 In Step 3, how did the surface of the balloon vary? What happened when you pushed the pin into the bottom? Why?

a) the bottom was thicker, less stretched

b) it didn't pop

c) the latex was not under much stress

4 Explain why every team's balloon exploded in Step 1, but most balloons didn't explode in Step 2 or Step 3.

In Step 1, the pins punctured high stress areas; in Steps 2 and 3 the pins punctured low stress areas.

5 Describe how adding a piece of adhesive tape changed the balloon's ability to handle stress.

Adding adhesive tape gave the balloon backing and support.

What Happened

Review the section with students. Emphasize bold-face words that identify key concepts and introduce new vocabulary.

An inflated balloon normally pops when a pin hits it. This is because its tightly stretched latex surface is under a lot of **stress**! *(In this case, the stress comes from the* **force** *of the air you* **pushed** *into the balloon.) When a pin makes a hole, the stressed latex can't deal with the rapidly rushing air, so it tears and the balloon explodes!*

Some **materials** *can handle a lot of stress. Others can be modified to increase their ability to handle stress. Sometimes stress areas can be bypassed altogether.*

In Step 2, you increased an area's ability to handle stress. By adding the adhesive tape, you gave the latex some backing and support. In Step 3, you bypassed the stressed areas, focusing on a spot where the latex was not as stressed (stretched). When the pin made a hole, the material didn't tear, and the balloon didn't pop!

What We Learned

Answers will vary. Suggested responses are shown at left.

Conclusion

Read this section aloud to the class to summarize the concepts learned in this activity.

Food for Thought

Read the Scripture aloud to the class. Talk about the importance of trusting God's word. Discuss ways we can get closer to the source of all knowledge.

Journal

If time permits, have a general class discussion about notes and drawings various students added to their journal pages. Discuss correct and incorrect predictions, and remind students that this "trial and error" process is part of the scientific process.

CONCLUSION

Stretching a material creates stress. Some materials handle stress well. Others can be modified to increase their stress-handling ability.

FOOD FOR THOUGHT

Daniel 6:3-24 Before this activity, everyone in your class probably thought that pins always pop balloons. But your teacher knew that wasn't true. The end result didn't fool your teacher, but it probably was a big surprise for you!

Daniel's enemies (and even his friends) were certain he would be eaten by those hungry lions. But God knew that wasn't true. God had other plans for Daniel. In the end, it was Daniel's enemies who became lunch for the lions! Which is more trustworthy — what everyone thinks is true, or what God says is true?

JOURNAL My Science Notes

Extended Teaching

1. Challenge students to interview someone born before 1940. Have them compare today's containers (mostly plastic) with containers from when they were young. Have students report their findings to the class.

2. Become "polymer predators." Challenge students to find and list as many polymer-based products as possible around school and at home. Combine their findings (and samples) to create a polymer bulletin board.

3. Using the Internet, have teams research recycling plastic. Challenge each team to create a plastics recycling poster based on their findings. Post these posters around the school.

4. Have teams discuss what life would be like without polymers. Have students write a story about how their lives would be different in a polymer-free world.

5. Invite a nurse to visit your classroom. Find out what the term "stress" means in medical terms. Have students write about how this is similar or different from the way the term is used in this lesson.

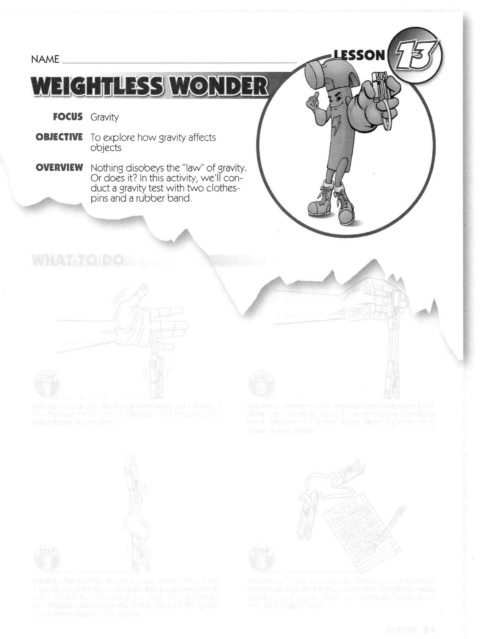

WEIGHTLESS WONDER

FOCUS Gravity

OBJECTIVE To explore how gravity affects objects

OVERVIEW Nothing disobeys the "law" of gravity. Or does it? In this activity, we'll conduct a gravity test with two clothespins and a rubber band.

LESSON 13

WHAT TO DO

Category

Physical Science
Forces

Focus

Gravity

Objective

To explore how gravity affects objects

National Standards

A1, A2, B1, B2, B3, G1, G2

Materials Needed

clothespins - 2
rubber band

Safety Concerns

Additional Comments

Students may need assistance in seeing that the rubber band in Step 3 is not as tight as in Step 2. Monitor teams to make sure every student has a turn to "drop" and a turn to "watch."

Overview

Read the overview aloud to your students. The goal is to create an atmosphere of curiosity and inquiry.

WHAT TO DO

Monitor student research teams as they complete each step.

WEIGHTLESS WONDER

FOCUS Gravity

OBJECTIVE To explore how gravity affects objects

OVERVIEW Nothing disobeys the "law" of gravity. Or does it? In this activity, we'll conduct a gravity test with two clothespins and a rubber band.

WHAT TO DO

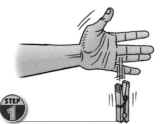

STEP 1

Pick up a clothespin. **Hold** your arm straight out in front of you. **Release** the clothespin. **Observe** what happens, and **make notes** in your journal.

STEP 2

Clip two clothespins onto a rubber band (see illustration). **Hold** one clothespin, letting the other hang by the rubber band. **Observe** the rubber band. **Draw** a picture of its shape in your journal.

STEP 3

Predict what will happen to the shape of the rubber band if you let go of the top clothespin. **Ask** a team member to watch closely from the side as you drop the top clothespin. **Discuss** what happened to the shape of the rubber band. **Make notes** in your journal.

STEP 4

Review each step in this activity. **Discuss** why the bottom clothespin appeared to be momentarily weightless. **Make notes** in your journal. **Share** and **compare** observations with your research team.

FORCES **61**

Teacher to Teacher

Newton's Second Law of Motion states that the larger the object or greater the acceleration, the greater the force produced. The formula for weight is Fw=mg. Fw is the symbol for weight or gravitional force, m is mass, and g is the acceleration rate. In general, the more there is of you (mass), the greater the weight.

WHAT HAPPENED?

When you dropped the top clothespin, it began to fall immediately. But the bottom clothespin hesitated — apparently weightless for a moment! What really happened is that **inertia** (and the **pull** of the rubber band) came into play. **Gravity** pulled on the clothespins equally. But since you let go of the top clothespin first, gravity pulled it down first while other forces kept the bottom clothespin in place a moment longer.

Let's look at this again. Before you released the clothespin, your upward pull was exactly equal to gravity's downward pull. That's why the clothespins didn't move. But when you let go of the top clothespin, the upward pulling force was gone! The result was a chain reaction. The top clothespin fell, the rubber band returned to its original shape, this pulled on the bottom clothespin, and the combination of pull and inertia made the bottom clothespin hesitate before falling.

WHAT WE LEARNED

1. Describe what happened to the clothespin in Step 1. What force affected it?

a) it fell straight down

b) gravity

2. Why didn't the clothespins fall in Step 2? What were the two opposing forces involved?

a) because the rubber band was holding it

b) gravity and your hand

3. What did you predict in Step 3? How did this prediction reflect what actually happened?

Answers will vary, but should reflect logical comparisons.

4. In Step 3, what force caused the rubber band to stretch? What two things caused it to bulge out?

a) gravity

b) inertia; action/reaction

5. Describe how various forces made the bottom clothespin appear momentarily weightless.

The rubber band and both clothespins were falling at the same rate, but the top clothespin started falling first, because the rubber band pulled up a little on the bottom clothespin.

What Happened

Review the section with students. Emphasize bold-face words that identify key concepts and introduce new vocabulary.

When you dropped the top clothespin, it began to fall immediately. But the bottom clothespin hesitated — apparently weightless for a moment! What really happened is that **inertia** *(and the* **pull** *of the rubber band) came into play.* **Gravity** *pulled on the clothespins equally. But since you let go of the top clothespin first, gravity pulled it down first, while other forces kept the bottom clothespin in place a moment longer.*

Let's look at this again. Before you released the clothespin, your upward pull was exactly equal to gravity's downward pull. That's why the clothespins didn't move.

But when you let go of the top clothespin, the upward pulling force was gone! The result was a chain reaction. The top clothespin fell, the rubber band returned to its original shape, this pulled on the bottom clothespin, and the combination of pull and inertia made the bottom clothespin hesitate before falling.

What We Learned

Answers will vary. Suggested responses are shown at left.

Conclusion

Read this section aloud to the class to summarize the concepts learned in this activity.

Food for Thought

Read the Scripture aloud to the class. Talk about what it takes to develop a relationship with God. Discuss how you can know that God is always with you.

Journal

If time permits, have a general class discussion about notes and drawings various students added to their journal pages. Discuss correct and incorrect predictions, and remind students that this "trial and error" process is part of the scientific process.

CONCLUSION

Forces can create the illusion of momentary weightlessness, but gravity and inertia still affect everything on Earth.

FOOD FOR THOUGHT

Job 26:7-14 Everything must obey the law of gravity. In this activity, gravity was exerting a constant pull on every object. No matter where you go in the Universe, gravity is present to some degree, constantly pulling you.

This Scripture reminds us that God is present everywhere. Like gravity, God is constantly pulling everyone closer, seeking to draw them into a relationship with him. Remember, no matter what happens, no matter how frightened or sad or lonely you become, God is always there for you.

JOURNAL My Science Notes

Extended Teaching

1. Invite a parachutist to visit your classroom. Discuss the sport and how a "free fall" feels. Have students write a paragraph about one thing they learn.

2. Using the Internet, have teams research gravity and "g forces." Challenge each team to create a poster depicting one thing they learn.

3. Take a field trip to a scuba shop. Find out how scuba divers deal with buoyancy (which is similar to weightlessness). Have students write a paragraph about one thing they learn.

4. Ask students, "Would your weight be the same on another planet?" Have teams discuss the difference between weight (pull of gravity) and mass (the amount of matter in an object).

5. Have teams research the effects of long-term weightlessness on astronauts. What are some of the problems associated with this (bone loss, muscle loss, etc.)? Have students write about one thing they learn.

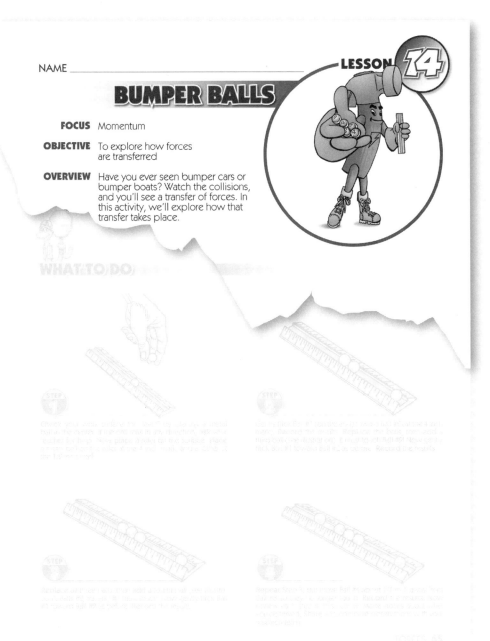

NAME _____

BUMPER BALLS

FOCUS Momentum

OBJECTIVE To explore how forces are transferred

OVERVIEW Have you ever seen bumper cars or bumper boats? Watch the collisions, and you'll see a transfer of forces. In this activity, we'll explore how that transfer takes place.

Category

Physical Science
Forces

Focus

Momentum

Objective

To explore how forces are transferred

National Standards

A1, A2, B1, B2, B3, E1, E2, F5, G1, G2

Materials Needed

metal balls - 5
ruler

Safety Concerns

4. Slipping
If balls fall on the floor, there is a potential for slipping. Remind students to exercise caution.

4. Other
Don't allow students to put the balls in their mouth. They can pose a choking hazard!

Additional Comments

Use the type of ruler that has a groove down the middle. If a work surface isn't level, put folded paper under a leg or thin pieces of paper under the ruler. Remind students to flick the balls *gently*! Too much force and the activity will not work properly.

Overview

Read the overview aloud to your students. The goal is to create an atmosphere of curiosity and inquiry.

WHAT TO DO

Monitor student research teams as they complete each step.

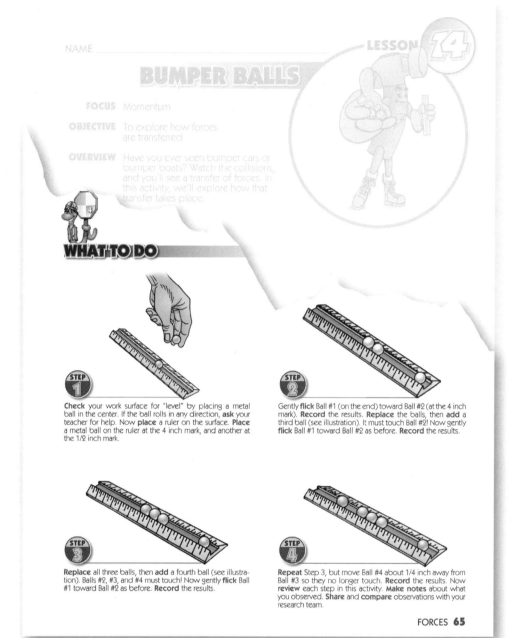

Teacher to Teacher

This activity demonstrates all three of Newton's "Laws of Motion." First, the ball moved when force was applied and kept moving until another force stopped it. That's inertia. Second, there was an observable relationship between mass, acceleration, and applied force. That's F = ma. Third, an action (flicking) created a reaction (balls moving). That's action/ reaction.

WHAT HAPPENED?

Did you find the results surprising? When the moving ball hit the target (transferring its momentum), only the last ball in line moved! No matter how many balls were in line, only the last one took off. That's because each stationary ball simply transferred the original momentum to the next one in line. Since the last ball had nothing to hold it back, it rolled away. Notice that the balls had to be touching, or the **force** couldn't transfer.

Any moving object has **momentum**. Momentum is a combination of how big an object is (**size**) and how fast it's moving (**speed**). If two objects are identical, then the faster one has more momentum. But a small object moving extremely fast (like a bullet) could have much more momentum than a large object moving slowly (like a sumo wrestler).

WHAT WE LEARNED

1 Why is it important for the work surface to be level for this activity? What might happen if it slanted slightly?

Answers should reflect the need to measure force from the ball, not from any rolling.

2 What happened to Ball #2 in the first part of Step 2? What happened in the second part of Step 2? Why were the results different?

a) Ball #2 rolled away

b) Ball #2 stayed put

c) force was transferred to Ball #3

3 Describe what happened in Step 3. Why didn't Ball #2 and Ball #3 move much? What happened to Ball #4? Why?

a) similar answers to #2

b) #4 rolled away when #1 struck the pile

c) force was transferred to the end ball

4 Why was it important for the balls to be touching in Step 2, Step 3, and Step 4? What would have happened to the momentum if there were gaps between the balls?

If balls are not touching, force can't be transferred, end ball will not move much (although middle one would move a little).

5 Momentum is a combination of what two factors? How can a small object have more momentum than a large one?

a) how big an object is and how fast it's moving

b) if the small object is moving much faster

What Happened

Review the section with students. Emphasize bold-face words that identify key concepts and introduce new vocabulary.

Did you find the results surprising? When the moving ball hit the target (transferring its momentum), only the last ball in line moved! No matter how many balls were in line, only the last one took off. That's because each stationary ball simply transferred the original momentum to the next one in line. Since the last ball had nothing to hold it back, it rolled away. Notice that the balls had to be touching, or the **force** *couldn't transfer.*

Any moving object has **momentum**. *Momentum is a combination of how big an object is (***size***) and how fast it's moving (***speed***). If two objects are identical, then the faster one has more momentum. But a small object moving extremely fast (like a bullet) could have much more momentum than a large object moving slowly (like a sumo wrestler).*

What We Learned

Answers will vary. Suggested responses are shown at left.

Conclusion

Read this section aloud to the class to summarize the concepts learned in this activity.

Food for Thought

Read the Scripture aloud to the class. Talk about the importance of God controlling our lives. Discuss ways we can "listen" to God and learn to follow his instructions.

Journal

If time permits, have a general class discussion about notes and drawings various students added to their journal pages. Discuss correct and incorrect predictions, and remind students that this "trial and error" process is part of the scientific process.

CONCLUSION

Momentum can be transferred between objects. Momentum is a combination of an object's size and its speed.

FOOD FOR THOUGHT

Isaiah 30:18, 21 Once you understood the principles involved, you were able to control the direction of momentum. By setting up the balls just so, you were able to transfer forces effectively and keep the balls from falling off the work surface.

This Scripture reminds us that God is waiting for us to let him take control of our lives. God understands and controls the forces around us. When we trust ourselves to his care, he is able to guide us to the correct path and keep us from falling. Our part is to learn to listen to God and follow his instructions.

JOURNAL My Science Notes

Extended Teaching

1. Repeat this activity with three balls at the 4 inch mark, and flicking two balls from the end. Have students compare the results with the original activity. How were they similar? How were they different?

2. Have someone bring a croquet set to school. Have them demonstrate how the game works. Have teams discuss how the behavior of the balls demonstrates momentum and the transfer of forces.

3. Invite a state trooper to visit your classroom. Ask him/her to explain the importance of seatbelts.

Discuss how momentum plays a role. Have students write a paragraph about one thing they learn.

4. Have teams discuss ways we protect ourselves from the laws of motion (seatbelts, helmets, padding, bumpers, etc.). Challenge each team to create a poster showing a specific safety device and how it works.

5. Take a field trip to a racquetball court. Watch how the players use momentum and force to control the ball. Have students write a paragraph about one thing they learn.

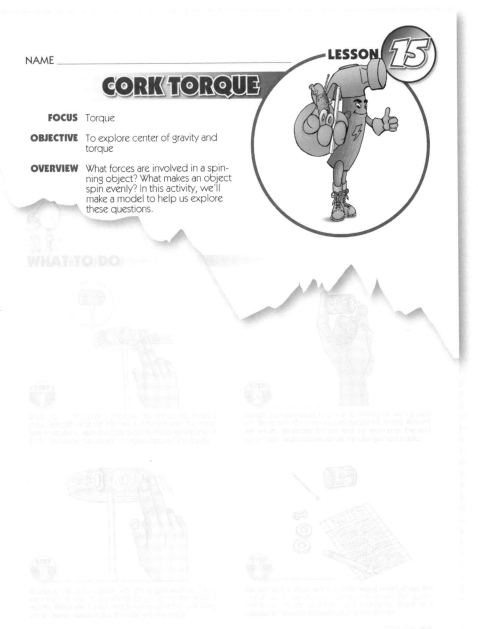

NAME _____

CORK TORQUE

FOCUS Torque

OBJECTIVE To explore center of gravity and torque

OVERVIEW What forces are involved in a spinning object? What makes an object spin evenly? In this activity, we'll make a model to help us explore these questions.

WHAT TO DO

Category
Physical Science
Forces

Focus
Torque

Objective
To explore center of gravity and torque

National Standards
A1, A2, B1, B2, B3, E1, E2, F5, G1, G2

Materials Needed
small cork
soda straw
straight pin
push pin
small washer
large washer

Safety Concerns
4. Sharp Object
Remind students to exercise caution with the straight pin and push pin.

Additional Comments

This activity includes two separate problems to solve. To avoid confusion, make sure students follow the instructions sequentially . Remind students to spin the cork gently. Too much force interferes with efficient action.

Overview

Read the overview aloud to your students. The goal is to create an atmosphere of curiosity and inquiry.

WHAT TO DO

Monitor student research teams as they complete each step.

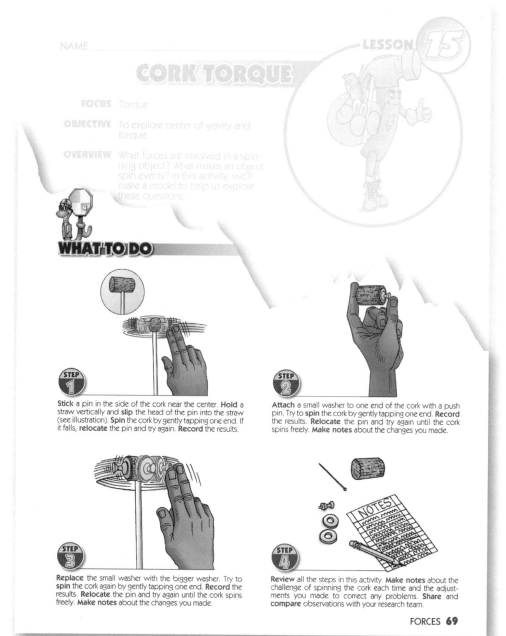

CORK TORQUE

FOCUS Torque

OBJECTIVE To explore center of gravity and torque

OVERVIEW What forces are involved in a spinning object? What makes an object spin evenly? In this activity, we'll make a model to help us explore these questions.

WHAT TO DO

STEP 1

Stick a pin in the side of the cork near the center. **Hold** a straw vertically and **slip** the head of the pin into the straw (see illustration). **Spin** the cork by gently tapping one end. If it falls, **relocate** the pin and try again. **Record** the results.

STEP 2

Attach a small washer to one end of the cork with a push pin. Try to **spin** the cork by gently tapping one end. **Record** the results. **Relocate** the pin and try again until the cork spins freely. **Make notes** about the changes you made.

STEP 3

Replace the small washer with the bigger washer. Try to **spin** the cork again by gently tapping one end. **Record** the results. **Relocate** the pin and try again until the cork spins freely. **Make notes** about the changes you made.

STEP 4

Review all the steps in this activity. **Make notes** about the challenge of spinning the cork each time and the adjustments you made to correct any problems. **Share** and **compare** observations with your research team.

FORCES **69**

Teacher to Teacher

Ever driven a car with an out-of-balance tire? The wobble and vibration you feel occur because the wheel's center of gravity is off center. When small lead weights are added to one side of the rim, they effectively relocate the center of gravity so that the tire is "balanced."

WHAT HAPPENED?

A twisting **force** is called **torque**. To **balance** torque, you have to find the **center of gravity**. Putting a pin in the exact center of the cork helped it spin freely. But when you added weight to one side, the center of gravity changed. You had to move the pin to get the cork to spin freely again.

An object's center of gravity is related to its **shape** and **mass**. A ruler balances easily at the center because it's almost identical on both sides of that point. But a baseball bat is much heavier on one end. You have to move toward the heavy end of the bat to find its center of gravity. Balancing a teeter-totter is similar, except instead of moving the balance point, we move the **weight** toward or away from the middle to shift the center of gravity.

WHAT WE LEARNED

1 Compare Step 1 with Step 2. How were they similar? How were they different? What did you change to rebalance the cork?

a) similar: same procedure

b) different: added washer

c) changed location of pin

2 Describe Step 3. What did you do with the support pin to make the cork spin freely? Why?

a) answers will vary

b) relocated it

c) to reflect the new center of gravity

3 What is a "twisting force" called? What might happen if this force is not balanced?

a) torque

b) things wobble, vibrate, don't spin smoothly, etc.

4 If you added an even bigger washer in Step 3, which way would the support pin need to move? Why?

a) closer to the washer

b) the added weight would shift the center of gravity

5 Using what you've learned in this activity, explain why the spinning parts of an engine must be balanced.

Without balanced parts, an engine can't run smoothly, it vibrates, it may rattle apart, etc.

What Happened

Review the section with students. Emphasize bold-face words that identify key concepts and introduce new vocabulary.

*A twisting **force** is called **torque**. To **balance** torque, you have to find the **center of gravity**. Putting a pin in the exact center of the cork helped it spin freely. But when you added weight to one side, the center of gravity changed. You had to move the pin to get the cork to spin freely again.*

*An object's center of gravity is related to its **shape** and **mass**. A ruler balances easily at the center because it's almost identical on both sides of that point. But a baseball bat is much heavier on one end. You have to move toward the heavy end of the bat to find its center of gravity. Balancing a teeter-totter is similar, except instead of moving the balance point, we move the **weight** toward or away from the middle to shift the center of gravity.*

What We Learned

Answers will vary. Suggested responses are shown at left.

Conclusion

Read this section aloud to the class to summarize the concepts learned in this activity.

Food for Thought

Read the Scripture aloud to the class. Talk about the importance of learning to trust God. Discuss ways we can share God's love and compassion with those in need.

Journal

If time permits, have a general class discussion about notes and drawings various students added to their journal pages. Discuss correct and incorrect predictions, and remind students that this "trial and error" process is part of the scientific process.

CONCLUSION

Twisting force is called torque. Balancing torque requires locating the center of gravity — the point around which a spinning object turns freely.

FOOD FOR THOUGHT

Proverbs 12:25 Once you understand how torque works, balancing the cork isn't too hard. But the pin only has to be pushed a little bit off center to start creating problems again!

Many people face tragedies (a death, an accident, etc.) that throw them off balance. But this Scripture reminds us that a word of encouragement does wonders! As God's children, we must always be ready to share his love and caring compassion with others — especially when their hearts are heavy. Kind words don't make a tragedy go away, but they can often help someone recover that needed balance.

JOURNAL My Science Notes

Extended Teaching

1. Take a field trip to a tire shop. Find out how tires are balanced. What makes some tires wear until they can't be balanced? Have students write a paragraph about one thing they learn.

2. Invite a local coach to visit your classroom. Have him/her describe how adjusting their center of gravity helps athletes in sports. Ask him/her to demonstrate. Have students write a paragraph about one thing they learn.

3. Challenge teams to find the center of gravity of various objects by balancing them on the tip of a pencil. Have them record the results, then share their findings with the class.

4. Winter weather can cause chunks of ice to freeze on a tire's rim. Challenge teams to explain why this could cause vibration. Encourage them to create drawings to support their ideas.

5. Using the Internet, research back problems in children caused by heavy bookpacks. Challenge teams to explain how this relates to center of gravity. Encourage them to come up with possible solutions.

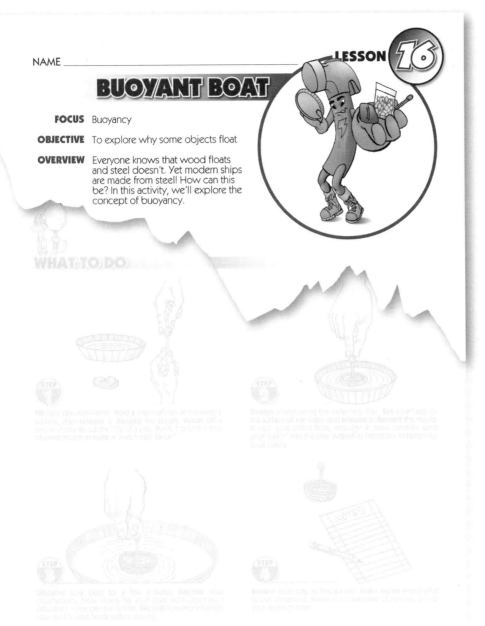

NAME _____

BUOYANT BOAT

LESSON **16**

FOCUS Buoyancy

OBJECTIVE To explore why some objects float

OVERVIEW Everyone knows that wood floats and steel doesn't. Yet modern ships are made from steel! How can this be? In this activity, we'll explore the concept of buoyancy.

WHAT TO DO

FORCES **73**

Category

Physical Science
Forces

Focus

Buoyancy

Objective

To explore why some objects float

National Standards

A1, A2, B1, B2, B3, E1, E2, F5, G1, G2

Materials Needed

clay
matchstick
popcorn seeds
pie pan
water
paper towels

Safety Concerns

4. **Slipping**
There is a potential for spills with this activity. Remind students to exercise caution.

Additional Comments

Use large wooden matches for the "sailor" in this activity. (Be sure to remove the flammable heads in advance!) Clay pieces should be the same size so research teams can compare final results accurately.

Overview

Read the overview aloud to your students. The goal is to create an atmosphere of curiosity and inquiry.

WHAT TO DO

Monitor student research teams as they complete each step.

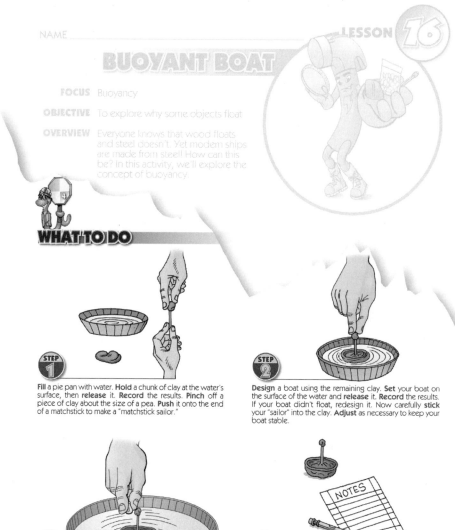

BUOYANT BOAT

FOCUS Buoyancy

OBJECTIVE To explore why some objects float

OVERVIEW Everyone knows that wood floats and steel doesn't. Yet modern ships are made from steel! How can this be? In this activity, we'll explore the concept of buoyancy.

WHAT TO DO

STEP 1
Fill a pie pan with water. **Hold** a chunk of clay at the water's surface, then **release** it. **Record** the results. **Pinch** off a piece of clay about the size of a pea. **Push** it onto the end of a matchstick to make a "matchstick sailor."

STEP 2
Design a boat using the remaining clay. **Set** your boat on the surface of the water and **release** it. **Record** the results. If your boat didn't float, redesign it. Now carefully **stick** your "sailor" into the clay. **Adjust** as necessary to keep your boat stable.

STEP 3
Observe your boat for a few minutes. **Record** your observations. Now slowly **fill** your boat with unpopped popcorn — one piece at a time. **Record** how many kernels your team's boat holds before sinking.

STEP 4
Review each step in this activity. **Make notes** about what you've observed. **Share** and **compare** observations with your research team.

FORCES **73**

Teacher to Teacher

This activity demonstrates the "trial and error" method common among inventors. Using persistance, patience, and observation, an inventor tries something, analyzes the results, makes changes, then tries again. Many scientific discoveries, from vulcanization to velcro to Post-It® notes, have come as a result of such a process.

WHAT HAPPENED?

All **matter** on Earth is constantly being **pulled** downward by **gravity**. To keep an object from sinking in the water, gravity has to be overcome. (**pushed**) by another **force**. The opposing force we see pushing in this activity is called **buoyancy**.

When you dropped the chunk of clay in Step 1, it sank. When you molded the same clay into a boat shape, it began to float! How is this possible? The boat shape allowed the clay to **displace** (shove aside) the water. If the water displaced **weighs** more than boat and its contents, the boat floats. But if the boat and contents weigh more than the water (as it did when you added enough corn), then the boat sinks.

WHAT WE LEARNED

1 What were the two opposing forces in this activity? What determined which force won?

a) gravity, buoyancy

b) buoyancy at first, but gravity always wins in the end

2 Compare the clay used in Step 1 and Step 2. How was it the same? How was it different?

a) same: it was the same clay

b) different: small piece used in Step 1, large in Step 2; dry in Step 1, wet in Step 2, etc.

3 How much corn did your boat hold before sinking? How were the more successful boats different from the others?

a) answers will vary

b) answers will vary but should reflect logical arguments

4 When a boat builder talks about the boat's "displacement," what does this mean?

The amount of water that the hull of the boat replaces.

5 Based on what you've learned, why would a boat sink if a hole let water in?

Water is heavier than air, making the boat heavier so it sinks.

What Happened

Review the section with students. Emphasize bold-face words that identify key concepts and introduce new vocabulary.

*All **matter** on Earth is constantly being **pulled** downward by **gravity**. To keep an object from sinking in the water, gravity has to be overcome (**pushed**) by another **force**. The opposing force we see pushing in this activity is called **buoyancy**.*

*When you dropped the chunk of clay in Step 1, it sank. When you molded the same clay into a boat shape, it began to float! How is this possible? The boat shape allowed the clay to **displace** (shove aside) the water. If the water displaced **weighs** more than boat and its contents, the boat floats. But if the boat and contents weigh more than the water (as it did when you added enough popcorn seeds), then the boat sinks.*

What We Learned

Answers will vary. Suggested responses are shown at left.

Conclusion

Read this section aloud to the class to summarize the concepts learned in this activity.

Food for Thought

Read the Scripture aloud to the class. Talk about God's love and how it supports us. Discuss ways we can get closer to the source of love and power.

Journal

If time permits, have a general class discussion about notes and drawings various students added to their journal pages. Discuss correct and incorrect predictions, and remind students that this "trial and error" process is part of the scientific process.

CONCLUSION
The displacement of water can create buoyancy. Buoyancy and gravity are opposing forces.

FOOD FOR THOUGHT
Acts 27:39-41 Your clay boat was hardly seaworthy, but it did manage to float in your pie pan pond. As long as the force of buoyancy kept holding it up, your popcorn cargo survived. When the boat was overloaded, water poured in and it sank.

Scripture tells of a frightening shipwreck Paul experienced. As the ship struck the rocks, water began to rush in. The ship no longer had the support of buoyancy and it sank. People can be like that, too. Without God's support, the burdens of life can overload them as trials and obstacles rush in and drag them down. Only God's love can help us weather the storms of life!

JOURNAL My Science Notes

Extended Teaching

1. The "sailor" in this activity helps expand the torque concept from our last lesson. Have teams compare a standing sailor to one lying down, then explain the role torque plays on a boat's stability.

2. Take a field trip to a boat dealer. Compare different kinds of boats (pontoons, canoes, V-hull, etc.) and what makes them float. Find out about displacement. Have students write a paragraph about one thing they learn.

3. Invite a boat builder to visit your classroom. Ask him/her to talk about the process, and what is needed to make a boat seaworthy. Have students write a paragraph about one thing they learn.

4. Use the Internet to research famous shipwrecks and their causes. Challenge each team to create a poster describing one such wreck. Find out what was done to help prevent the same thing from happening again.

5. Use the Internet to find historic examples of trial-and-error research (Thomas Edison and filaments for light bulbs, Charles Goodyear and vulcanization, etc.). Challenge teams to present their findings to the class.

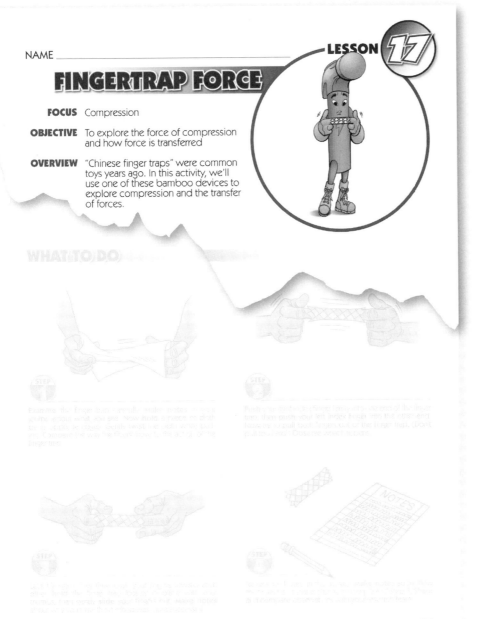

NAME _____

FINGERTRAP FORCE

LESSON 17

FOCUS Compression

OBJECTIVE To explore the force of compression and how force is transferred

OVERVIEW "Chinese finger traps" were common toys years ago. In this activity, we'll use one of these bamboo devices to explore compression and the transfer of forces.

Category

Physical Science
Forces

Focus

Compression

Objective

To explore compression and how force is transferred

National Standards

A1, A2, B1, B2, B3, E1, E2, F5, G1, G2

Materials Needed

chinese finger trap
piece of cloth

Safety Concerns

Additional Comments

Chinese finger traps were popular toys in our grandparents' day, but today's tech-oriented students may never have seen one. Don't let them pull too hard or they may hurt themselves or damage the toy. *(Warning: Stay away from Internet research on this one! The terms "fingercuff" or "finger trap" are counter-culture slang for sexually-deviant behavior.)*

Overview

Read the overview aloud to your students. The goal is to create an atmosphere of curiosity and inquiry.

WHAT TO DO

Monitor student research teams as they complete each step.

NAME

FINGERTRAP FORCE

LESSON 17

FOCUS Compression

OBJECTIVE To explore the force of compression and how force is transferred

OVERVIEW "Chinese finger traps" were common toys years ago. In this activity, we'll use one of these bamboo devices to explore compression and the transfer of forces.

WHAT TO DO

STEP 1

Examine the finger trap carefully. **Make notes** in your journal about what you see. Now **hold** a piece of cloth by its opposite edges. Gently **twist** the cloth while pulling. **Compare** the way the fibers move to the action of the finger trap.

STEP 2

Push your right index finger firmly into one end of the finger trap, then **push** your left index finger into the other end. Now try to **pull** both fingers out of the finger trap. (Don't pull too hard!) **Observe** what happens.

STEP 3

Let's try again. This **time** push your fingers toward each other, **hold** the finger trap loosely in place with your thumbs, then gently **slide** your fingers out. **Make notes** about why you think this method was more successful.

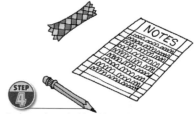

STEP 4

Review each step in this activity. **Make notes** about how the finger trap's shape changed in Step 2 and Step 3. **Share** and **compare** observations with your research team.

FORCES **77**

Teacher to Teacher

This activity demonstrates how forces can be transferred and absorbed. The structure of the finger trap allows the relatively weak straw to absorb and transfer tremendous force! Examples of materials designed to absorb or transfer force include the cartilage between joints, the foam in a bicycle helmet, and the webbing of a seat belt.

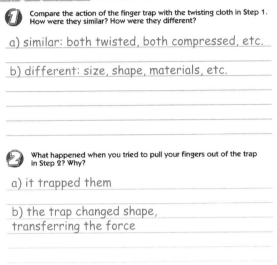

WHAT HAPPENED?

When you **pushed** your fingers into the trap, it changed shape slightly to let them in. But when you started to **pull** them out again, the trap changed shape to grab your fingers! As you pulled harder, the **force** of your **muscles** was **transferred** to the trap, causing it to **twist** and compress even more tightly around your fingers.

The trap works because of the interlocking, woven strips. Pushing in separates the strips slightly, but pulling out binds them more tightly together. As you discovered, the only way to get out was to understand the forces involved and work with them, not against them!

WHAT WE LEARNED

1 Compare the action of the finger trap with the twisting cloth in Step 1. How were they similar? How were they different?

a) similar: both twisted, both compressed, etc.

b) different: size, shape, materials, etc.

2 What happened when you tried to pull your fingers out of the trap in Step 2? Why?

a) it trapped them

b) the trap changed shape, transferring the force

3 What happened when you tried to pull your fingers out of the trap in Step 3? Why?

a) they came out

b) pushing the trap in kept it from twisting

4 How did the shape of the finger trap change in each step? What caused this to occur?

a) answers will vary, but should accurately reflect steps

b) the interlocking, woven strips

5 Describe how this activity demonstrated a transfer of force. Where did the force originate?

a) pulling force converted to a strong push against fingers

b) muscles, arms, etc.

What Happened

Review the section with students. Emphasize bold-face words that identify key concepts and introduce new vocabulary.

*When you **pushed** your fingers into the trap, it changed shape slightly to let them in. But when you started to **pull** them out again, the trap changed shape to grab your fingers! As you pulled harder, the **force** of your **muscles** was **transferred** to the trap, causing it to **twist** and compress even more tightly around your fingers.*

The trap works because of the interlocking, woven strips. Pushing in separates the strips slightly, but pulling out binds them more tightly together. As you discovered, the only way to get out was to understand the forces involved and work with them, not against them!

What We Learned

Answers will vary. Suggested responses are shown at left.

Conclusion

Read this section aloud to the class to summarize the concepts learned in this activity.

Food for Thought

Read the Scripture aloud to the class. Talk about the difference between working on our problems ourselves versus working on our relationship with God and placing our problems in his hands.

Journal

If time permits, have a general class discussion about notes and drawings various students added to their journal pages. Discuss correct and incorrect predictions, and remind students that this "trial and error" process is part of the scientific process.

CONCLUSION

Forces can be transferred from one place to another.

FOOD FOR THOUGHT

Galatians 3:21-22 With a finger trap, the harder you try to force your way out, the more you're trapped! You can only be set free by understanding the forces involved and following the rules.

Life is like a finger trap. The harder we try without God's help, the more difficult things become. We're quickly caught in the awful grip of sin! But by spending time with God, we learn to understand the forces involved. Give in to the finger trap, and your fingers are free. Give in to God, and your soul is free!

JOURNAL My Science Notes

_____
_____
_____
_____
_____
_____
_____
_____
_____
_____
_____
_____
_____
_____
_____
_____

80 FORCES

Extended Teaching

1. Have teams test paper towels for strength by placing a large washer on a wet paper towel, then lifting. How do woven towels compare to non-woven? Do layers help? Have teams share and compare their findings.

2. Invite a police officer to visit your classroom. Find out about restraints (physcial and mechanical) used in law enforcement. Discuss forces and leverage. Have students write a paragraph about one thing they learn.

3. Bulletproof vests are made of a woven material called Kevlar. Have teams research this amazing material. Challenge teams to create a poster showing how Kevlar works.

4. Take a field trip to a location where textiles are woven or baskets are made. Find out how woven layers increase the strength of the final product. Have students write a paragraph about one thing they learn.

5. Have teams research various ways forces are transferred. Have them share their findings with the class. Challenge teams to draw pictures or write descriptions for a class bulletin board on the transfer of forces.

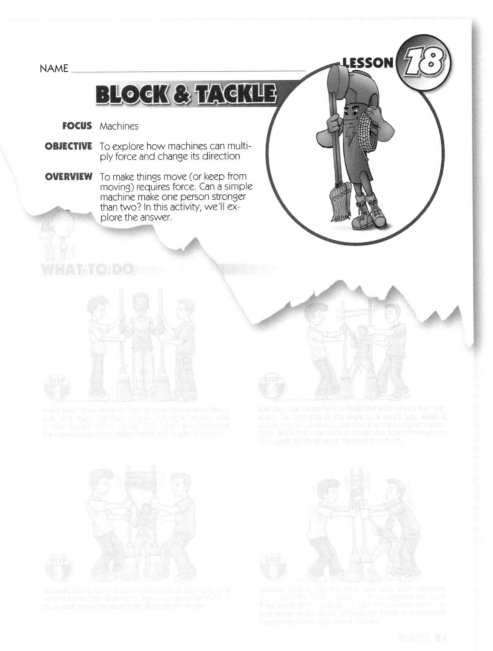

BLOCK & TACKLE

LESSON 18

FOCUS Machines

OBJECTIVE To explore how machines can multiply force and change its direction

OVERVIEW To make things move (or keep from moving) requires force. Can a simple machine make one person stronger than two? In this activity, we'll explore the answer.

WHAT TO DO

Category

Physical Science
Forces

Focus

Machines

Objective

To explore how machines can multiply force and change its direction

National Standards

A1, A2, B1, B2, B3, E1, E2, F5, G1, G2

Materials Needed

brooms - 2
rope - 20 feet

Safety Concerns

4. Other
See cautions under "Additional Comments" below.

Additional Comments

Focus on the fact that a block and tackle arrangement allows one student (on the rope) to exert more force than two students (on the broomsticks). Depending on your students, you may wish to do this activity as a demonstration. Too much force can break a broomstick, cause students to lose their balance, or lead to rope burns!

Overview

Read the overview aloud to your students. The goal is to create an atmosphere of curiosity and inquiry.

WHAT TO DO

Monitor student research teams as they complete each step.

NAME

BLOCK & TACKLE

LESSON 18

FOCUS Machines

OBJECTIVE To explore how machines can multiply force and change its direction

OVERVIEW To make things move (or keep from moving) requires force. Can a simple machine make one person stronger than two? In this activity, we'll explore the answer.

WHAT TO DO

STEP 1

Hold two broomsticks in front of you, one in each hand. **Ask** one team member to grab the right broom, and another the left. When you say "Go!" have them gently **pull** the broomsticks apart. **Make notes** about what happens.

STEP 2

Ask two team members to **hold** the sticks about two feet apart. **Tie** one end of the rope to a stick's top, **wrap** it around the second stick, then back to the first (see illustration). **Hold** the rope tight and **ask** your team members to try to **pull** the sticks apart. **Record** the results.

STEP 3

Repeat Step 2, but this time **wrap** the rope back and forth several times (see illustration). **Ask** your team members to try to **pull** the sticks apart again. **Record** the results.

STEP 4

Repeat Step 3, but this time have your team members try to hold the sticks steady while you **tighten** the rope. **Take up** as much rope as you can. Now **review** each step and **make notes** about differences. **Share** and **compare** observations with your research team.

FORCES **81**

Teacher to Teacher

There are six simple machines: lever, inclined plane, wheel and axle, wedge, screw, and pulley. A block and tackle is a compound machine because it's like a complex pulley that uses more than one wheel and axle. Though not complex, this machine can greatly multiply human force, allowing a person to easily lift items weighing several times their own weight.

WHAT HAPPENED?

The "block and tackle" you created is actually a **compound machine** made from two **simple machines** — two different **wheels** and **axles**. In this activity, the broomsticks played the role of two axles and the rope acted like a set of wheels. Machines with block and tackle arrangements can lift or hold tremendous amounts of **weight** with minimal amounts of **force**.

Notice that in addition to increasing the force, the machine changed the **direction** of the force. (The two people on the broomsticks were **pulling** in different directions from the person controlling the rope.) A car jack is a similar example. A relatively light downward **push** will raise up a very heavy car. The force provided by a person's muscles is both **multiplied** *and* sent in a different direction.

WHAT WE LEARNED

1 Compare Step 2 and Step 3. How were they similar? How were they different?

a) same procedure, same people

b) rope looped different giving rope-person more force

2 Compare Step 3 and Step 4. How were they similar? How were they different?

a) same materials, same people

b) stick people pulling in Step 3; rope person pulling in Step 4

82 FORCES

3 Describe what happened in Step 4. How did this demonstrate the transfer of forces?

a) one rope person was able to overpower two stick holders

b) answers will vary

4 What two simple machines did the rope/broomstick arrangement imitate? How did it change the direction of a force?

a) wheel and axle; pulley

b) rope person and stick people were pulling different directions

5 Give another example of a machine that either multiplies force or changes its direction. Tell how it works.

answers will vary (car jack, can opener, teeter-totter, etc.)

What Happened

Review the section with students. Emphasize bold-face words that identify key concepts and introduce new vocabulary.

The "block and tackle" you created is actually a **compound machine** *made from two* **simple machines** *— two different* **wheels** *and* **axles**. *In this activity, the broomsticks played the role of two axles and the rope acted like a set of wheels. Machines with block and tackle arrangements can lift or hold tremendous amounts of* **weight** *with minimal amounts of* **force**.

Notice that in addition to increasing the force, the machine changed the **direction** *of the force. (The two people on the broomsticks were* **pulling** *in different directions from the person controlling the rope.) A car jack is a similar example. A relatively light downward* **push** *will raise up a very heavy car. The force provided by a person's muscles is both* **multiplied** *and sent in a different direction.*

What We Learned

Answers will vary. Suggested responses are shown at left.

Conclusion

Read this section aloud to the class to summarize the concepts learned in this activity.

Food for Thought

Read the Scripture aloud to the class. Talk about the importance of spending time with God each day. Discuss things we can do to set aside this special time with God.

Journal

If time permits, have a general class discussion about notes and drawings various students added to their journal pages. Discuss correct and incorrect predictions, and remind students that this "trial and error" process is part of the scientific process.

CONCLUSION

Machines can multiply force. They can also change the direction of a force.

FOOD FOR THOUGHT

Isaiah 40:29-31 In this activity, we saw how a simple machine was able to multiply the force of one person so they could overpower the strength of two. Machines are wonderful devices to help us increase our force.

Of course, no machine can equal the amazing power that comes from God! This Scripture reminds us that we all have times when we're tired or weak, ready to give up. But if you spend time every day learning to trust him, God can fill you with life-giving strength.

JOURNAL My Science Notes

Extended Teaching

1. Have teams research the six different types of simple machines. Challenge teams to create a six-part poster describing each machine and showing an example of each.

2. Take a field trip to an automotive repair facility or machine shop. Ask them to demonstrate the use of a chain hoist (a type of block and tackle). Have students write a paragraph about at least one thing they learn.

3. Invite a carpenter to visit your classroom and bring a selection of hand tools. Challenge teams to examine each tool and apply something they've learned (screwdriver = torque; hammer = lever; etc.).

4. Have teams search the school for examples of simple machines. Record the results. Challenge teams to create drawings and descriptions for a "Simple Machines" bulletin board.

5. Have students write a story telling at least three ways their day would be different without simple machines.

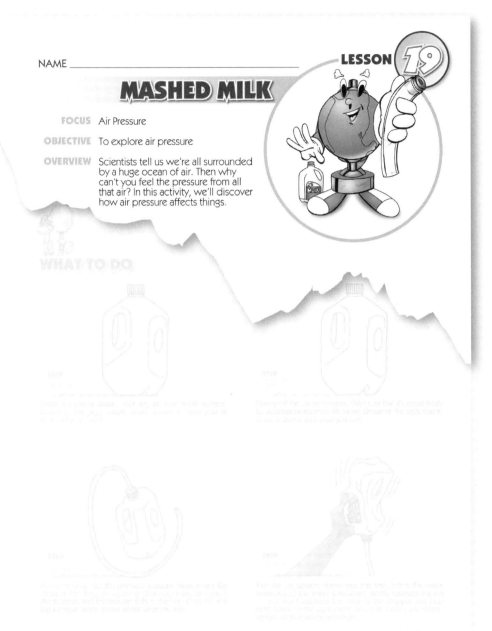

NAME _____

MASHED MILK

FOCUS Air Pressure

OBJECTIVE To explore air pressure

OVERVIEW Scientists tell us we're all surrounded by a huge ocean of air. Then why can't you feel the pressure from all that air? In this activity, we'll discover how air pressure affects things.

Category
Earth Science

Focus
Air Pressure

Objective
To explore air pressure

National Standards
A1, A2, B1, B2, B3, D1, G1, G2

Materials Needed
clear hose
one-hole stopper
milk jug
water
sink

Safety Concerns
4. Slipping
There is a potential for spills. Remind students to exercise caution with water.

Additional Comments

The sink (or container) should have sides high enough to contain the flowing water. Encourage students to squeeze the jug very gently if the water doesn't immediately begin draining out.

Overview

Read the overview aloud to your students. The goal is to create an atmosphere of curiosity and inquiry.

WHAT TO DO

Monitor student research teams as they complete each step.

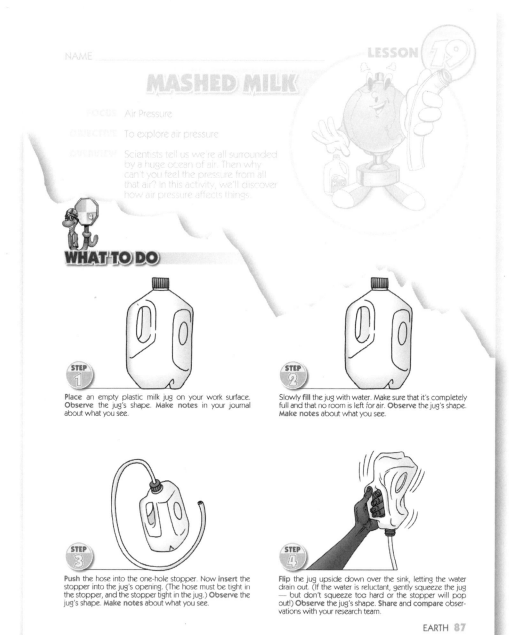

LESSON 19

MASHED MILK

FOCUS   Air Pressure

OBJECTIVE   To explore air pressure

OVERVIEW   Scientists tell us we're all surrounded by a huge ocean of air. Then why can't you feel the pressure from all that air? In this activity, we'll discover how air pressure affects things.

WHAT TO DO

STEP 1
Place an empty plastic milk jug on your work surface. **Observe** the jug's shape. **Make notes** in your journal about what you see.

STEP 2
Slowly **fill** the jug with water. Make sure that it's completely full and that no room is left for air. **Observe** the jug's shape. **Make notes** about what you see.

STEP 3
Push the hose into the one-hole stopper. Now **insert** the stopper into the jug's opening. (The hose must be tight in the stopper, and the stopper tight in the jug.) **Observe** the jug's shape. **Make notes** about what you see.

STEP 4
Flip the jug upside down over the sink, letting the water drain out. (If the water is reluctant, gently squeeze the jug — but don't squeeze too hard or the stopper will pop out!) **Observe** the jug's shape. **Share** and **compare** observations with your research team.

EARTH **87**

Teacher to Teacher

Gases and liquids are fluids. Fluids have "pressure" — the force pushing or pulling on a given unit of area. In this activity, gravity not only pulled the water out of the jug, it took the pressure with it.

This activity also demonstrates the fact that air pressure is all around us. It helped crush the jug!

WHAT HAPPENED?

The empty jug didn't crush because the **pressure** of the air (**atmosphere**) was the same inside and out. Scientists call this kind of balance **equilibrium**. You could tell the air pressure was equal because the jug didn't collapse. Then you filled the jug with water. Although the air was completely removed, the jug still didn't collapse since the air pressure outside was the same as the water pressure inside.

Then you flipped the jug upside down, and the plastic tubing let the water escape. This caused the water pressure inside to begin dropping. No air could get back in to equalize the pressure! As the pressure **pushing** out became weaker and weaker, it allowed the pressure outside to push in and crush the container.

 WHAT WE LEARNED

1 Describe the jug in Step 1, Step 2, and Step 3. How did it look similar? How did it look different?

Step 1: empty, normal
Step 2: full of water, normal
Step 3: full of water, hose in top, normal

2 Why didn't air pressure crush the jug in Step 1? Why didn't it crush the jug in Step 2?

In both steps, there was equal air pressure inside and outside the jug.

88 EARTH

3 Explain why the jug crushed in Step 4.

Water pulled air out of jug as it drained; low pressure inside/high pressure outside crushed jug.

4 If you opened a large hole in the bottom of the upside-down jug while it was emptying, would it still have crushed? Why or why not?

a) no

b) air could get into the jug to equalize pressure

5 Based on what you've learned, why do most gasoline cans have a small hole opposite the spout?

So air can get in to equalize the pressure inside and outside the can as you pour.

What Happened

Review the section with students. Emphasize bold-face words that identify key concepts and introduce new vocabulary.

The empty jug didn't crush because the **pressure** *of the air (**atmosphere**) was the same inside and out. Scientists call this kind of balance* **equilibrium**. *You could tell the air pressure was equal because the jug didn't collapse. Then you filled the jug with water. Although the air was completely removed, the jug still didn't collapse since the air pressure outside was the same as the water pressure inside.*

Then you flipped the jug upside down, and the plastic tubing let the water escape. This caused the water pressure inside to begin dropping. No air could get back in to **equalize** *the pressure! As the pressure* **pushing** *out became weaker and weaker, it allowed the pressure outside to push in and crush the container.*

What We Learned

Answers will vary. Suggested responses are shown at left.

Conclusion

Read this section aloud to the class to summarize the concepts learned in this activity.

Food for Thought

Read the Scripture aloud to the class. Talk about problems and pressures students feel. Discuss how we can learn to rely on God to make us strong inside.

Journal

If time permits, have a general class discussion about notes and drawings various students added to their journal pages. Discuss correct and incorrect predictions, and remind students that this "trial and error" process is part of the scientific process.

? CONCLUSION

Balanced pressures create equilibrium. Major differences in pressure can create strong forces.

FOOD FOR THOUGHT

Psalm 29:11 Your milk jug is a good example of what happens when pressures push in. When the inside becomes weak and the pressure from the outside is strong, the jug collapses.

People are a lot like that milk jug. We live in a world full of problems and pressures. Unless we learn to rely on God to make us strong inside, those outside pressures can crush us. Spend time getting to know God better, and he will fill you with the strength to withstand the world.

JOURNAL, My Science Notes

Extended Teaching

1. Repeat this activity. As water begins to drain, poke a large hole in the top of the jug. Have students compare the results with the original activity. How were they similar? How were they different?

2. Using the Internet, have teams research the difference in air pressure between mountain tops and sea level. Discuss why mountain climbing equipment includes oxygen tanks.

3. Challenge teams to find and list examples of balanced forces working against each other (teeter-totter, tightrope walker, etc.). Have them share their findings with the class.

4. Invite a diver to visit your classroom. Talk about differences in pressure and how this affects diving. Have students write a paragraph about one thing they learn.

5. Take a field trip to a factory that uses air-powered equipment. Find out how the air pressure is produced and how it is used to perform work. Have students write a paragraph about one thing they learn.

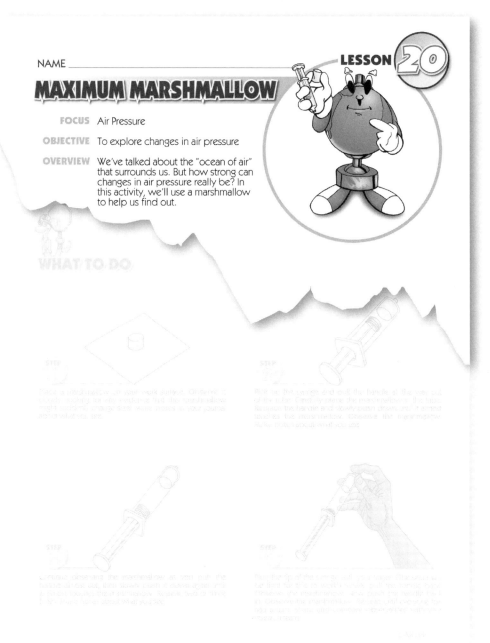

MAXIMUM MARSHMALLOW

LESSON 20

FOCUS Air Pressure

OBJECTIVE To explore changes in air pressure

OVERVIEW We've talked about the "ocean of air" that surrounds us. But how strong can changes in air pressure really be? In this activity, we'll use a marshmallow to help us find out.

WHAT TO DO

Category
Earth Science

Focus
Air Pressure

Objective
To explore changes in air pressure

National Standards
A1, A2, B1, B2, B3, D1, G1, G2

Materials Needed
syringe
mini-marshmallow

Safety Concerns
3. Hygiene
Don't allow students to eat marshmallows!

Additional Comments

Wash and dry the syringes well after you complete this activity. Monitor students to make sure they take turns. Multiple repetitions of Step 4 by the same person can blister a sensitive fingertip!

Overview

Read the overview aloud to your students. The goal is to create an atmosphere of curiosity and inquiry.

WHAT TO DO

Monitor student research teams as they complete each step.

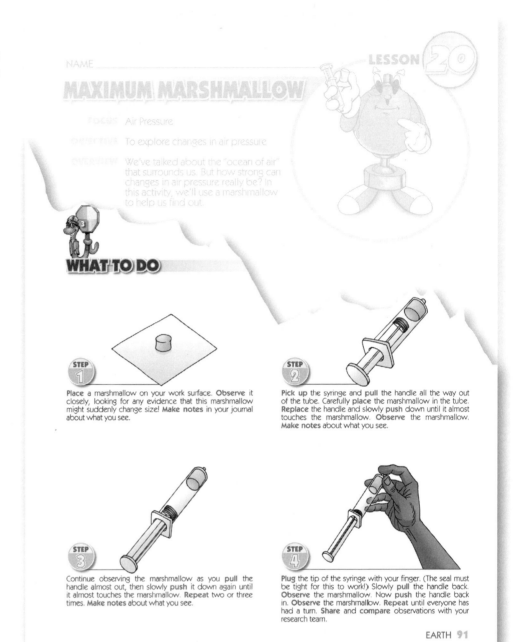

MAXIMUM MARSHMALLOW

LESSON 20

FOCUS Air Pressure

OBJECTIVE To explore changes in air pressure

OVERVIEW We've talked about the "ocean of air" that surrounds us. But how strong can changes in air pressure really be? In this activity, we'll use a marshmallow to help us find out.

WHAT TO DO

STEP 1
Place a marshmallow on your work surface. **Observe** it closely, looking for any evidence that this marshmallow might suddenly change size! **Make notes** in your journal about what you see.

STEP 2
Pick up the syringe and **pull** the handle all the way out of the tube. Carefully **place** the marshmallow in the tube. **Replace** the handle and slowly **push** down until it almost touches the marshmallow. **Observe** the marshmallow. **Make notes** about what you see.

STEP 3
Continue observing the marshmallow as you **pull** the handle almost out, then slowly **push** it down again until it almost touches the marshmallow. **Repeat** two or three times. **Make notes** about what you see.

STEP 4
Plug the tip of the syringe with your finger. (The seal must be tight for this to work!) Slowly **pull** the handle back. **Observe** the marshmallow. Now **push** the handle back in. **Observe** the marshmallow. **Repeat** until everyone has had a turn. **Share** and **compare** observations with your research team.

EARTH **91**

Teacher to Teacher

The most visible effect of air pressure on Earth is our weather. High pressure is like a dome or mountain of air and low pressure is like a valley. Clouds (and their attendant moisture) tend to flow "downhill," leaving high pressure areas clear and low pressure areas filled with clouds.

WHAT HAPPENED?

Air pressure is the **force** of the air constantly **pushing** all around us. Except during violent weather, we usually don't have an opportunity to see big changes in air pressure. That's because the **atmosphere** is huge, and air pressure changes normally happen very slowly.

By using the syringe, we shrank the "atmosphere" to the size of the tube. This allowed us to change air pressure very quickly. Since a marshmallow is mostly air (that's why it's so soft), it's a good indicator of big changes in air pressure. When we **pulled** the syringe handle out, there was less air pressure in the tube, so the marshmallow **expanded** (because of the air trapped inside it). When we **pushed** the handle in, air pressure increased, so the marshmallow (and the air inside it) was **compressed** into a smaller size.

WHAT WE LEARNED

1 Compare the marshmallow in Step 2 and Step 4. How was it similar? How was it different?

a) similar: same marshmallow

b) different: size changed in Step 4

2 Why was it important to push the handle close to the marshmallow in Step 2? What did this allow us to better control?

a) to remove as much air as possible before beginning

b) air pressure

3 What is the name of the "ocean of air" that surrounds us? Why don't we see air pressure changes in it?

a) the atmosphere

b) because it's so huge and changes usually happen slowly

4 How did the syringe help us see changes in air pressure? How did the marshmallow help?

a) small space allowed air pressure to change quickly

b) its behavior helped us see the changes

5 Would a peanut have worked just as well for this activity? Why or why not?

a) no

b) a peanut is not mostly air, so it wouldn't change shapes

What Happened

Review the section with students. Emphasize bold-face words that identify key concepts and introduce new vocabulary.

Air pressure is the force of the air constantly pushing all around us. Except during violent weather, we usually don't have an opportunity to see big changes in air pressure. That's because the atmosphere is huge, and air pressure changes normally happen very slowly.

By using the syringe, we shrank the "atmosphere" to the size of the tube. This allowed us to change air pressure very quickly. Since a marshmallow is mostly air (that's why it's so soft), it's a good indicator of big changes in air pressure. When we pulled the syringe handle out, there was less air pressure in the tube, so the marshmallow expanded (because of the air trapped inside it). When we pushed the handle in, air pressure increased, so the marshmallow (and the air inside it) was compressed into a smaller size.

What We Learned

Answers will vary. Suggested responses are shown at left.

Conclusion

Read this section aloud to the class to summarize the concepts learned in this activity.

Food for Thought

Read the Scripture aloud to the class. Talk about the kinds of pressures that surround us each day. Discuss how God's invisible force helps us deal with these pressures.

Journal

If time permits, have a general class discussion about notes and drawings various students added to their journal pages. Discuss correct and incorrect predictions, and remind students that this "trial and error" process is part of the scientific process.

? CONCLUSION

Changes in air pressure can create movement. Huge changes in air pressure can have a tremendous effect our weather.

FOOD FOR THOUGHT

Judges 16:28-30 In this activity, your pushing and pulling definitely had an effect on the marshmallow. Although you couldn't see the force itself, the effects of the force were clearly visible from the changes that occurred.

Scripture tells us Samson turned away from God. He was deceived, weakened, imprisoned, and even blinded, But in his weakest hour, Samson remembered the invisible force of God that always surrounds us. Through prayer, he harnessed God's mighty power one final time — and the results were clearly visible in the huge changes that occurred.

JOURNAL My Science Notes

Extended Teaching

1. Repeat this activity but plug the syringe tip first, drop in a marshmallow, then replace the handle and push in. Have students compare the results with the original activity. How were they similar? How were they different?

2. Invite a meteorologist to visit your classroom. Ask him/her to talk about how air pressure affects the weather. Have students write a paragraph about one thing they learn.

3. Visit an automotive repair shop. Have a mechanic demonstrate various air tools and explain how they are used. Have students write a paragraph about one thing they learn.

4. Using the Internet, have teams research how our lungs are affected by air pressure changes. Challenge each team to create a poster showing at least one thing they learned.

5. Obtain a simple barometer and explain how it indicates air pressure. Have students record readings twice each day for one week. Compare readings with the weather each day. What conclusions can be drawn?

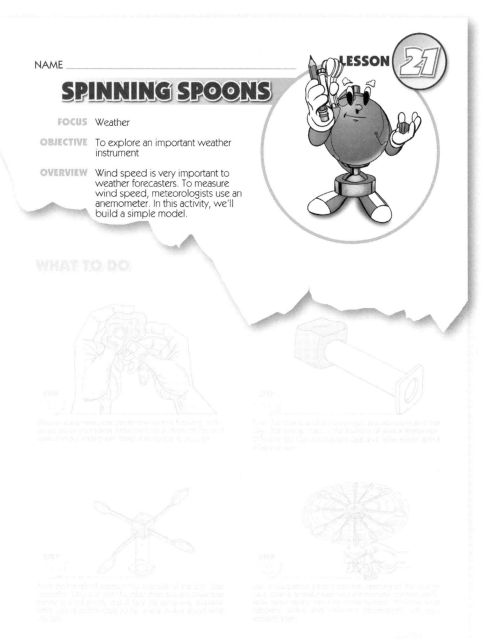

NAME _____

SPINNING SPOONS

LESSON 21

FOCUS Weather

OBJECTIVE To explore an important weather instrument

OVERVIEW Wind speed is very important to weather forecasters. To measure wind speed, meteorologists use an anemometer. In this activity, we'll build a simple model.

WHAT TO DO

Category

Earth Science

Focus

Weather

Objective

To explore an important weather instrument

National Standards

A1, A2, B1, B2, B3, D1, E1, E2, F5, G1, G2

Materials Needed

clay
syringe
spoons - 4
pencil

Safety Concerns

Additional Comments

If the device doesn't turn smoothly, it isn't balanced properly. Spoons must be an even distance apart and pushed into the clay the same amount. Help students make adjustments as needed.

Overview

Read the overview aloud to your students. The goal is to create an atmosphere of curiosity and inquiry.

WHAT TO DO

Monitor student research teams as they complete each step.

NAME _____

SPINNING SPOONS

FOCUS Weather

OBJECTIVE To explore an important weather instrument

CHALLENGE Wind speed is very important to weather forecasters. To measure wind speed, meteorologists use an anemometer. In this activity, we'll build a simple model.

WHAT TO DO

STEP 1
Discuss some ways you can tell the wind is blowing. Make notes about your ideas. Now pick up a chunk of clay and form it into a small cube. Keep it as square as you can.

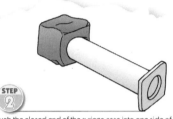

STEP 2
Push the closed end of the syringe case into one side of the clay. The syringe case is the bottom of your anemometer. Observe the clay and syringe case and make notes about what you see.

STEP 3
Push the handle of a spoon into one side of the clay. (See illustration.) Repeat with the other three spoons. Make sure they're spaced evenly and all face the same way. Examine what you've constructed so far. Make notes about what you see.

STEP 4
Slip a sharpened pencil into the opening of the syringe case. Check to make sure your anemometer can turn easily. Now blow gently into one of the spoons. Observe what happens. Share and compare observations with your research team.

EARTH 95

Teacher to Teacher

The science of weather study is called meteorology. Meteorologists use many different instruments to gather the data needed to accurately predict weather. Even then, the slightest change can cause tremendous shifts in a forecast. Even in this age of sophistocated computer models, most people still consider weather forecasting as much an art as a science!

WHAT HAPPENED?

An **anemometer** is a spinning device designed to measure **wind speed**. Each air cup (a spoon in your model) catches the passing air and changes it into a circular motion. In simple versions, you can get a rough idea of wind speed by watching how fast the anemometer spins. More sophisticated versions actually measure the speed of the wind in tiny increments, making them amazingly accurate.

Notice that the anemometer changes the **direction** of the **force** coming toward it. Straight wind (**linear motion**) is changed by the cups into spinning (**rotary motion**). This provides the **torque** (twisting force) that is necessary in order to take accurate measurements.

WHAT WE LEARNED

 1 What is the name of the device used to measure wind speed? Describe how it works.

a) anemometer

b) air cups catch passing air, changing linear motion into a circular motion

 2 Describe your ideas for measuring wind from Step 1. How were they similar to an anemometer? How were they different?

Answers will vary, but should reflect logical comparisons.

 3 Describe the purpose of the clay, the syringe case, and the spoons in this model. What was the purpose of each?

clay: to hold spoons
syringe case: part of the wheel/axle
spoons: to catch air

 4 Why is careful spoon placement important in Step 3? What might occur if they were off balance or pointing in different directions?

a) so the device is balanced

b) the device wouldn't turn smoothly

5 Would the model you built provide an accurate measurement of wind speed? Why or why not?

a) no

b) it's too simple; it needs more parts; etc.

What Happened

Review the section with students. Emphasize bold-face words that identify key concepts and introduce new vocabulary.

*An **anemometer** is a spinning device designed to measure **wind speed**. Each air cup (a spoon in your model) catches the passing air and changes it into a circular motion. In simple versions, you can get a rough idea of wind speed by watching how fast the anemometer spins. More sophisticated versions actually measure the speed of the wind in tiny increments, making them amazingly accurate.*

*Notice that the anemometer changes the **direction** of the **force** coming toward it. Straight wind (**linear motion**) is changed by the cups into spinning (**rotary motion**). This provides the **torque** (twisting force) that is necessary in order to take accurate measurements.*

What We Learned

Answers will vary. Suggested responses are shown at left.

Conclusion

Read this section aloud to the class to summarize the concepts learned in this activity.

Food for Thought

Read the Scripture aloud to the class. Discuss times when students have been frightened. Share a time you have been frightened, too! Talk about how trusting in God can help calm our fears.

Journal

If time permits, have a general class discussion about notes and drawings various students added to their journal pages. Discuss correct and incorrect predictions, and remind students that this "trial and error" process is part of the scientific process.

CONCLUSION
Wind has force and helps transfer energy around the Earth. Wind speed can be measured using an anemometer.

FOOD FOR THOUGHT
Mark 4:35-41 Wind is often gentle and cooling, but sometimes it can be wild and destructive! Knowing the wind speeds across broad areas helps forecasters predict tomorrow's weather. Yet even the greatest forecaster can't change the weather!

This Scripture tells how a great storm terrified the disciples and threatened to sink their boat. But when they woke Jesus, he commanded the storm to stop. Suddenly, all was peaceful again! Remember, the power that calmed that raging storm is the same power that can calm our hearts. Look to Jesus, and you can find peace.

JOURNAL My Science Notes

Extended Teaching

1. Using the Internet, have teams research weather history. How did ancient cultures try to influence the weather? In what ways did weather impact ancient cultures? Have teams share their findings with the class.

2. Invite an agricultural extension agent to visit your classroom. Find out how weather affects agriculture in your area. What role does wind play? Have students write a paragraph about one thing they learn.

3. Take a field trip to a television station. Have a meteorologist demonstrate the tools he/she uses to gather data and predict the weather. Have students write a paragraph about one thing they learn.

4. Have teams research weather-related disasters that have occured in the U.S. over the past century. Challenge each team to create a poster about one of these disasters and its cause.

5. Challenge students to write a story about how a massive shift in your area's weather patterns would change their daily lives. Share some of these stories with the class.

NAME _____

POROUS PUMICE

FOCUS Geology

OBJECTIVE To explore properties of igneous rock

OVERVIEW Everyone knows that rocks "sink like a rock" — or do they? This is another activity that teaches us that things are not always as simple as they seem!

WHAT TO DO

Category

Earth Science

Focus

Geology

Objective

To explore properties of igneous rock

National Standards

A1, A2, B1, B2, D1, G1, G2

Materials Needed

pumice stone
whipping cream
whisk
water
bowl

Safety Concerns

4. **Slipping**
There is a potential for spills. Remind students to exercise caution with water.

Additional Comments

Monitor to make sure students are not eating the whipped cream. To avoid the potential for mold, the pumice must be completely dry before storing.

Overview

Read the overview aloud to your students. The goal is to create an atmosphere of curiosity and inquiry.

WHAT TO DO

Monitor student research teams as they complete each step.

NAME _____

LESSON 22

POROUS PUMICE

FOCUS Geology

OBJECTIVE To explore properties of igneous rock

OVERVIEW Everyone knows that rocks "sink like a rock" — or do they? This is another activity that teaches us that things are not always as simple as they seem!

WHAT TO DO

STEP 1
Pour some whipping cream into a bowl. **Pick up the whisk** and begin whipping the cream. **Whip** the cream until something starts to happen. **Make notes** in your journal about what you see.

STEP 2
Carefully **observe** the piece of pumice stone. **Make notes** about similarities and differences to other rocks that you are familiar with. Now **predict** what will happen if you drop this rock into water.

STEP 3
Fill a bowl with water. Gently **place** the pumice stone in the water. **Observe** what happens.

STEP 4
Compare the whipped cream you made in Step 1 with the pumice stone. How are they similar. How are they different. **Make notes** on your journal page, then **share** and **compare** observations with your research team.

EARTH 99

Teacher to Teacher

Pumice is a product of volcanoes. Most volcanoes are located along the rim of the Pacific Ocean in the so-called "Ring of Fire." Volcanoes release tremendous energy when they erupt — many times that of the most powerful atomic bomb!

WHAT HAPPENED?

Like whipped cream, your **pumice** contains a lot of air. Since air is less dense than water (and there's so much trapped) you end up with a floating rock! Other kinds of rocks are much more **dense**, so they're the ones that "sink like a rock."

Pumice is one type of **igneous rock** (melted rock from volcanoes). Imagine a bottle of soda pop. As long as it's under **pressure**, there are no bubbles. But shake it up, open the cap — and as pressure falls bubbles shoot everywhere!

Pumice is created in a similar fashion. Deep underground there is enormous pressure. During a volcanic eruption, **magma** (melted rock) is forced to the surface and violently ejected. The instant drop in pressure results in violent expansion of **volcanic gasses**. The combination of these forces creates bubbles in the liquid rock. As the rock cools, these bubbles become trapped inside, creating pumice.

WHAT WE LEARNED

1 Describe the cream in Step 1 before and after whipping. How did it look similar? How did it look different? What caused the change?

a) answers will vary

b) similar: same material

c) different: fluffy after whipping

d) the added air

2 What did you predict in Step 2? How did this prediction reflect what actually happened in Step 3?

Answers will vary, but should reflect logical comparisons.

3 Compare the whipped cream and the pumice. How were they similar? How were they different?

a) similar: both filled with air

b) different: pumice hard, cream soft, pumice grey, cream white, etc.

4 Explain how pumice was made. What do scientists call the melted rock inside the Earth?

a) answers should reflect the soda pop comparison in "What Happened"

b) magma

5 Why does pumice float? How does density relate to buoyancy?

a) it contains a lot of air

b) less density equals more buoyancy

What Happened

Review the section with students. Emphasize bold-face words that identify key concepts and introduce new vocabulary.

*Like whipped cream, your **pumice** contains a lot of air. Since air is less dense than water (and there's so much trapped), you end up with a floating rock! Other kinds of rocks are much more **dense**, so they're the ones that "sink like a rock."*

*Pumice is one type of **igneous rock** (melted rock from volcanoes). Imagine a bottle of soda pop. As long as it's under **pressure**, there are no bubbles. But shake it up, open the cap — and as pressure falls, bubbles shoot everywhere!*

*Pumice is created in a similar fashion. Deep underground there is enormous pressure. During a volcanic eruption, **magma** (melted rock) is forced to the surface and violently ejected. The instant drop in pressure results in violent expansion of **volcanic gasses**. The combination of these forces creates bubbles in the liquid rock. As the rock cools, these bubbles become trapped inside, creating pumice.*

What We Learned

Answers will vary. Suggested responses are shown at left.

Conclusion

Read this section aloud to the class to summarize the concepts learned in this activity.

Food for Thought

Read the Scripture aloud to the class. Talk about what it feels like to be lost or alone. Discuss the concept that nothing on Earth can separate us from the love of God.

Journal

If time permits, have a general class discussion about notes and drawings various students added to their journal pages. Discuss correct and incorrect predictions, and remind students that this "trial and error" process is part of the scientific process.

? CONCLUSION

Igneous rocks are formed by melting, then hardening. Some igneous rocks, like pumice, are filled with spaces caused by volcanic gasses.

FOOD FOR THOUGHT

Romans 8:38-39 It's easy to separate pumice from other kinds of rocks. Just drop them all in the water! Other more serious separations happen too easily in this world. Circumstances may separate you from your friends, your possessions, or even your family.

Yet this Scripture reminds us that absolutely nothing can separate us from God's love! No force or power, not the devil nor the angels, not the highest mountain nor the deepest ocean . . . not even death itself can separate us from God's endless love — the most powerful force in the universe! Be sure to take time today to thank God for his amazing love.

JOURNAL My Science Notes

Extended Teaching

1. Have teams check the density of other materials (a styrofoam pellet, a pencil, a "normal" rock, a paperclip, etc.) by repeating Step 4. Make sure they record the results. Encourage teams to share their findings.

2. Using the Internet, have teams research famous volcanoes. Challenge each team to create a poster mapping and describing one of these volcanoes. Make sure they include dates of major eruptions!

3. Invite a geologist to visit your classroom. Have him/her show samples of igneous rocks. Discuss how these differ from metamorphic and sedimentary rocks. Have students write a paragraph about one thing they learn.

4. Take a field trip to a store that specializes in lawn and garden supplies. List the various kinds of landscaping stone available and the ways it is used. Challenge each team to prepare a presentation on one type of stone.

5. Have teams research the volcanoes of Hawaii. How large are they? How active are they? Have students write several paragraphs describing their findings.

NAME _____

LEAKY LIMESTONE

FOCUS   Chemical Weathering

OBJECTIVE   To explore a unique form of erosion

OVERVIEW   Limestone is often used in buildings, roads, and statues. Yet even this hard stone can be destroyed by something as simple as rain! In this activity, we'll explore how this happens.

WHAT TO DO

Category
Earth Science

Focus
Chemical Weathering

Objective
To explore a unique form of erosion

National Standards
A1, A2, B1, D1, G1, G2

Materials Needed
limestone
paper cup
hydrochloric acid
pipette
paper towels

Safety Concerns

1. Goggles
Always protect the eyes when working with chemicals.

2. Corrosion
Avoid direct contact of chemicals with bare skin.

4. Slipping
There is a potential for spills with this activity. Remind students to exercise caution.

Additional Comments

The dilute hydrochloric acid used in this activity is relatively safe, but goggles and gloves will help students develop good safety habits. Rinse and dry the limestone thoroughly before storing.

Overview

Read the overview aloud to your students. The goal is to create an atmosphere of curiosity and inquiry.

WHAT TO DO

Monitor student research teams as they complete each step.

LESSON 23

LEAKY LIMESTONE

FOCUS: Chemical Weathering

OBJECTIVE: To explore a unique form of erosion

OVERVIEW: Limestone is often used in buildings, roads, and statues. Yet even this hard stone can be destroyed by something as simple as rain! In this activity, we'll explore how this happens.

WHAT TO DO

STEP 1
Closely **examine** a piece of limestone. With your research team, **discuss** some ways you might break this rock down into smaller pieces. **Record** these ideas in your journal.

STEP 2
Examine the items in your materials kit. Could any of these items have an effect on a piece of limestone? **Make notes** about why or why not.

STEP 3
Place the limestone in a plastic cup. Carefully **add** hydrochloric acid one drop at a time. **Make notes** about how the liquid is affecting the rock. (Keep paper towels handy in case of a mess.)

STEP 4
Carefully clean your work area following instructions from your teacher. Now review each step in this activity. **Make notes** about any adjustments in your thinking. **Share** and **compare** observations with your research team.

EARTH **103**

Teacher to Teacher

A chemical change occurs when a process results in a different substance. In this activity, for instance, the hydrochloric acid changed the limestone (calcium carbonate) into carbon dioxide, water, and a bit of calcium chloride — all of which are different substances than the limestone you began with.

By contrast, a physical change occurs when the form of a substance changes, but not the substance itself. A good example is breaking limestone rocks into gravel.

WHAT HAPPENED?

Erosion is a process that breaks things down over time. There are many different kinds of erosion. For example, you've probably seen ditches or gullies that streams or rain water have cut through soil. The erosion **modeled** in this activity is **chemical erosion**. It's the breakdown of material through a chemical process.

In Step 3, the bubbling came from **carbon dioxide** released by a chemical reaction between the **hydrochloric acid** and **calcium carbonate** (limestone). So are people going around pouring hydrochloric acid on statues? In a way, that's what is happening. The **air pollution** people produce reacts with **water** in the **atmosphere** to produce **acid rain**. While the acid in this rain is too **dilute** for you to feel, over time it can create serious problems in the **environment** — not only for rivers and streams, but even for buildings or statues!

WHAT WE LEARNED

1 Describe the ideas you had for breaking down the limestone. How were they similar to chemical weathering? How were they different?

answers will vary, but should reflect logical comparisons.

2 What items in your materials kit did you think might help break down the limestone? How?

answers will vary, but should reflect logical assumptions.

104 EARTH

 Describe what happened in Step 3. What caused the bubbles? What three chemical substances were involved?

a) answers will vary.

b) carbon dioxide

c) calcium carbonate, hydrochloric acid, carbon dioxide.

4 Name at least two types of erosion. How are they similar? How are they different?

a) examples of physical or chemical erosion.

b) physical erosion changes form, but not substance; chemical changes substance.

5 Why is acid rain a problem? What steps might be taken to eliminate acid rain?

a) acid rain damages the environment.

b) anything that lessens air pollution.

What Happened

Review the section with students. Emphasize bold-face words that identify key concepts and introduce new vocabulary.

*Erosion is a process that breaks things down over time. There are many different kinds of erosion. For example, you've probably seen ditches or gullies that streams or rain water have cut through soil. The erosion **modeled** in this activity is **chemical erosion**. It's the breakdown of material through a chemical process.*

*In Step 3, the bubbling came from **carbon dioxide** released by a chemical reaction between the hydrochloric acid and calcium carbonate (limestone). So are people going around pouring hydrochloric acid on statues? In a way, that's what is happening. The **air pollution** people produce reacts with **water** in the **atmosphere** to produce **acid rain**. While the acid in this rain is too **dilute** for you to feel, over time it can create serious problems in the **environment** — not only for rivers and streams, but even for buildings or statues!*

What We Learned

Answers will vary. Suggested responses are shown at left.

Conclusion

Read this section aloud to the class to summarize the concepts learned in this activity.

Food for Thought

Read the Scripture aloud to the class. Talk about how worry and stress can erode our faith. Discuss ways we can spend more time building our relationship with God.

Journal

If time permits, have a general class discussion about notes and drawings various students added to their journal pages. Discuss correct and incorrect predictions, and remind students that this "trial and error" process is part of the scientific process.

CONCLUSION

There are many kinds of erosion. Chemical weathering is a form of erosion caused by acid rain.

FOOD FOR THOUGHT

Psalm 46:1-3 Although we don't often see big changes in our short lifetimes, nothing on this Earth will last forever. Earthquakes, volcanic eruptions, storms (and even little things like acid rain and erosion) continue to take their toll. Eventually, everything on Earth will wear away and be destroyed.

Scripture tells us that God's children don't need to worry — even if the world blows up and the mountains all fall into the sea! That goes for our day-to-day living too. Like acid rain on limestone, there are many little things that will erode our faith over time if we ignore them. But spending time with God each day will make us strong and keep us safe in his loving arms.

JOURNAL My Science Notes

106 EARTH

Extended Teaching

1. Divide a bulletin board into two sides with the headings "Physical Change" and "Chemical Change." Challenge teams to collect and post pictures that demonstrate such changes.

2. Invite an environmentalist or agricultural extension agent to visit your classroom. Discuss acid rain and its effect on the local environment. Have students write a paragraph about one thing they learn.

3. Challenge students to go on an "Erosion Expedition" looking for signs of erosion around home and school. (Gravel washing from a driveway is a good example.) Have them report their findings to the class.

4. Have teams research the "Dust Bowl." Look for its causes and what was done to avoid it happening again. Challenge each team to create a poster showing at least one result of this disaster.

5. Challenge teams to find examples of chemical weathering around the school (rust on a flagpole, bricks beginning to crumble, etc.). Have each team share their findings with the class.

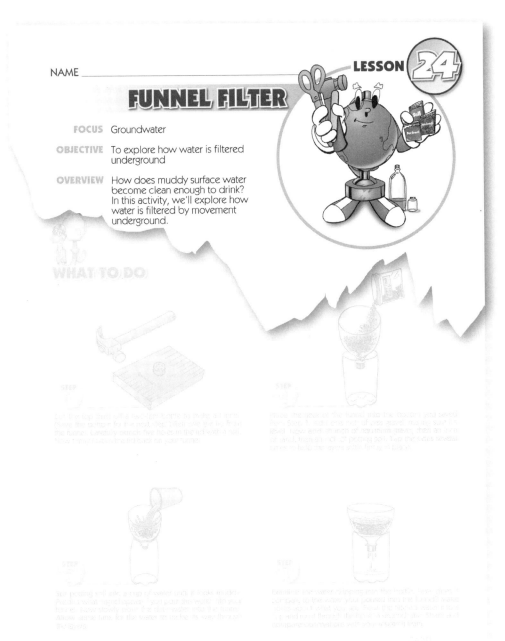

NAME _____

FUNNEL FILTER

FOCUS Groundwater

OBJECTIVE To explore how water is filtered underground

OVERVIEW How does muddy surface water become clean enough to drink? In this activity, we'll explore how water is filtered by movement underground.

WHAT TO DO

STEP

STEP

STEP

STEP

Category
Earth Science

Focus
Groundwater

Objective
To explore how water is filtered underground

National Standards
A1, A2, B1, B2, B3, D1, F1, F2, F3, F4, G1, G2

Materials Needed
nail
jar
pea gravel
aquarium gravel
paper cup
sand
potting soil
two-liter bottle
hammer
water

Safety Concerns
4. Slipping
There is a potential for spills. Remind students to exercise caution with water.

Additional Comments

To avoid smashed fingers, you may want to make the lids in advance. Materials need to be packed tightly. Make sure students agitate the "muddy water" to insure plenty of "impurities" go into the funnel. Don't let students drink the filtered water.

Overview

Read the overview aloud to your students. The goal is to create an atmosphere of curiosity and inquiry.

WHAT TO DO

Monitor student research teams as they complete each step.

NAME

LESSON 24

FUNNEL FILTER

FOCUS Groundwater

OBJECTIVE To explore how water is filtered underground

QUESTION How does muddy surface water become clean enough to drink? In this activity, we'll explore how water is filtered by movement underground.

WHAT TO DO

STEP 1

Cut the top third off a two-liter bottle to make a funnel. (Save the bottom for the next step.) **Remove** the lid from the funnel. Carefully **punch** five holes in the lid with a nail. Now firmly **fasten** the lid back on your funnel.

STEP 2

Place the neck of the funnel into the bottom you saved from Step 1. **Add** one inch of pea gravel, making sure it's level. Now **add** an inch of aquarium gravel, then an inch of sand, then an inch of potting soil. **Tap** the sides several times to help the layers settle firmly in place.

STEP 3

Stir potting soil into a cup of water until it looks muddy. **Predict** what might happen if you pour this water into your funnel. Now slowly **pour** the dirty water into the funnel. **Allow** some time for the water to trickle its way through the layers.

STEP 4

Examine the water dripping into the bottle. How does it compare to the water your poured into the funnel? Make notes about what you see. **Pour** the filtered water into a cup and run it through the funnel a second time. **Share** and compare observations with your research team.

EARTH **107**

Teacher to Teacher

Groundwater is the major source of water for all human needs. But groundwater accounts for only .6% of the water found on Earth! Most of the rest is bound up in the ocean, glaciers, and polar ice caps, making it essentially unavailable for meeting our needs. That's why groundwater purity is such an important issue.

What Happened

Review the section with students. Emphasize bold-face words that identify key concepts and introduce new vocabulary.

*Although this water still isn't clean enough to drink (there may be **bacteria** or other harmful **microbes**), your Funnel Filter did a pretty good job of removing the largest particles!*

*In the Earth's **water cycle**, soil, sand, and rocks perform a similar function on a much bigger scale. **Surface water** trickles down deep into the ground (now it's called **groundwater**) and **impurities** are **filtered** out in the process. For thousands of years, the Earth has been renewing water supplies this way.*

*However, don't assume that any clear, cold spring water is safe to drink! Modern man has introduced so many new **pollutants** into the **environment**, almost all water now requires special filters and treatments to make it safe to drink.*

What We Learned

Answers will vary. Suggested responses are shown at left.

 WHAT HAPPENED?

Although this water still isn't clean enough to drink (there may be bacteria or other harmful microbes), your Funnel Filter did a pretty good job of removing the largest particles!

In the Earth's water cycle, soil, sand, and rocks perform a similar function on a much bigger scale. Surface water trickles down deep into the ground (now it's called groundwater) and impurities are filtered out in the process. For thousands of years, the Earth has been renewing water supplies this way.

However, don't assume that any clear, cold spring water is safe to drink! Modern man has introduced so many new pollutants into the environment, almost all water now requires special filters and treatments to make it safe to drink.

 WHAT WE LEARNED

1 Describe the layers in your Funnel Filter. How do the particle sizes differ from layer to layer?

a) answers will vary

b) they get smaller and smaller toward the top

2 What did you predict in Step 3? How did this prediction reflect what actually happened?

Answers will vary, but should reflect logical comparisons.

---

 3 Compare the water you poured in your Funnel Filter in Step 3 with the water dripping out in Step 4. What caused the difference?

a) muddy in Step 3, clear in Step 4

b) the filtering process

 4 Early Americans often settled near abundant supplies of clear spring water. Is this usually a safe source for drinking water today? Why or why not?

a) not usually

b) enviromental pollutants require most water to be purified to be safe

5 Why is it important to control dump sites? How might something dumped on the ground miles away affect the water we drink?

a) to avoid pollution and contaminants

b) impurities might travel though the groundwater

Conclusion

Read this section aloud to the class to summarize the concepts learned in this activity.

Food for Thought

Read the Scripture aloud to the class. Talk about the concept of "living water." Discuss ways we can make sure we have an abundant supply.

Journal

If time permits, have a general class discussion about notes and drawings various students added to their journal pages. Discuss correct and incorrect predictions, and remind students that this "trial and error" process is part of the scientific process.

CONCLUSION

Earth works like a giant filter to clean groundwater. Keeping these groundwater supplies pure helps provide safe drinking water.

FOOD FOR THOUGHT

Psalm 1:1-3 Pure, clean water is vital to all living things. Water is so important to human survival that it's often used as an illustration of our spiritual and emotional well-being.

In this Scripture, the psalmist compares those who follow God to a tree planted by a stream. Because it is so close, it always has an abundant source of water. The same is true in our lives. As long as we stay close to Jesus, spending time learning to trust him each day, we'll always have an abundant source of "living" water!

JOURNAL My Science Notes

Extended Teaching

1. Demonstrate how a coffee filter is used to make coffee. How are the results similar to the original activity? How are they different?

2. Using the Internet, have teams research how our lungs and kidneys work like filters. Challenge each team to create a poster showing at least one aspect of this process.

3. Take a field trip to a water treatment plant. Find out what steps are taken to make water safe to drink. Have students write a paragraph about one thing they learn.

4. Invite a nurse to visit your classroom. Have him/her talk about some of the ways our bodies filter fluids and air. Have students write a paragraph about one thing they learn.

5. Contact your state's Department of Natural Resources. Find out what kind of pollutants are a concern in your area. Challenge students to write a story about how this might affect their lives if not corrected.

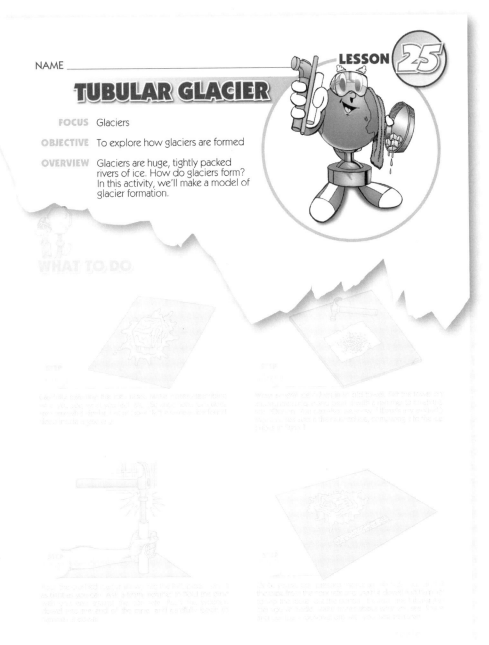

NAME

TUBULAR GLACIER

FOCUS Glaciers

OBJECTIVE To explore how glaciers are formed

OVERVIEW Glaciers are huge, tightly packed rivers of ice. How do glaciers form? In this activity, we'll make a model of glacier formation.

Category
Earth Science

Focus
Glaciers

Objective
To explore how glaciers are formed

National Standards
A1, A2, B1, B3, D1, D2, G1, G2

Materials Needed
PVC pipe
wooden dowel
ice cubes
towel
hammer

Safety Concerns

2. Thermal Burn
Remind students that holding ice too long can "burn" the skin.

4. Slipping
There is a potential for spills. Remind students to exercise caution with water.

4. Other
Remind students to exercise caution when using the hammer.

Additional Comments

If possible, schedule this activity for outdoors since it can be very messy. A winter day offers the option of packing snow into the tube instead of crushed ice! To avoid potential problems, collect hammers immediately after use.

Overview

Read the overview aloud to your students. The goal is to create an atmosphere of curiosity and inquiry.

WHAT TO DO

Monitor student research teams as they complete each step.

TUBULAR GLACIER

FOCUS Glaciers

OBJECTIVE To explore how glaciers are formed

OVERVIEW Glaciers are huge, tightly packed rivers of ice. How do glaciers form? In this activity, we'll make a model of glacier formation.

WHAT TO DO

STEP 1

Carefully **examine** the ice cubes. **Make notes** describing what you see, what you feel, etc. (Science note: Ice cubes are somewhat similar, but not exactly the same as ice found deep inside a glacier.)

STEP 2

Wrap several ice cubes in an old towel. **Set** the towel on a concrete surface and **beat** it with a hammer to crush the ice. (Option: You can also use snow if there's any around.) **Make notes** about the crushed ice, comparing it to the ice cubes in Step 1.

STEP 3

Pour the crushed ice (or snow) into the PVC pipe. **Pack** it as tight as you can! **Ask** a team member to hold the pipe with one end against the concrete. **Push** the wooden dowel into the end of the pipe, and carefully begin to **hammer** it down.

STEP 4

Once you've compressed the ice as much as you can, **lift** the pipe from the concrete and use the dowel and hammer to **tap** the "core" out the bottom. **Examine** the tubular glacier you've made. **Make notes** about what you see. **Share** and **compare** observations with your research team.

EARTH **111**

Teacher to Teacher

Scientists refer to glaciers as having a "budget." If more snow falls than melts, the glacier's budget is positive. If more snow melts than falls, the budget is negative. When the budget is positive, glaciers form and advance. (An excessively positive budget can even produce a "galloping glacier" — one which moves several feet in a year.) If the budget is negative, then the glacier recedes.

WHAT HAPPENED?

The pressure created by the hammer compressed the loose ice tightly together. This imitated the creation of glaciers, which are formed by enormous weight compressing snow into ice. Most glaciers begin high in mountain valleys. Falling snow piles up each winter, but doesn't all melt in the summer. Year by year, the snow pile grows higher and heavier, building up so much pressure that snow begins to compress into ice. Over time, thousands of tons of ice are created. As this massive ice mass (now called a glacier) continues to push down, the pressure causes the bottom layers to try to move, making the glacier slowly creep downhill.

Depending on global climate, glaciers may grow or shrink, changing the surface of the Earth beneath them. Some modern glaciers are over a mile thick! Scientists tell us the enormous weight of a huge glacier can actually push the crust of the Earth down several feet.

 WHAT WE LEARNED

1 Compare the ice cubes in Step 1 with the crushed ice or snow in Step 2. How are they similar? How are they different?

a) similar: both the same material

b) different: Step 1 is solid and hard; Step 2 is loose and crumbly

2 Describe the process by which most glaciers are formed.

answers should reflect the description in "What Happened?"

112 EARTH

3 How was the hammer and pipe process we used in this activity similar to the process that creates a glacier? How was it different?

a) similar: it allowed pressure and packing, etc.

b) different: glaciers aren't made in pipes, etc.

4 Compare the "glacier core" from Step 4 with the crushed ice or snow from Step 2. How are they similar? How are they different?

a) similar: the same material

b) different: Step 2 is loose and crumbly; Step 4 is packed and hard

5 Core samples from glaciers sometimes show pollution deep within the ice. Based on what you've learned about glaciers, how is this possible?

Air pollution gets into the snow that falls and eventually becomes a glacier.

EARTH 113

What Happened

Review the section with students. Emphasize bold-face words that identify key concepts and introduce new vocabulary.

*The **pressure** created by the hammer **compressed** the loose ice tightly together. This imitated the creation of **glaciers**, **which** are formed by enormous **weight** compressing snow into ice. Most glaciers begin high in mountain valleys. Falling snow piles up each winter, but doesn't all melt in the summer. Year by year, the snow pile grows higher and heavier, building up so much pressure that snow begins to compress into ice. Over time, thousands of tons of ice are created. As this massive **ice mass** (now called a glacier) continues to push down, the pressure causes the bottom layers to try to move, making the glacier slowly creep downhill.*

*Depending on global climate, glaciers may grow or shrink, changing the surface of the Earth beneath them. Some modern glaciers are over a mile thick! Scientists tell us the enormous weight of a huge glacier can actually push the **crust** of the Earth down several feet.*

What We Learned

Answers will vary. Suggested responses are shown at left.

Conclusion

Read this section aloud to the class to summarize the concepts learned in this activity.

Food for Thought

Read the Scripture aloud to the class. Talk about problems and hard times students have experienced. Share some of your own challenges. Discuss how God uses trials and obstacles to help us grow and make us stronger.

Journal

If time permits, have a general class discussion about notes and drawings various students added to their journal pages. Discuss correct and incorrect predictions, and remind students that this "trial and error" process is part of the scientific process.

CONCLUSION

Glaciers are formed when falling snow piles up year after year, creating enormous weight that compresses snow into layers of ice. A glacier's incredible weight also causes it to move slowly downhill.

FOOD FOR THOUGHT

2 Corinthians 1:8-9 As you put the crushed ice or snow under great pressure with your hammer, changes occurred. The soft, pliable ice or snow became a chunk of solid ice!

In this Scripture, Paul writes about a time of tremendous physical, spiritual, and mental pressure. He and Timothy felt crushed and overwhelmed by the obstacles and problems they faced — until they put their whole trust in God! Sometimes God lets us experience hard times to help us learn to rely completely on him. Like the snow, the right kind of pressure only makes us stronger!

JOURNAL My Science Notes

Extended Teaching

1. Have students research how ancient glaciers affected the United States. (The "Loess Hills" of western Iowa and lakes dotting Minnesota are just two examples.) Challenge teams to create a poster based on their findings.

2. Invite a geologist to visit your classroom. Discuss unique geological formations (like "horn" mountains) that were formed by ancient glaciers. Have students write a paragraph about one thing they learn.

3. Using the Internet, have teams research modern glaciers. Where are they found? How big are they? Challenge each team to prepare a report for the class describing a specific glacier.

4. Take a field trip to an ice plant. Find out how this "man-made" ice is created and where it is used. Have students write a paragraph about one thing they learn.

5. There are two major types of glaciers — valley (also known as "alpine") and continental (also known as "ice sheets"). Challenge teams to research glacier types, then create a poster showing the difference.

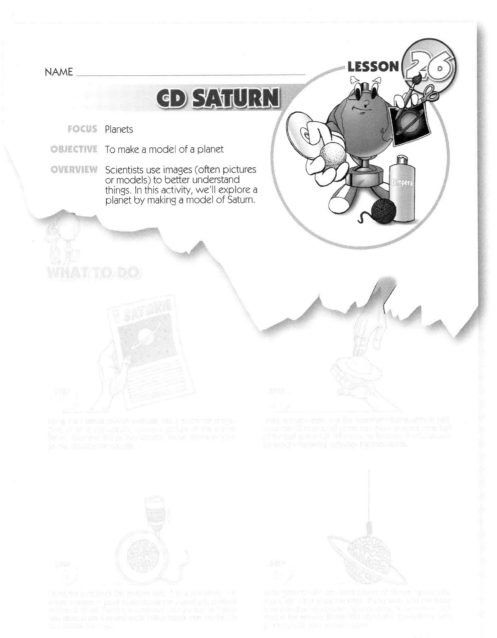

CD SATURN

FOCUS Planets

OBJECTIVE To make a model of a planet

OVERVIEW Scientists use images (often pictures or models) to better understand things. In this activity, we'll explore a planet by making a model of Saturn.

WHAT TO DO

Category
Earth Science

Focus
Planets

Objective
To make a model of a planet

National Standards
A1, A2, B1, B2, D1, G1, G2

Materials Needed
styrofoam ball
black yarn
old CD
glitter
picture of Saturn
knife
glue
markers
paint
toothpick

Safety Concerns
4. Sharp Objects
Remind students to exercise caution when using the knife.

Additional Comments

To avoid students using knives, you may wish to cut the styrofoam balls in advance. Any damaged or unwanted CDs will work fine for this activity. Junk mail from computer and online advertisers is another good source for CDs.

Overview

Read the overview aloud to your students. The goal is to create an atmosphere of curiosity and inquiry.

WHAT TO DO

Monitor student research teams as they complete each step.

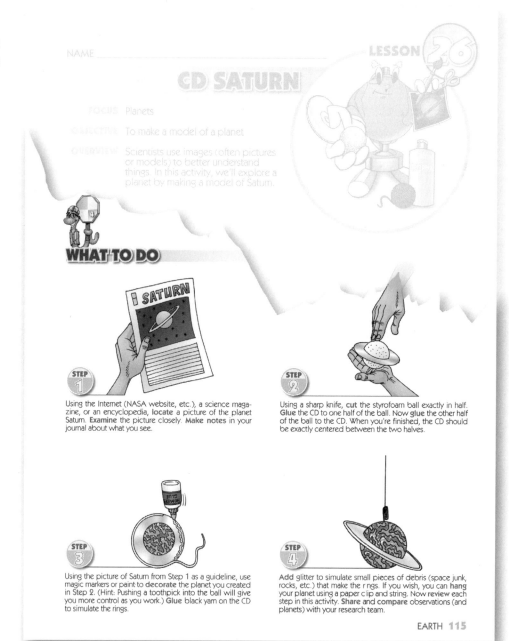

Teacher to Teacher

Saturn is an interesting planet for research. Saturn's "day" is about 10 Earth hours, but its "year" is almost 30 Earth years long. Scientists tell us that Saturn has at least 17 moons, and its surface experiences storms so severe, that by comparison, Earth's hurricanes are just a light breeze!

WHAT HAPPENED?

The first hint **Saturn** wasn't simply a spherical **planet** (like **Earth**) came from a discovery made by **Galileo** in 1610. The first **telescopes** were very weak. Galileo modified the design, creating a powerful telescope that allowed him to see farther and clearer. Since then, scientists have discovered many amazing things about planets!

Your **model** resembles the view early **astronomers** might have had of Saturn. The "rings" they thought were **solid** (like your CD) are actually made from millions of pieces of broken rock and frozen debris. The rings only look solid because the Sun's light **reflects** from the particles' surfaces. Saturn's surface is extremely stormy, often with winds of over a thousand miles per hour, and its **atmosphere** is toxic to life as we know it. Even with a very inexpensive telescope, Saturn is fun to watch in the night sky.

WHAT WE LEARNED

 1 Describe the model you made in this activity. How is it similar to Saturn? How is it different?

a) answers will vary, but should reflect logical comparisons

 2 Who first discovered that Saturn wasn't similar to Earth? What device helped him in this discovery, and where did it come from?

a) Galileo

b) a telescope

c) Galileo modified the design of earlier, weaker telescopes

 3 What are the rings of Saturn made from? Why did early astronomers think the rings were solid?

a) broken rock, frozen debris, etc.

b) weak telescopes made particle groups look solid

4 How did the invention of telescopes help scientific discovery? Name other "scope" devices with lenses, and tell what they're used for.

a) scientists could see better

b) microscopes, cameras, glasses, etc.

5 Based on present technology, could astronauts visit the surface of Saturn? Why or why not?

a) no

b) distance, toxic atmosphere, violent storms, etc.

What Happened

Review the section with students. Emphasize bold-face words that identify key concepts and introduce new vocabulary.

*The first hint **Saturn** wasn't simply a spherical **planet** (like **Earth**) came from a discovery made by **Galileo** in 1610. The first **telescopes** were very weak. Galileo modified the design, creating a powerful telescope that allowed him to see farther and clearer. Since then, scientists have discovered many amazing things about planets!*

*Your **model** resembles the view early **astronomers** might have had of Saturn. The "**rings**" they thought were **solid** (like your CD) are actually made from millions of pieces of broken rock and frozen debris. The rings only look solid because the Sun's light **reflects** from the particles' surfaces. Saturn's surface is extremely stormy, often with winds of over a thousand miles per hour, and its **atmosphere** is toxic to life as we know it. Even with a very inexpensive telescope, Saturn is fun to watch in the night sky.*

What We Learned

Answers will vary. Suggested responses are shown at left.

Conclusion

Read this section aloud to the class to summarize the concepts learned in this activity.

Food for Thought

Read the Scripture aloud to the class. Talk about the immensity and complexity of God's universe. Discuss how this awesome creator cares for mankind, and knows and loves every individual.

Journal

If time permits, have a general class discussion about notes and drawings various students added to their journal pages. Discuss correct and incorrect predictions, and remind students that this "trial and error" process is part of the scientific process.

☉CONCLUSION

Each planet in our solar system has special and unique features. Devices like telescopes help scientists expand our knowledge through new discoveries.

🍴FOOD FOR THOUGHT

Genesis 1:14-15 Your model was designed to help you better understand Saturn. Saturn is only one planet in a universe full of wonders! Step outside on a clear night, and you can see thousands of stars. Scripture tells us God created these wonderful lights in the sky. When we think of the millions of stars, planets, moons, comets, constellations, and galaxies, our minds are overwhelmed at the immensity of God's work! Isn't it amazing that despite the vastness of God's mighty creation, he still knows each one of us personally? Remember, God not only knows you, but also loves you with an endless love!

📓JOURNAL My Science Notes

Extended Teaching

1. Using the Internet, have students research NASA's Voyager project. Challenge each team to create a poster showing at least one way Voyager increased our knowledge of this amazing planet.

2. Invite an amateur astronomer to visit your classroom. Have him/her demonstrate the use of a telescope and talk about the different kinds. Have students write a paragraph about one thing they learn.

3. Take a field trip to a planetarium. Find out how it works and how planetariums help us better understand the universe. Have students write a paragraph about one thing they learn.

4. Take a field trip to an observatory (check with your local university). Have students write a few paragraphs comparing an observatory with a planetarium. How are they similar? How are they different?

5. Have teams research the Hubbell Telescope. What does it do? Who was it named for? Challenge each team to create a poster about one aspect of this amazing piece of technology.

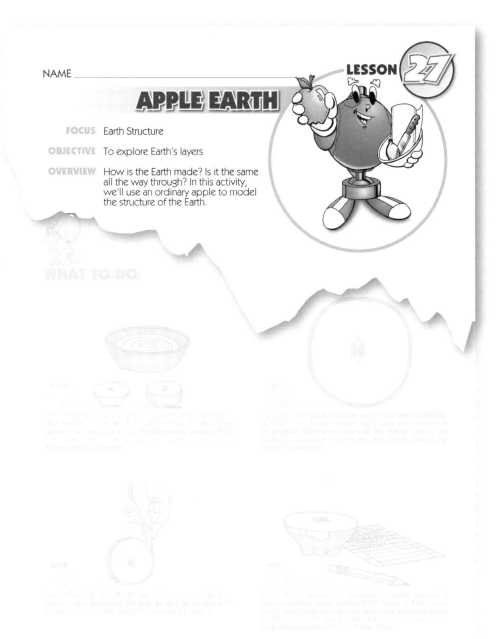

NAME _____

APPLE EARTH

FOCUS Earth Structure

OBJECTIVE To explore Earth's layers

OVERVIEW How is the Earth made? Is it the same all the way through? In this activity, we'll use an ordinary apple to model the structure of the Earth.

WHAT TO DO

Category
Earth Science

Focus
Earth Structure

Objective
To explore Earth's layers

National Standards
A1, A2, B1, D1, D3, G1, G2

Materials Needed
lemon juice
bowl
knife
apple

Safety Concerns

3. Hygiene
Don't allow students to eat any part of the apple.

4. Sharp Objects
Remind students to exercise caution when using the knife.

Additional Comments

To avoid students using knives, you may wish to cut the apple for each team. Don't do this in advance or Step 1 will not work! For hygiene reasons, don't allow students to eat any portion of the apple (especially seeds which contain traces of cyanide).

Overview

Read the overview aloud to your students. The goal is to create an atmosphere of curiosity and inquiry.

WHAT TO DO

Monitor student research teams as they complete each step.

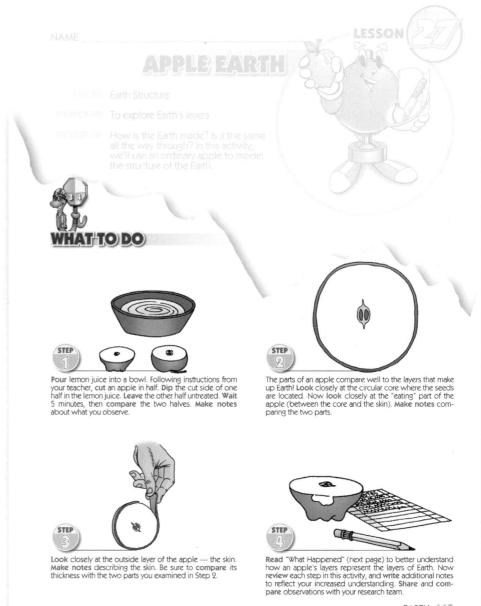

NAME _____

LESSON 27

APPLE EARTH

FOCUS   Earth Structure

OBJECTIVE   To explore Earth's layers

OVERVIEW   How is the Earth made? Is it the same all the way through? In this activity, we'll use an ordinary apple to model the structure of the Earth.

WHAT TO DO

STEP 1
Pour lemon juice into a bowl. Following instructions from your teacher, **cut** an apple in half. **Dip** the cut side of one half in the lemon juice. Leave the other half untreated. **Wait** 5 minutes, then **compare** the two halves. **Make notes** about what you observe.

STEP 2
The parts of an apple compare well to the layers that make up Earth! **Look** closely at the circular core where the seeds are located. Now **look** closely at the "eating" part of the apple (between the core and the skin). **Make notes** comparing the two parts.

STEP 3
Look closely at the outside layer of the apple — the skin. **Make notes** describing the skin. Be sure to **compare** its thickness with the two parts you examined in Step 2.

STEP 4
Read "What Happened" (next page) to better understand how an apple's layers represent the layers of Earth. Now **review** each step in this activity, and **write** additional notes to reflect your increased understanding. **Share** and **compare** observations with your research team.

EARTH **119**

Teacher to Teacher

How do scientists know about the Earth's structure beneath the crust? An earthquake produces P and S waves which can travel through the planet. By recording the behavior of these waves on the other side of the world, scientists can tell what kind of material (liquid or solid) they encountered along the way.

WHAT HAPPENED?

The thickness of the apple parts provides a good comparison to the relative thickness of **Earth's layers**. The core of the apple represents the **core** of Earth. The main part of the apple (between the core and skin) represents the **mantle** of Earth. The apple skin represents the thinnest layer, the **crust** of Earth.

Scientists believe that Earth's core is mostly molten iron. The mantle is made of **minerals** in a state between **liquid** and **solid** that scientists refer to as **plastic**. The crust (the part you walk on) is mostly made of **rock**, **soil**, **sand**, and similar materials. Compared to the other layers, it's relatively solid. But the crust is **brittle** and subject to violent **forces** like **earthquakes** and **volcanoes**, as well as simple (but still active) forces like **erosion**.

WHAT WE LEARNED

1 Compare the three parts of the apple. How were they similar? How were they different? How does the thickness of the parts compare?

answers should reflect the description from "What Happened?"

2 Using the apple as a model, name and describe the innermost (center) layer of Earth. What is it composed of?

a) the core

b) mostly molten iron

3 Name and describe the middle layer of Earth. What is it composed of?

a) the mantle

b) various minerals in a "plastic" state between liquid and solid

4 Name and describe the outer layer of Earth. What is it composed of?

a) the crust

b) rock, soil, sand, and similar materials

5 What kind of forces affect the crust of Earth? Why do these forces rarely affect the core or mantle?

a) earthquakes, volcanoes, etc.

b) it is made of iron, relatively solid

What Happened

Review the section with students. Emphasize bold-face words that identify key concepts and introduce new vocabulary.

The thickness of the apple parts provides a good comparison to the relative thickness of **Earth's layers.** *The core of the apple represents the* **core** *of Earth. The main part of the apple (between the core and skin) represents the* **mantle** *of Earth. The apple skin represents the thinnest layer, the* **crust** *of Earth.*

Scientists believe that Earth's core is mostly molten iron. The mantle is made of **minerals** *in a state between* **liquid** *and* **solid** *that scientists refer to as* **plastic.** *The crust (the part you walk on) is mostly made of* **rock**, **soil**, **sand**, *and similar materials. Compared to the other layers, it's relatively solid. But the crust is* **brittle** *and subject to violent* **forces** *like* **earthquakes** *and* **volcanoes**, *as well as simple (but still active) forces like* **erosion**.

What We Learned

Answers will vary. Suggested responses are shown at left.

Conclusion

Read this section aloud to the class to summarize the concepts learned in this activity.

Food for Thought

Read the Scripture aloud to the class. Talk about how our actions can be a reflection of God's love. Discuss ways our behavior can show God's character to the world.

Journal

If time permits, have a general class discussion about notes and drawings various students added to their journal pages. Discuss correct and incorrect predictions, and remind students that this "trial and error" process is part of the scientific process.

? CONCLUSION

The Earth is composed of three main layers: the core, the mantle, and the crust. The relative thickness of these layers is similar to the parts of an apple.

FOOD FOR THOUGHT

2 Thessalonians 3:6-10 Models are useful in helping us understand the world around us. In this Scripture, Paul writes about the importance of being a good model to others.

Think about the way you treat those around you. Are you being a good model? Does the way you relate to others reflect the love of God? The more time you spend learning about God, the more you'll be able to truly reflect God's character to the world.

JOURNAL My Science Notes

Extended Teaching

1. Discuss how models increase our understanding. Have teams list other types of models (globes, anatomy models, model airplanes, etc.). Have them share their conclusions with the class.

2. Take a field trip to the geology department of a local university. Find out about seismometers and how they work. Have students write a paragraph about one thing they learn.

3. Using the Internet, have teams research major earthquakes. How often do they occur? Where do they happen most?

Challenge each team to create a poster depicting their findings.

4. Invite a geologist to visit your classroom. Ask him/her to discuss the relationship of plate boundaries and earthquakes. Have students write a paragraph about one thing they learn.

5. Using the Internet, have teams research major historical earthquakes. How do these relate to earthquakes today, both in location and intensity? Challenge each team to present one such earthquake event to the class.

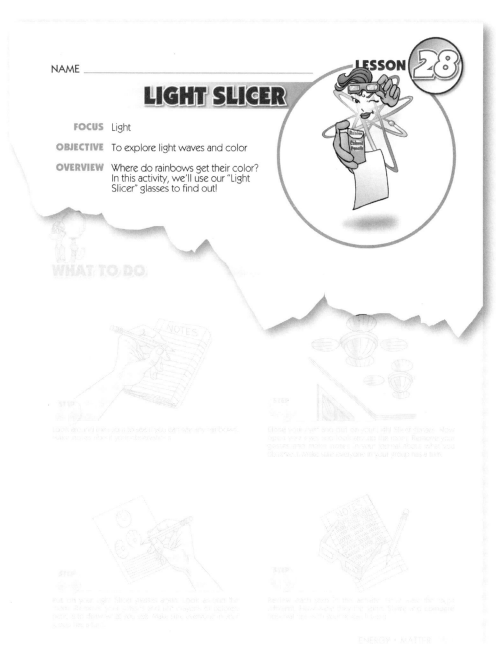

NAME _____

LIGHT SLICER

FOCUS Light

OBJECTIVE To explore light waves and color

OVERVIEW Where do rainbows get their color? In this activity, we'll use our "Light Slicer" glasses to find out!

LESSON 28

Category

Physical Science
Energy/Matter

Focus

Light

Objective

To explore light waves and color

National Standards

A1, A2, B1, B2, B3, E1, E2, F5, G1, G2

Materials Needed

Light Slicer glasses
crayons/colored pencils
art paper

Safety Concerns

4. Other
Glasses are for indoor use only. Do not allow students to look at the sun!

Additional Comments

Although standard bulbs work well for this activity, fluorescent lights provide a wider, more vibrant range of colors. Under no circumstances should students be allowed to look at the sun! These glasses do not provide protection from strong solar light.

Overview

Read the overview aloud to your students. The goal is to create an atmosphere of curiosity and inquiry.

WHAT TO DO

Monitor student research teams as they complete each step.

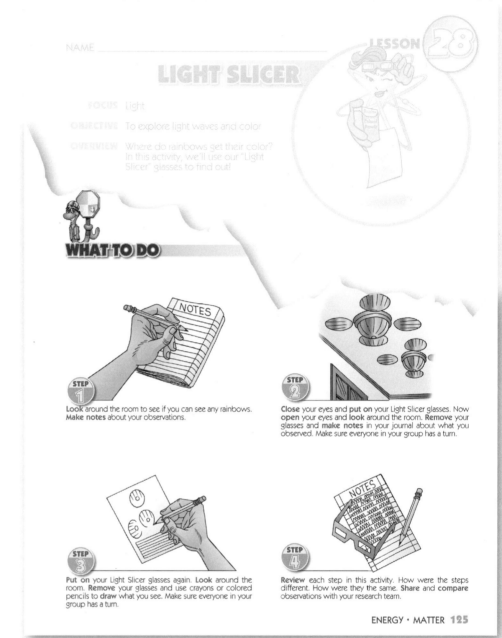

Teacher to Teacher

The electromagnetic spectrum includes wavelengths as small as a trillionth of a meter and as large as a football field! Frequencies vary just as widely. Although some living creatures can "see" frequencies humans can't (rattlesnakes detect infrared light, and honeybees use ultraviolet light to find flowers), human eyes only detect about 1% of the electromagnetic spectrum. That means most of the "light" in the universe is unseen by mankind.

WHAT HAPPENED?

Light travels in **waves**. Waves come in different lengths (called **wavelengths**). Like a **prism**, your **Light Slicer** glasses can **bend** light. Bending light in this fashion separates it into different wavelengths in a process known as **refraction**. Our eyes see these different wavelengths as different **colors**.

Rainbows make colors the same way because water droplets act like miniature prisms. Do you know the colors of the rainbow in order? A great way to remember them is with the name "Roy G. Biv." That's an acronym for Red, Orange, Yellow, Green, Blue, Indigo, and Violet.

There are many kinds of waves in our world — like **light** waves, **sound** waves, and **heat** waves — but we'll save that for other lessons!

WHAT WE LEARNED

1 Compare what you saw in Step 1 with what you saw in Step 2. How were the views similar? How were they different?

Answers will vary, but should reflect logical comparisons.

2 Make a list of the colors you saw in Step 2. What's an easy way to remember the colors of the rainbow in order?

a) red, orange, yellow, green, blue, indigo, violet

b) Roy G. Biv

3 Explain how your "Light Slicer" glasses change the way your eyes see light. What is the process called?

a) bending light separated it into different wavelengths

b) refraction

4 Explain how a rainbow creates colors.

Water droplets act as miniature prisms, refraction creates colors.

5 Other than light, name as least three other kinds of waves. (Hint: What kitchen appliance uses a special kind of wave to heat food quickly?)

microwaves, heat waves, sound waves, etc.

What Happened

Review the section with students. Emphasize bold-face words that identify key concepts and introduce new vocabulary.

Light travels in waves. Waves come in different lengths (called wavelengths). Like a prism, your Light Slicer glasses can bend light. Bending light in this fashion separates it into different wavelengths in a process known as refraction. Our eyes see these different wavelengths as different colors.

Rainbows make colors the same way because water droplets act like miniature prisms. Do you know the colors of the rainbow in order? A great way to remember them is with the name "Roy G. Biv." That's an acronym for Red, Orange, Yellow, Green, Blue, Indigo, and Violet.

There are many kinds of waves in our world — like light waves, sound waves, and heat waves — but we'll save that for other lessons!

What We Learned

Answers will vary. Suggested responses are shown at left.

Conclusion

Read this section aloud to the class to summarize the concepts learned in this activity.

Food for Thought

Read the Scripture aloud to the class. Talk about unkept promises and how they make us feel. Compare this to the trustworthiness of God. Discuss specific promises from Scripture.

Journal

If time permits, have a general class discussion about notes and drawings various students added to their journal pages. Discuss correct and incorrect predictions, and remind students that this "trial and error" process is part of the scientific process.

CONCLUSION

Prisms can bend light, separating it into different wavelengths. Visible light has several wavelengths that humans perceive as colors.

FOOD FOR THOUGHT

Genesis 9:13 In this activity, you had an opportunity to explore light and see rainbows. A rainbow is one of the more amazing forms of light on Earth.

But rainbows are more than just a pretty sky coloring. Every rainbow represents a promise from God. Scripture tells us that after the Flood, God promised to never again cover the Earth with water. God placed the rainbow in the sky as a sign of this promise. And unlike people, God never makes a promise he doesn't intend to keep!

JOURNAL   My Science Notes

Extended Teaching

1. Repeat this activity using different types of light (full spectrum bulbs, flashlights, computer screens, etc.) Have students compare results with the original activity. How are they similar? How are they different?

2. Using the Internet, have students research "invisible" light (infrared, x-rays, ultraviolet, etc.). Challenge each team to create a poster of the electromagnetic spectrum showing various types of light.

3. Invite an electric company representative to your classroom. Ask him/her to demonstrate how houses are tested for infrared (heat) waves and energy loss. Have students write a paragraph about one thing they learn.

4. Take a field trip to a hospital. Ask a technician to explain different forms of light that are used in the diagnoses and treatment of medical problems. Have students write a paragraph about one thing they learn.

5. Have teams research creatures that can detect light humans can't (rattlesnakes, honeybees, etc.). Challenge each team to contribute material for a bulletin board on this topic.

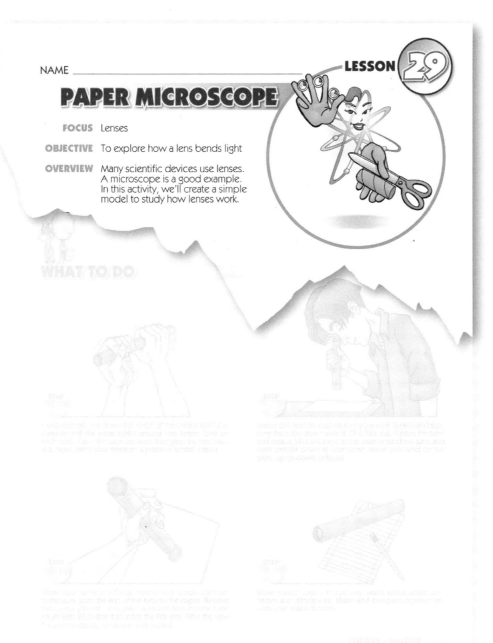

PAPER MICROSCOPE

LESSON 29

FOCUS Lenses

OBJECTIVE To explore how a lens bends light

OVERVIEW Many scientific devices use lenses. A microscope is a good example. In this activity, we'll create a simple model to study how lenses work.

WHAT TO DO

Category

Physical Science
Energy/Matter

Focus

Lenses

Objective

To explore how a lens bends light

National Standards

A1, A2, B1, B3, E1, E2, F5, G1, G2

Materials Needed

lenses - 2
scissors
cardboard tube
tape
paper
ruler

Safety Concerns

4. Sharp Objects
Remind students to exercise caution when using scissors.

Additional Comments

Remind students that the microscope is only for looking at objects, not at any light source! For some really unique images, let teams experiment with adding a third lens.

Overview

Read the overview aloud to your students. The goal is to create an atmosphere of curiosity and inquiry.

WHAT TO DO

Monitor student research teams as they complete each step.

NAME _____

PAPER MICROSCOPE

FOCUS   Lenses

OBJECTIVE   To explore how a lens bends light

OVERVIEW   Many scientific devices use lenses. A microscope is a good example. In this activity, we'll create a simple model to study how lenses work.

LESSON 29

WHAT TO DO

STEP 1

Using scissors, **cut** down the length of the cardboard tube. Carefully **roll** the tube tightly around two lenses (one on each end). **Tape** the tube securely, then **pop** the lens back out. Now, **print** your name on a piece of scratch paper.

STEP 2

Insert one lens by placing it on your work surface and slipping the tube down over it. (If it falls out, tighten the tube and retape.) Put your eye to the open end of the tube and **look** straight down at your name. **Move** your head (or the tube) up or down to focus.

STEP 3

When your name is in focus, **freeze!** **Ask** a team member to measure from the end of the tube to the paper. **Record** this in your journal. Now **push** a second lens into the tube (as in Step 2) so that it touches the first lens. **Find** the new focusing distance, **measure**, and **record**.

STEP 4

Review each step in this activity. **Make notes** about similarities and differences. **Share** and **compare** observations with your research team.

ENERGY · MATTER **129**

Teacher to Teacher

Concave lenses are thicker at the edges. They're also called "diverging" lenses because they spread light, bending it away from the center of the lens. Convex lenses are thicker in the middle. They're also called "converging" lenses because they concentrate light, bending it toward the center of the lens.

WHAT HAPPENED?

A **lens** is a piece of curved glass or plastic that causes **light** to **bend** as it passes through. Some of the earliest-known lenses were made by glass craftsmen in Venice. Some of these "spectacles" were made over 650 years ago! Because people thought these little glass disks resembled lentils (a kind of legume), they became known as "lentils of glass." The Latin word for this phrase is "lenses."

Moving a lens back and forth allows you to adjust (**focus**) the amount of light hitting a particular spot and the degree it bends. This focusing makes an **image** easier to see. Today, lenses are used in many devices — microscopes, eye glasses, contact lenses, cameras, telescopes, binoculars — the list is almost endless! But every lens works on the same principle of bending light.

WHAT WE LEARNED

1 Compare the views through the tube in Step 1 and Step 2. How were they similar? How were they different?

Answers will vary, but should reflect logical comparisons.

2 Describe the surface of a lens. What happens to light when it goes through a lens?

a) the surface is curved

b) it bends

3 What can we do to improve the image seen through a lens? What is this called?

a) move the lens back and forth to adjust the light

b) focus

4 Name three common devices that use lenses and tell what each is used for.

Eye glasses improve vision; cameras focus and record images; binoculars magnify distant images; etc.

5 Explain some of the history of lenses. When were the first lens made? Where were they made? Where did they get their name?

a) over 650 years ago

b) Venice

c) From the phrase, "lentils of glass"

What Happened

Review the section with students. Emphasize bold-face words that identify key concepts and introduce new vocabulary.

*A **lens** is a piece of curved glass or plastic that causes **light** to **bend** as it passes through. Some of the earliest-known lenses were made by glass craftsmen in Venice. Some of these "spectacles" were made over 650 years ago! Because people thought these little glass disks resembled lentils (a kind of legume), they became known as "lentils of glass." The Latin word for this phrase is "lenses."*

*Moving a lens back and forth allows you to adjust (**focus**) the amount of light hitting a particular spot and the degree it bends. This focusing makes an **image** easier to see. Today, lenses are used in many devices — microscopes, eye glasses, contact lenses, cameras, telescopes, binoculars — the list is almost endless! But every lens works on the same principle of bending light.*

What We Learned

Answers will vary. Suggested responses are shown at left.

Conclusion

Read this section aloud to the class to summarize the concepts learned in this activity.

Food for Thought

Read the Scripture aloud to the class. Discuss how God's Word can give us new insights and keep us on the right path.

Journal

If time permits, have a general class discussion about notes and drawings various students added to their journal pages. Discuss correct and incorrect predictions, and remind students that this "trial and error" process is part of the scientific process.

CONCLUSION
A lens is curved piece of glass or plastic used to bend light. Focus means adjusting the distance between a lens and an object to get a clearer view of an image.

FOOD FOR THOUGHT
Psalms 119:105 Your microscope model provided a simple way to make things easier to see. Real microscopes help scientists get a clearer understanding of how things work, and discover the answers to important questions.

While scientific tools are great for some kinds of questions, they can't provide answers to our every personal question. That's why God has given us the Scriptures! As we spend time each day reading or listening to God's Word, we discover new insights that show us the right path and keep us from stumbling.

JOURNAL My Science Notes

Extended Teaching

1. Repeat this activity using a longer cardboard tube. Have students compare the results to the original activity. How were they similar? How were they different?

2. Visit an optometrist. Ask him/her to demonstrate how eyes are tested. Discuss how correct lenses can help people see better. Have students write a paragraph about one thing they learn.

3. Invite a photographer to visit your classroom. Ask him/her to demonstrate how a camera works, and how different lenses produce different images. Have students write a paragraph about one thing they learn.

4. Using the Internet, have students research telescopes, binoculars, rifle scopes and similar devices. How do they magnify images? Challenge each team to create a poster showing one device and how it works.

5. Using a real microscope, examine cork cells. (The slices of cork must be very thin! A local high school biology teacher may have some prepared cork slides you could borrow for this.)

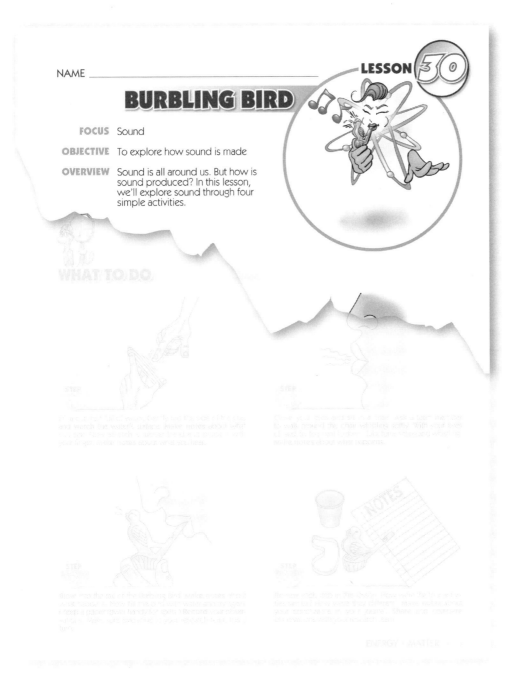

NAME _____

BURBLING BIRD

LESSON 30

FOCUS Sound

OBJECTIVE To explore how sound is made

OVERVIEW Sound is all around us. But how is sound produced? In this lesson, we'll explore sound through four simple activities.

WHAT TO DO

Category

Physical Science
Energy/Matter

Focus

Sound

Objective

To explore how sound is made

National Standards

A1, A2, B1, B2, B3, E1, E2, F5, G1, G2

Materials Needed

paper cup
rubber band
burbling bird
pipette
water

Safety Concerns

3. Hygiene
Wipe the mouthpiece with an antiseptic wipe between uses.

4. Slipping
There is a potential for spills with this activity. Remind students to exercise caution.

Additional Comments

Blowing too hard is a common mistake. It requires the correct combination of air speed and water to make the whistle "warble like a bird." After the activity if over, be sure to clean and disinfect the bird before storing.

Overview

Read the overview aloud to your students. The goal is to create an atmosphere of curiosity and inquiry.

WHAT TO DO

Monitor student research teams as they complete each step.

WHAT TO DO

BURBLING BIRD

FOCUS Sound

OBJECTIVE To explore how sound is made

OVERVIEW Sound is all around us. But how is sound produced? In this lesson, we'll explore sound through four simple activities.

STEP 1
Fill a cup half full of water. Gently tap the side of the cup and watch the water's surface. Make notes about what you see. Now stretch a rubber band and pluck it with your finger. Make notes about what you hear.

STEP 2
Close your eyes and sit in a chair. Ask a team member to walk around the chair whistling softly. With your eyes closed, try to point to them. Take turns sitting and whistling. Make notes about what happens.

STEP 3
Blow into the tail of the Burbling Bird. Make notes about what happens. Now fill the bird with water and try again. (Keep a paper towel handy for spills.) Record your observations. Make sure everyone in your research team has a turn.

STEP 4
Review each step in this lesson. How were the four activities similar? How were they different? Make notes about your conclusions in your journal. Share and compare observations with your research team.

ENERGY · MATTER **133**

Teacher to Teacher

Sound with a frequency (vibration rate) lower than humans can hear is called infrasound. Whales and elephants use infrasound to communicate over great distances.

Sound with a frequency higher than humans can hear is called ultrasound. Dolphins and bats use these very high vibration rates to find food.

❓WHAT HAPPENED?

Sound travels in **waves** produced by rapid back-and-forth movements that are called **vibrations**. It requires **energy** to make something vibrate. In this case, the energy was provided by your lungs. As you began to blow, the **air** in the plastic bird began to vibrate, creating sound. Adding water changed the amount of air trapped in the bird. This changed the length of the wave and how fast it vibrated. This different vibration rate created the different sound you heard.

Almost anything that creates sound works in the same way whether it's a musical instrument (buzzing reed, plucked string, banged drum), your voice (vibrating vocal chords), or even the television or radio (vibrating speaker). The combination that produces sound is always the same — energy, vibration, sound.

❓WHAT WE LEARNED

 1 How does sound travel? What are the rapid back-and-forth movements called? What is required to make this happen?

a) in waves

b) vibrations

c) energy

2 Compare the two activities in Step 1. How were they similar? How were they different?

answers will vary, but should reflect logical comparisons.

3 How was the activity from Step 2 similar to the activities in Step 1? How was it different?

Answers will vary, but should reflect logical comparisons.

4 Compare the sound from the empty bird with the sound after you added water. How were they similar? How were they different?

a) similar: a whistling noise

b) different: water caused it to warble

5 List three things that produce sound. Explain how vibration is involved with each.

guitar, vibrating strings; voice, vibrating vocal cords; radio, vibrating speaker; etc.

What Happened

Review the section with students. Emphasize bold-face words that identify key concepts and introduce new vocabulary.

Sound travels in *waves* produced by rapid back-and-forth movements that are called *vibrations*. It requires *energy* to make something vibrate. In this case, the energy was provided by your lungs. As you began to blow, the *air* in the plastic bird began to vibrate, creating sound. Adding water changed the amount of air trapped in the bird. This changed the length of the wave and how fast it vibrated. This different vibration rate created the different sound you heard.

Almost anything that creates sound works in the same way whether it's a musical instrument (buzzing reed, plucked string, banged drum), your voice (vibrating vocal chords), or even the television or radio (vibrating speaker). The combination that produces sound is always the same — energy, vibration, sound.

What We Learned

Answers will vary. Suggested responses are shown at left.

Conclusion

Read this section aloud to the class to summarize the concepts learned in this activity.

Food for Thought

Read the Scripture aloud to the class. Talk about how prayer becomes easier and more natural with practice. Discuss ways we can set time aside for meditation and prayer.

Journal

If time permits, have a general class discussion about notes and drawings various students added to their journal pages. Discuss correct and incorrect predictions, and remind students that this "trial and error" process is part of the scientific process.

CONCLUSION
It takes energy to make something vibrate. When vibration occurs, sound is the result.

FOOD FOR THOUGHT
Mark 1:35 At first, you may have had a little trouble getting the Burbling Bird to sing properly. But after a little practice, you could warble away!

Prayer is a lot like that. The more we pray, the easier it becomes. While you can pray anywhere, earnest prayer (and listening) takes time alone with God away from the world's distractions. In spite of his hectic schedule, in spite of the press of the daily crowds, Jesus took "quality time" to meditate and pray every day. We can too!

JOURNAL My Science Notes

Extended Teaching

1. Have teams research onomatopoeia (words that imitate sounds) and similar descriptives (like "warble," "burble," or "chortle"). Have them make lists, then share their findings with the class.

2. Play a recording of different bird sounds. See which ones students can identify. Have teams research why birds sing. Have them present their findings to the class.

3. Take a field trip to listen to a high school band. Ask the musicians to explain how their instruments work. Have students write a paragraph about one thing they learn.

4. Invite a professional musician to visit your classroom. Discuss variations in sound like pitch, timbre, and volume. Find out how these affect performance. Have students write a paragraph about one thing they learn.

5. Using the Internet, have teams research how animals use sound (communication, finding food, etc.). Challenge each team to contribute material for a classroom bulletin board on this topic.

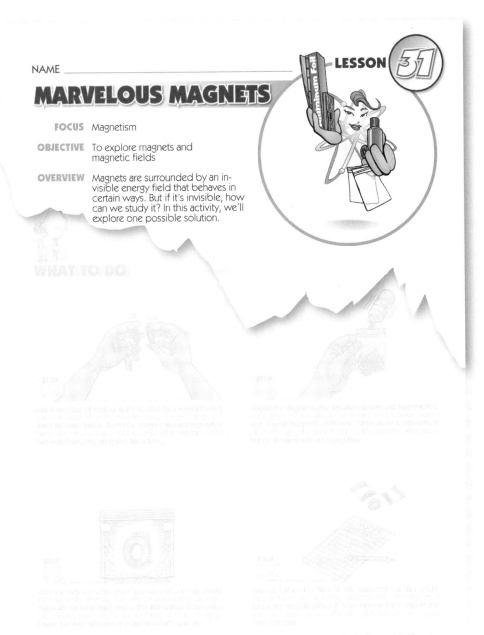

NAME _____

MARVELOUS MAGNETS

LESSON 31

FOCUS Magnetism

OBJECTIVE To explore magnets and magnetic fields

OVERVIEW Magnets are surrounded by an invisible energy field that behaves in certain ways. But if it's invisible, how can we study it? In this activity, we'll explore one possible solution.

WHAT TO DO

Category

Physical Science
Energy/Matter

Focus

Magnetism

Objective

To explore magnets and magnetic fields

National Standards

A1, A2, B1, B2, D1, E1, E2, F5, G1, G2

Materials Needed

magnets-2
wooden dowel rod
PVC pipe
nail
iron filings
sealable bags-2
aluminum foil

Safety Concerns

4. Other
Magnets can pinch fingers when they snap together.

Additional Comments

Don't let iron filings come into direct contact with magnets or clean up will be very difficult. Also, remind students to keep the magnets completely away from any computers and similar electronic devices.

Overview

Read the overview aloud to your students. The goal is to create an atmosphere of curiosity and inquiry.

WHAT TO DO

Monitor student research teams as they complete each step.

MARVELOUS MAGNETS

FOCUS Magnetism

OBJECTIVE To explore magnets and magnetic fields

OVERVIEW Magnets are surrounded by an invisible energy field that behaves in certain ways. But if it's invisible, how can we study it? In this activity, we'll explore one possible solution.

WHAT TO DO

STEP 1
Ask a member of another team to hold their magnet while you hold yours. **Hold** the magnets close to each other, but don't let them touch. **Turn** one magnet around and **bring** them close again. **Make notes** about what happens. (Be sure everyone on both teams has a turn.)

STEP 2
Touch the magnet to the wooden dowel rod, then the PVC pipe, then the aluminum foil, then the nail. **Make notes** about what happens each time. Now **pour** a tablespoon of iron filings in the plastic bag. **Leave** a little air and **seal** it tightly. **Repeat** with a second bag.

STEP 3
Stick the magnet to the center (outside!) of one bag. **Shake** the bag gently, then **hold** it with the sealed end up. **Make notes** about what happens to the iron filings. Now **place** the second bag next to the first bag with the magnet. **Shake** the bags gently and **observe** what happens.

STEP 4
Repeat the end of Step 3 until everyone has had a turn. Be sure the bags stay tightly closed so the iron filings don't touch the magnet directly! Now **review** each step in this activity. **Share** and **compare** observations with your research team.

ENERGY · MATTER **137**

Teacher to Teacher

Some students may ask, "What causes magnetism?" The most current view is the Domain Theory, which states that magnetism is the result of the arrangement and spinning motion of the electrons within atoms. The effectiveness of a magnetic field is determined by the number of electrons spinning in each direction.

WHAT HAPPENED?

Since iron filings are attracted by **magnetic fields**, their behavior helped you see how these fields surround a magnet. By watching the filings, we can see that magnetic fields are not flat — their influence is **multi-dimensional**. This means they affect things above or below, in front or in back, or on either side.

When you put two magnets close to each other, their behavior depended on which way you were holding them. This is because magnets have two **poles** known as **north** and **south**. Similar poles (like north and north) **push** apart or **repel** each other. Opposite poles (like north and south) **pull** together or **attract**.

WHAT WE LEARNED

 1 Describe what happened to the magnets in Step 1. Why did they behave differently depending on how you held them?

a) magnets pushed away or pulled together.

b) the way they were aligned with each other.

2 Describe the reaction of each material in Step 2 to the magnet. What can we conclude from this?

a) attracted to nail; not attracted to other materials.

b) a nail contains iron, which is magnetic.

3 Based on what you discovered in Step 2, what would happen if the bag contained only sawdust or paper? Why?

a) nothing

b) sawdust and paper are not magnetic.

4 Describe the magnetic field shown by the iron filings' behavior in Step 3. What additional behavior occurred in Step 4. What can we conclude from this?

a) answers will vary.

b) similar arrangement on both sides.

c) magnetic field is multi-directional.

5 What are the two ends of a magnet called? How do these two ends react to each other? What are these two reactions called?

a) north and south poles

b) like poles repel; opposites attract.

c) pull together = attract; push apart = repel.

What Happened

Review the section with students. Emphasize bold-face words that identify key concepts and introduce new vocabulary.

Since iron filings are attracted by **magnetic fields**, *their behavior helped you see how these fields surround a magnet. By watching the filings, we can see that magnetic fields are not flat — their influence is* **multi-dimensional**. *This means they affect things above or below, in front or in back, or on either side.*

When you put two magnets close to each other, their behavior depended on which way you were holding them. This is because magnets have two **poles** *known as* **north** *and* **south**. *Similar poles (like north and north)* **push** *apart or* **repel** *each other. Opposite poles (like north and south)* **pull** *together or* **attract**.*

What We Learned

Answers will vary. Suggested responses are shown at left.

Conclusion

Read this section aloud to the class to summarize the concepts learned in this activity.

Food for Thought

Read the Scripture aloud to the class. Talk about what happens when God fills our hearts. Discuss ways others can tell he is working in our lives.

Journal

If time permits, have a general class discussion about notes and drawings various students added to their journal pages. Discuss correct and incorrect predictions, and remind students that this "trial and error" process is part of the scientific process.

CONCLUSION

Magnets have invisible fields. Similar poles of a magnet repel each other. Opposite poles attract each other.

FOOD FOR THOUGHT

Acts 4:31 Until the magnet arrived, the iron filings were lifeless. They didn't show any movement or activity. But when the power of the magnet came near, things changed dramatically! The iron filings really became active, and they helped us see the power that was present.

Scripture tells us something special happens when God fills our lives. We may feel dull, ordinary, and powerless — but when the Spirit of God begins working in our lives, we can begin to make a real difference in the world. Like the filings made the magnet's power visible, so we can make God's power and love visible to others.

JOURNAL My Science Notes

Extended Teaching

1. Repeat the activity using different shaped magnets. Have students compare the field shapes formed with the original activity. How are they similar? How are they different?

2. Find someone who owns a GPS system (surveyor, hiker, hobbiest, etc.). Invite him/her to visit your classroom and demonstrate how this device works. Have students write a paragraph about one thing they learn.

3. Have teams create an electromagnet by wrapping insulated wire around a nail and hooking the ends to a D cell battery. Challenge them to touch the nail to various objects and record the results. (Avoid computers!)

4. Have teams research the magnetic force of the North and South Poles. Challenge each team to contribute material for a classroom bulletin board on planetary magnetism.

5. Take a field trip into the woods with an outdoor enthusiast. Ask him/her to demonstrate the proper use of a compass. Have students write a paragraph about one thing they learn.

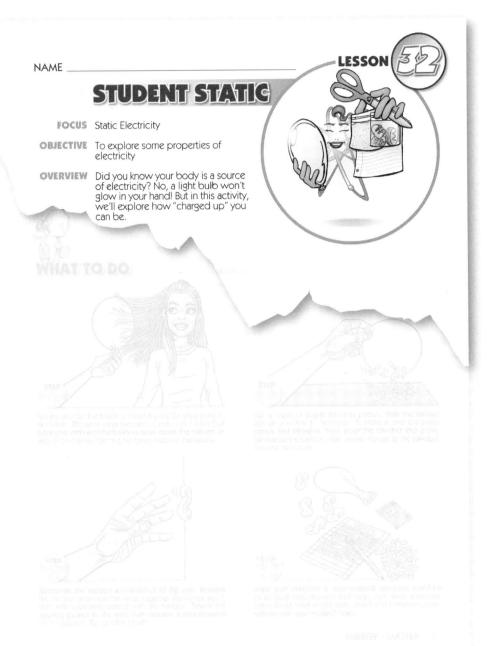

STUDENT STATIC

FOCUS Static Electricity

OBJECTIVE To explore some properties of electricity

OVERVIEW Did you know your body is a source of electricity? No, a light bulb won't glow in your hand! But in this activity, we'll explore how "charged up" you can be.

WHAT TO DO

Category

Physical Science
Energy/Matter

Focus

Static Electricity

Objective

To explore some properties of electricity

National Standards

A1, A2, B1, B2, B3, E1, E2, F5, G1, G2

Materials Needed

balloon
sawdust
packing pellet
paper
scissors

Safety Concerns

4. Sharp Objects
Remind students to exercise caution when using scissors.

Additional Comments

To avoid an undue mess, keep the sawdust in the bag until ready for use, then clean up immediately afterward. Students with fine, straight hair and no hair spray make the best "chargers" for the balloon. Keep extra balloons on hand in case of breakage.

Overview

Read the overview aloud to your students. The goal is to create an atmosphere of curiosity and inquiry.

WHAT TO DO

Monitor student research teams as they complete each step.

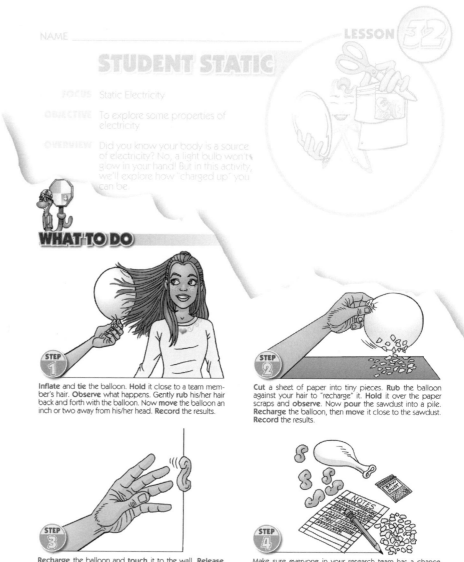

NAME _____

LESSON 32

STUDENT STATIC

FOCUS Static Electricity

OBJECTIVE To explore some properties of electricity

OVERVIEW Did you know your body is a source of electricity? No, a light bulb won't glow in your hand! But in this activity, we'll explore how "charged up" you can be.

WHAT TO DO

STEP 1
Inflate and tie the balloon. Hold it close to a team member's hair. Observe what happens. Gently rub his/her hair back and forth with the balloon. Now move the balloon an inch or two away from his/her head. Record the results.

STEP 2
Cut a sheet of paper into tiny pieces. Rub the balloon against your hair to "recharge" it. Hold it over the paper scraps and observe. Now pour the sawdust into a pile. Recharge the balloon, then move it close to the sawdust. Record the results.

STEP 3
Recharge the balloon and touch it to the wall. Release the balloon and observe what happens. Recharge again, then rub a packing peanut with the balloon. Touch the packing peanut to the wall, then release it and observe what happens. Record the results.

STEP 4
Make sure everyone in your research team has a chance to try each step. Review each step, then write additional notes about what you've seen. Share and compare observations with your research team.

ENERGY · MATTER 141

Teacher to Teacher

There are three basic subatomic particles: protons, neutrons, and electrons. Only electrons move freely. When large numbers of electrons move, it creates electricity — either static or current. This activity is an example of static electricity (also found in clinging clothes and lightning bolts!). Current electricity, of course, is what powers our homes, factories, and schools.

⟨❓WHAT HAPPENED?⟩

Rubbing the balloon back and forth captured **electrons** from your hair. Their **negative charges** (trapped on the balloon's surface) caused objects to be **attracted** to the balloon. In Step 3, you were even able to **transfer** the electrons from your hair to the balloon, then on to a packing peanut!

But just because you have an "electric personality," don't plan to light up the room! While all **electricity** is made of electrons, there are two different kinds of electricity. **Current** electricity (the kind that powers most household devices) is based on electrons that are moving. **Static** electricity (like you produced) is based on electrons that are not moving.

⟨❓WHAT WE LEARNED⟩

 1 Compare what happened in Step 1 before you rubbed the balloon with what happened after. How were they similar? How were they different?

answers will vary, but should reflect
logical comparisons.

2 Describe what happened in Step 2. How did the balloon affect the paper? How did it affect the sawdust?

both the paper and the sawdust stuck to
the balloon.

3 Describe what happened in Step 3. What transferred from the balloon to the peanut? What was the result?

a) answers will vary.

b) electrons

c) the packing peanut stuck to the wall.

4 Name the two kinds of electricity. How are they similar? How are they different?

current: moving electrons; static: electrons
that are not moving.

5 Ten students walk across a fluffy carpet wearing wool socks. Based on what you've learned, could this generate enough electricity to light a small light bulb?

a) no

b) because it would generate static electricity,
not current electricity.

What Happened

Review the section with students. Emphasize bold-face words that identify key concepts and introduce new vocabulary.

*Rubbing the balloon back and forth captured **electrons** from your hair. Their **negative charges** (trapped on the balloon's surface) caused objects to be **attracted** to the balloon. In Step 3, you were even able to **transfer** the electrons from your hair to the balloon, then on to a packing peanut!*

*But just because you have an "electric personality," don't plan to light up the room! While all **electricity** is made of electrons, there are two different kinds of electricity. **Current** electricity (the kind that powers most household devices) is based on electrons that are moving. **Static** electricity (like you produced) is based on electrons that are not moving.*

What We Learned

Answers will vary. Suggested responses are shown at left.

Conclusion

Read this section aloud to the class to summarize the concepts learned in this activity.

Food for Thought

Read the Scripture aloud to the class. Discuss how learning more about God's care and compassion helps draw us deeper into his loving embrace.

Journal

If time permits, have a general class discussion about notes and drawings various students added to their journal pages. Discuss correct and incorrect predictions, and remind students that this "trial and error" process is part of the scientific process.

CONCLUSION

Electricity is based on electrons. There are two types of electricity. Current electricity means electrons are in motion. Static electricity means electrons are stationary.

FOOD FOR THOUGHT

John 12:32 The static electricity you created in this activity has an amazing power of attraction. Whenever the balloon was close to certain objects, they were immediately drawn to it.

This Scripture talks about another powerful attraction — the pull of God's love on the hearts of his children. By demonstrating God's incredible love, Jesus drew us to him in a powerful way. As we spend time each day learning more about God's care and compassion, we will be drawn deeper into his loving embrace.

JOURNAL My Science Notes

Extended Teaching

1. Have teams research how thunderstorms build up huge electrical charges. Find out about different types of lightning and how much energy is released. Challenge teams to contribute materials for a "lightning" bulletin board.

2. Invite a representative from the electric company to visit your classroom. Ask him/her to talk about different ways electricity is generated. Have students write a paragraph about one thing they learn.

3. Have students research what life in America was like before electricity. (Elderly friends or relatives are a great source!) Challenge them to write a story about how their life would be different without electricity.

4. Have teams research ways to conserve electricity. Challenge teams to apply their findings to their homes and the classroom. Have them create posters promoting energy conservation around your school.

5. Have teams research the difference between static electricity and current electricity. Challenge each team to contribute materials for a classroom bulletin board on this topic.

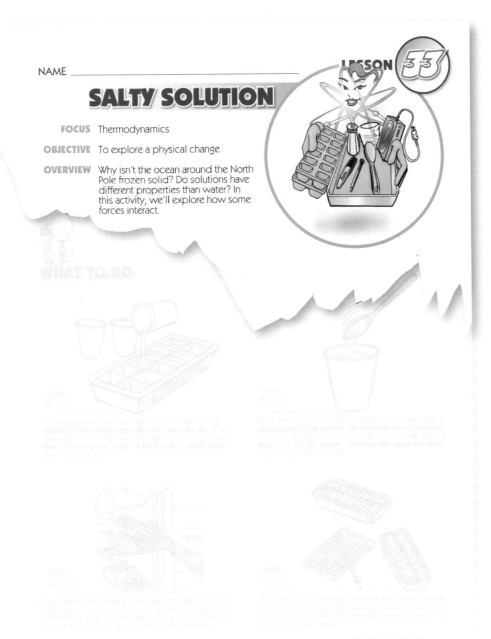

SALTY SOLUTION

LESSON 33

FOCUS Thermodynamics

OBJECTIVE To explore a physical change

OVERVIEW Why isn't the ocean around the North Pole frozen solid? Do solutions have different properties than water? In this activity, we'll explore how some forces interact.

WHAT TO DO

Category
Physical Science
Energy/Matter

Focus
Thermodynamics

Objective
To explore a physical change

National Standards
A1, A2, B1, B2, B3, E1, E2, F5, G1, G2

Materials Needed
paper cups-3
craft stick
salt
water
plastic ice trays-2
masking tape
tablespoon
freezer

Safety Concerns
4. Slipping
There is a potential for spills with this activity. Remind students to exercise caution.

Additional Comments

Begin this activity early in the day so that the freezing (Step 3) can be monitored closely. If metal ice cube trays are used, be careful that sweaty fingers don't get stuck to them!

Overview

Read the overview aloud to your students. The goal is to create an atmosphere of curiosity and inquiry.

Monitor student research teams as they complete each step.

NAME _____

SALTY SOLUTION

LESSON 33

FOCUS Thermodynamics

OBJECTIVE To explore a physical change

OVERVIEW Why isn't the ocean around the North Pole frozen solid? Do solutions have different properties than water? In this activity, we'll explore how some forces interact.

WHAT TO DO

STEP 1
Fill three paper cups with water from the sink. Carefully **empty** the cups into an ice cube tray. **Label** the tray "T" for "tap water." (Note: Masking tape makes a good temporary label.) **Observe** the water in the tray and **make notes** about what you see.

STEP 2
Refill the cups with water. Carefully **add** two heaping tablespoons of salt to each. **Stir** until the salt is completely dissolved. **Empty** the cups into a second ice cube tray and label it "S" for "salt water." **Observe** the water and **make notes** about what you see.

STEP 3
Place both ice cube trays in the freezer compartment of a refrigerator. **Predict** what effect if any the salt might have on the freezing point of the water. **Ask** a team member to check the trays every half hour. **Record** any changes.

STEP 4
[next day] **Remove** the two trays from the freezer. Carefully **examine** the contents and **record** the results. Now **review** each step in this activity. **Share** and **compare** observations with your research team.

ENERGY · MATTER **145**

Teacher to Teacher

The "salt" road crews spread on icy roads usually contains sand (for traction), sodium chloride (table salt), and calcium chloride. While many drivers believe this material melts ice, it actually just lowers water's freezing point. Depending on ground temperature, friction from tires usually does the rest.

WHAT HAPPENED?

The notes you recorded in your journal should indicate that the *fresh* water froze more quickly than the *salt* water. In fact, depending on how much salt you added, or how cold your freezer is, the salt solution may not have frozen at all!

Thermodynamics (thermo = heat) is the study of changes caused by **heat** and how heat moves from place to place. In this activity, **heat energy** was removed to cause a **physical change** — **freezing**. The **temperature** where a **liquid** becomes a **solid** (or vice versa) is its freezing (or **melting**) point. Liquids become solid when their **molecules** slow down so much that they stick together. The salt added to the water interfered with this process, lowering the freezing point.

Remember that freezing/thawing is a **physical change** — only the material's form changed. It's still the same material before freezing and after thawing.

WHAT WE LEARNED

 1 What does "thermodynamics" mean? Explain how it applies to this activity.

a) the study of changes caused by heat.

b) it studied what happens when heat is removed.

2 What did you predict in Step 3? How did this prediction reflect what actually happened?

answers will vary, but should reflect logical comparisons.

3 Explain how liquids become solids (and vice versa). What happens to their molecules?

liquids become solids when their molecules slow down and stick together (and vice versa).

4 Did this activity represent a physical change or a chemical change? Explain your answer.

a) physical change

b) only the material's form changed . . . it's still water.

5 Based on what you've learned, why does adding antifreeze change the freezing point of water in a car's radiator?

it interferes with the molecules' ability to stick together.

What Happened

Review the section with students. Emphasize bold-face words that identify key concepts and introduce new vocabulary.

The notes you recorded in your journal should indicate that the fresh water froze more quickly than the salt water. In fact, depending on how much salt you added, or how cold your freezer is, the salt solution may not have frozen at all!

***Thermodynamics** (thermo = heat) is the study of changes caused by **heat** and how heat moves from place to place. In this activity, **heat energy** was removed to cause a **physical change** — **freezing**. The **temperature** where a **liquid** becomes a **solid** (or vice versa) is its freezing (or **melting**) point. Liquids become solid when their **molecules** slow down so much that they stick together. The salt added to the water interfered with this process, lowering the freezing point.*

*Remember that freezing/thawing is a **physical change** — only the material's form changed. It's still the same material before freezing and after thawing.*

What We Learned

Answers will vary. Suggested responses are shown at left.

Conclusion

Read this section aloud to the class to summarize the concepts learned in this activity.

Food for Thought

Read the Scripture aloud to the class. Talk about how our words can be a positive reflection of God's love. Discuss things we can say to build up others.

Journal

If time permits, have a general class discussion about notes and drawings various students added to their journal pages. Discuss correct and incorrect predictions, and remind students that this "trial and error" process is part of the scientific process.

CONCLUSION

Thermodynamics is the study of changes caused by heat, and how heat moves from place to place. Dissolving materials in a solution can change its freezing point.

FOOD FOR THOUGHT

James 3:7-12 Looking at the water in the two ice trays, it was difficult to tell which was which before they froze. (That's why we needed the labels!) Yet even though they looked alike, the behaviors of the two were very different.

This Scripture talks about the effects of our tongue. The same mouth can say nice things, building someone up and making them feel better — or it can say mean things, hurting someone's feelings and making them feel bad. James reminds us that we need to "tame" our tongues! Before you speak, make sure the words you say are a positive reflection of the loving God you serve.

JOURNAL My Science Notes

Extended Teaching

1. Repeat this activity several times, adding different amounts of salt each time (start with 1/4 tsp.). Challenge teams to discover the exact amount of salt needed to keep the water from freezing. Keep careful records and graph the results.

2. Take a field trip to an automotive repair shop. Ask the mechanic to demonstrate how antifreeze is tested. Find out why freezing can damage an engine. Have students write a paragraph about one thing they learn.

3. If it's cold enough, even salt water can freeze. Have students research how ice made from salt water differs from ice made of fresh water. Challenge teams to share their findings with the class.

4. Using the Internet, have teams research how insects survive the winter without freezing. Challenge each team to create a poster showing one type of insect and how it survives freezing temperatures.

5. The Inuit people of the far North have many different names for ice based on its properties and formation. Have students research this, then write a paragraph or two about what they've learned.

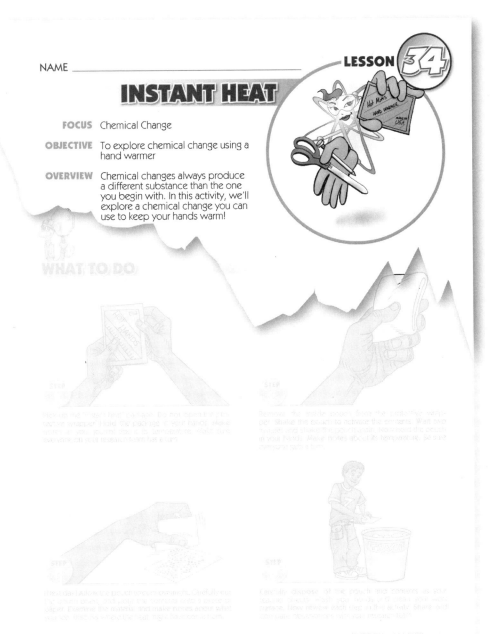

INSTANT HEAT

FOCUS Chemical Change

OBJECTIVE To explore chemical change using a hand warmer

OVERVIEW Chemical changes always produce a different substance than the one you begin with. In this activity, we'll explore a chemical change you can use to keep your hands warm!

WHAT TO DO

Category

Physical Science
Energy/Matter

Focus

Chemical Change

Objective

To explore a chemical change using a hand warmer

National Standards

A1, A2, B1, B2, B3, E1, E2, F5, G1, G2

Materials Needed

"instant heat" package
scissors
paper

Safety Concerns

2. Corrosion
Avoid direct contact of iron filings with skin.

3. Hygiene
Remind students to wash hands with soap and water after handling materials.

Additional Comments

Students should not open the inner package of the hand warmer until they are told to do so. Be sure to discard all materials immediately after Step 3 and carefully clean the work area. The oxidized iron filings can be a skin irritant.

Overview

Read the overview aloud to your students. The goal is to create an atmosphere of curiosity and inquiry.

WHAT TO DO

Monitor student research teams as they complete each step.

NAME _____

LESSON 34

INSTANT HEAT

FOCUS Chemical Change

OBJECTIVE To explore chemical change using a hand warmer

OVERVIEW Chemical changes always produce a different substance than the one you begin with. In this activity, we'll explore a chemical change you can use to keep your hands warm!

WHAT TO DO

STEP 1

Pick up the "instant heat" package. **Do not open** the protective wrapper! **Hold** the package in your hands. **Make notes** in your journal about its temperature. Make sure everyone on your research team has a turn.

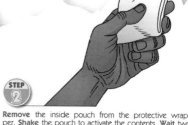

STEP 2

Remove the inside pouch from the protective wrapper. **Shake** the pouch to activate the contents. **Wait** two minutes and **shake** the pouch again. Now **hold** the pouch in your hands. **Make notes** about its temperature. Be sure everyone gets a turn.

STEP 3

[Next day] **Allow** the pouch to cool overnight. Carefully **cut** the pouch open, and **pour** the contents onto a piece of paper. **Examine** the material and **make notes** about what you see. **Discuss** where the heat might have come from.

STEP 4

Carefully **dispose** of the pouch and contents as your teacher directs. **Wash** your hands and **clean** your work surface. Now **review** each step in this activity. **Share** and **compare** observations with your research team.

ENERGY · MATTER **149**

Teacher to Teacher

Oxidation is normally a slow process. But because the iron in the packet is in tiny particles, the reaction happens quickly and energy (in the form of heat) is released. Scientists call a chemical reaction that gives off heat an "exothermic" reaction.

WHAT HAPPENED?

Inside this little package were **iron** filings. You couldn't see them, but you could tell by the feel of the package that they were very small. When you opened the outer wrapper, the **oxygen** in the air began to **react** with the filings in a **chemical change** called **oxidation**. This oxidation of the iron produced the **heat** you felt.

Remember, chemical change always results in a different substance. As oxidation changed the iron into a new compound (iron oxide, also known as rust), **energy** (in this case heat) was released.

Burning is another form of oxidation, only it happens much more quickly. The oxidation created in this activity is much slower than burning, but it can be very handy on a cold winter's morning!

WHAT WE LEARNED

1 Compare the Instant Heat pouch in Step 1 with the same pouch after Step 2. How were they similar? How were they different?

answers should reflect differences between the wrapped and unwrapped pouch.

2 What reacted with the filings in Step 2? What is this kind of reaction called? Name another form that happens more quickly.

a) oxygen

b) oxidation

c) burning

3 Describe the contents of the pouch from Step 3. What did the contents look like? Where might the heat have come from?

a) black, powdery, etc.

b) some sort of chemical reaction.

4 Did this activity demonstrate a physical or chemical change? Explain your answer.

a) chemical change

b) a different substance formed.

5 Scientists grind a block of wood into sawdust. Later, they set fire to another block of wood. Which activity is a physical change, and which is a chemical change? Explain your answer.

a) physical change = grinding wood into sawdust (same material, different form).

b) chemical change = burning wood (different substance).

What Happened

Review the section with students. Emphasize bold-face words that identify key concepts and introduce new vocabulary.

*Inside this little package were **iron** filings. You couldn't see them, but you could tell by the feel of the package that they were very small. When you opened the outer wrapper, the **oxygen** in the air began to **react** with the filings in a **chemical change** called **oxidation**. This oxidation of the iron produced the **heat** you felt.*

*Remember, chemical change always results in a different substance. As oxidation changed the iron into a new compound (iron oxide, also known as rust), **energy** (in this case heat) was released.*

***Burning** is another form of oxidation, only it happens much more quickly. The oxidation created in this activity is much slower than burning, but it can be very handy on a cold winter's morning!*

What We Learned

Answers will vary. Suggested responses are shown at left.

Conclusion

Read this section aloud to the class to summarize the concepts learned in this activity.

Food for Thought

Read the Scripture aloud to the class. Talk about the criteria we need to use in setting priorities. Discuss how spending time with God can help us keep our priorities in order.

Journal

If time permits, have a general class discussion about notes and drawings various students added to their journal pages. Discuss correct and incorrect predictions, and remind students that this "trial and error" process is part of the scientific process.

?CONCLUSION

Chemical change always produces a different substance. Some chemical changes release energy. Oxidation is a good example of a chemical change.

FOOD FOR THOUGHT

Matthew 6:10-21 The chemical reaction in this activity produced heat, but also caused the metal to corrode rapidly. Chemical and physical changes like rusting metal, crumbling stones, and rotting wood all serve to remind us that nothing in this world is permanent.

In this Scripture, Jesus points out that everything on Earth is temporary. Although material things like our car, our home, and our clothes seem pretty important, we must never let them become more important than God! If a friend accidently stains your favorite shirt, which is more important — the shirt or your friend's feelings? Spending time with God each day helps us keep our priorities in order.

JOURNAL   My Science Notes

Extended Teaching

1. Leave the iron filings out in the air for a few days. Observe them after the package has cooled down. Have students discuss what they find.

2. Obtain an "instant cold" pack from a coach or a sporting goods store. Follow the directions for using it and demonstrate it for the kids. How is this similar to the original activity? How is it different?

3. Have teams research how stainless steel is made. What it is made from. Why doesn't it rust as easily as an old nail? Have students write a paragraph or two about their findings.

4. Using the Internet, have students find out where and how iron is produced from ore or raw materials. Challenge each team to create a poster mapping some of these locations.

5. Take a field trip to a metal shop. Find out about different metals and methods used to attach one piece of metal to another. How does rust affect this process? Have students write a paragraph about one thing they learn.

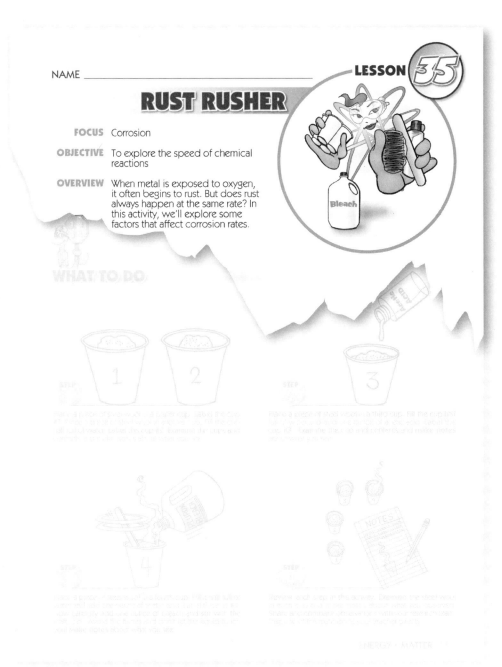

NAME _____

RUST RUSHER

LESSON 35

FOCUS Corrosion

OBJECTIVE To explore the speed of chemical reactions

OVERVIEW When metal is exposed to oxygen, it often begins to rust. But does rust always happen at the same rate? In this activity, we'll explore some factors that affect corrosion rates.

WHAT TO DO

Category
Physical Science
Energy/Matter

Focus
Corrosion

Objective
To explore the speed of chemical reactions

National Standards
A1, A2, B1, B3, G1, G2

Materials Needed
steel wool
paper cups - 4
craft stick
acetic acid
bleach
water

Safety Concerns

1. Goggles
Since chemicals are used in this activity, goggles are recommended.

2. Corrosion
Bleach is a skin, eye, nose, and lung irritant. Remind students to exercise caution.

3. Vapor
Bleach emits fumes. Remind students to exercise caution.

4. Slipping
There is a potential for spills with this activity. Remind students to exercise caution.

Additional Comments

Because of potential messes, you may wish to do this as a demonstration. Bleach and acetic acid will react vigorously (Step 3), so set the cup in a large pan or the sink. Remind students bleach can irritate skin, eyes, nose, and lungs — and also ruin clothes! After finishing, flush solutions down the drain and carefully dispose of the steel wool. Clean the activity area and wash hands thoroughly.

Overview

Read the overview aloud to your students. The goal is to create an atmosphere of curiosity and inquiry.

WHAT TO DO

Monitor student research teams as they complete each step.

RUST RUSHER

FOCUS Corrosion

OBJECTIVE To explore the speed of chemical reactions

OVERVIEW When metal is exposed to oxygen, it often begins to rust. But does rust always happen at the same rate? In this activity, we'll explore some factors that affect corrosion rates.

WHAT TO DO

STEP 1

Place a piece of steel wool in a paper cup. **Label** the cup #1. **Place** a piece of steel wool in another cup. **Fill** the cup half full of water. **Label** this cup #2. **Examine** the cups and contents and **make notes** about what you see.

STEP 2

Place a piece of steel wool in a third cup. **Fill** the cup half full of water and **add** one ounce of acetic acid. **Label** this cup #3. **Examine** the cup and contents and **make notes** about what you see.

STEP 3

Place a piece of steel wool in a fourth cup. **Fill** it half full of water and **add** one ounce of acetic acid. **Label** this cup #4. Now carefully **add** one ounce of bleach and **stir** with the craft stick. **Avoid** the fumes and don't let the liquid touch you! **Make notes** about what you see.

STEP 4

Review each step in this activity. **Examine** the steel wool in each cup and **make notes** about what you observed. **Share** and **compare** observations with your research team. **Dispose** of the materials as your teacher directs.

ENERGY · MATTER **153**

Teacher to Teacher

Given enough time, all three cups will produce iron oxide. The reactants in Cup 4 simply made the process faster! Scientists call the speed at which a chemical reaction occurs the "reaction rate." Factors affecting reaction rates include the nature of the reactants, the concentration of liquids, the temperature, and the presence of a catalyst. (Note: while a catalyst speeds up a reaction, it is not usually used up or consumed in the reaction process.)

WHAT HAPPENED?

Even though the steel wool (which is full of **iron**) was the same in every cup, the contents of Cup #4 corroded almost immediately! When iron and **oxygen** combine, we call the **corrosion** process **rusting**. In this activity, the bleach and acetic acid created a **chemical reaction** that greatly accelerated (sped up) the corrosion process.

Although the corrosion rate varies, eventually the steel wool in every cup will rust. Many people think water causes iron to rust, but actually water only speeds up the corrosion process by keeping the iron and oxygen in constant contact.

There are entire industries devoted to protecting metal from corrosion. Galvanizing, painting, plating, and alloying are just some of the methods used.

WHAT WE LEARNED

 1 Compare Cup #1 with Cup #2. How were they similar? How were they different?

identical except Cup 2 contained water

2 Compare Cup #3 with Cup #4. How were they similar? How were they different?

identical except Cup 4 contained bleach

3 Compare the corrosion rates of all four cups. How were they similar? How were they different?

Cups show increasing degrees of rust; Cup 1 = least, Cup 4 = most

4 When iron and oxygen combine, what is the corrosion process called? How does water accelerate this process?

a) rusting

b) by keeping iron and oxygen (in the water) in constant contact

5 Did this activity demonstrate a chemical or a physical change? Explain your answer.

a) chemical change

b) changed iron into iron oxide. (a different substance)

What Happened

Review the section with students. Emphasize bold-face words that identify key concepts and introduce new vocabulary.

*Even though the steel wool (which is full of **iron**) was the same in every cup, the contents of Cup #4 corroded almost immediately! When iron and **oxygen** combine, we call the **corrosion** process **rusting**. In this activity, the bleach and acetic acid created a **chemical reaction** that greatly accelerated (sped up) the corrosion process.*

Although the corrosion rate varies, eventually the steel wool in every cup will rust. Many people think water causes iron to rust, but actually water only speeds up the corrosion process by keeping the iron and oxygen in constant contact.

There are entire industries devoted to protecting metal from corrosion. Galvanizing, painting, plating, and alloying are just some of the methods used.

What We Learned

Answers will vary. Suggested responses are shown at left.

Conclusion

Read this section aloud to the class to summarize the concepts learned in this activity.

Food for Thought

Read the Scripture aloud to the class. Talk about how we change inside when we begin to actively care for others. Discuss specific things we can do to help those around us.

Journal

If time permits, have a general class discussion about notes and drawings various students added to their journal pages. Discuss correct and incorrect predictions, and remind students that this "trial and error" process is part of the scientific process.

CONCLUSION

The combination of iron and oxygen creates a kind of corrosion called rusting. Like other chemical reactions, the rate of the process can vary according to conditions.

FOOD FOR THOUGHT

1 Timothy 6:17-19 In this Scripture, the apostle Paul is writing to his young friend Timothy. His good advice echoes the words of Jesus that we read last week (Matthew 6: 10-21). No matter how much money someone has, no matter how many beautiful things they own, the only real treasure a person can have is what they've stored in Heaven.

How do we do this? Paul suggests that the more we do for others, the more we ourselves are changed to become like Jesus. The more we become like Jesus, reaching out to others in unselfish love, the more we invest in eternity. As someone once said, "The more you give to others, the more God gives to you!"

JOURNAL My Science Notes

Extended Teaching

1. Find a old piece of metal that has almost completely rusted. Bring it to class and let students see how crumbly iron oxide is. Have them write a paragraph about their impressions.

2. Using the Internet, have teams research ways to keep iron from rusting (galvanizing, painting, polymer coatings, etc.). Challenge each team to contribute material for a classroom bulletin board on this topic.

3. Older cars in the Northeast are often seriously rusted, while cars of the same age in the Southwest are not. Challenge teams to find out why, then make a presentation to the class explaining their findings.

4. Find a metal finishing shop (yellow pages under "plating"). Invite the manager to bring "before and after" samples, and to explain the plating process. Have students write a paragraph about one thing they learn.

5. Take a field trip to a shop that specializes in undercoating vehicles. Ask the manager to explain the process and its benefits. Have students write a paragraph about one thing they learn.

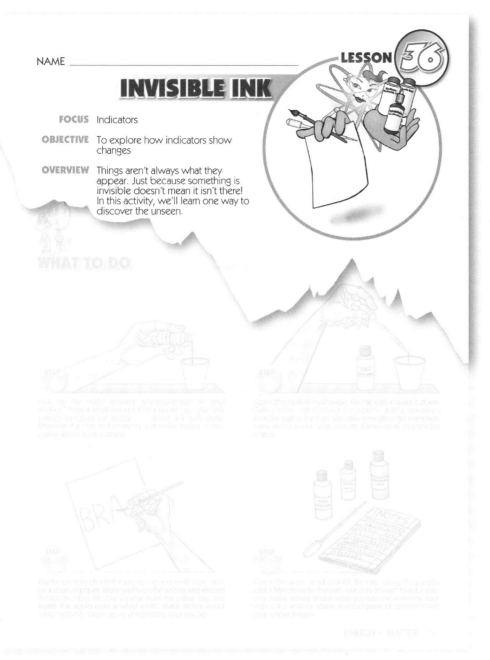

NAME _____

INVISIBLE INK

LESSON 36

FOCUS Indicators

OBJECTIVE To explore how indicators show changes

OVERVIEW Things aren't always what they appear. Just because something is invisible doesn't mean it isn't there! In this activity, we'll learn one way to discover the unseen.

WHAT TO DO

Category

Physical Science
Energy/Matter

Focus

Indicators

Objective

To explore how indicators show changes

National Standards

A1, A2, B1, G1, G2

Materials Needed

thymolphthalein
paper cup
sodium hydroxide
pipette
paint brush
white cloth
acetic acid
paper

Safety Concerns

1. Goggles
Since chemicals are used in this activity, goggles are recommended.

2. Corrosion
Sodium Hydroxide can be a severe skin irritant. Remind students to exercise caution.

3. Vapor
These chemicals emit fumes. Remind students to exercise caution.

Additional Comments

Since chemicals are used in this activity, you may wish to do it as a demonstration. Make sure there is plenty of ventilation. Be sure students wash hands and clean up carefully after Step 2 and Step 3. An old clean sock works well as the cloth in Step 3.

Overview

Read the overview aloud to your students. The goal is to create an atmosphere of curiosity and inquiry.

WHAT TO DO

Monitor student research teams as they complete each step.

NAME

INVISIBLE INK

FOCUS   Indicators

OBJECTIVE   To explore how indicators show changes

OVERVIEW   Things aren't always what they appear. Just because something is invisible doesn't mean it isn't there! In this activity, we'll learn one way to discover the unseen.

WHAT TO DO

STEP 1
Pick up the bottle labeled "thymolphthalein in ethyl alcohol." **Pour** a small amount into a paper cup. Use only enough to cover the bottom — about 1/4 inch deep. **Observe** the cup and contents and **make notes** in your journal about what you see.

STEP 2
Open the sodium hydroxide. **Fill** the cap and set it down. (Safety note: burns!) Using the pipette, **add** a few drops from the cap to the cup. Use only enough to get a reaction. **Make note**s about what you see. **Clean up** as your teacher directs.

STEP 3
Dip the paint brush into the paper cup and **write** your name on a sheet of paper. **Blow** gently on the writing and **record** the results. Now **fill** your pipette from the paper cup and **squirt** the liquid onto a white cloth. **Make notes** about what happens. **Clean up** as directed by your teacher.

STEP 4
Open the acetic acid and **fill** the cap. Using the pipette, **add** a few drops to the cup. Use only enough to get a reaction. **Make notes** about what you see. Now **review** each step in this activity. **Share** and **compare** observations with your research team.

ENERGY · MATTER **157**

Teacher to Teacher

Acid rain is a problem in many locations around the country. A common cause is devices which burn fuel and produce carbon dioxide (two oxygen atoms with one carbon atom connecting them). When this carbon dioxide combines with water (two hydrogen atoms and one oxygen atom), the result is carbonic acid. While carbonic acid is a relatively mild acid (soft drinks are a carbonic acid solution, for example), small amounts falling over a large period of time can eventually create serious problems in lakes and streams, as well as causing significant damage to trees and plants.

WHAT HAPPENED?

Thymolphthalein is a special chemical called an **indicator**. Indicators change color when **acid** or **base** levels change. Thymolphthalein is blue in a base, but clear in an acid. In Step 2, you added sodium hydroxide (a base), making a very blue solution. But when you painted this on the paper and blew on it gently, it began to disappear! This is because the **water** began to react with **carbon dioxide** in your breath to form a weak acid. Even though the **chemical change** was small, the indicator helped you discover it. In Step 4, the acetic acid neutralized the base, removing the color.

Acids and bases are measured with a system called a "**pH scale**." A reading of exactly 7 is **neutral** (neither acid nor base). Readings below 7 indicate an acid. Readings above 7 indicate a base. The pH scale is used in many ways, from environmental monitoring, to medical testing, to swimming pool tests — even checking a field's pH balance to produce better crops.

WHAT WE LEARNED

1 Compare the contents of the cup in Step 1 with the contents in Step 2. How were the solutions similar? How were they different?

solution in Cup 1 was clear; solution in Cup 2 turned blue

2 What chemical caused the color change in Step 2? Was this chemical an acid or a base? What property of thymolphthalein helped you determine this?

a) sodium hydroxide

b) base

c) it's a chemical indicator that changes color when acid or base levels change

3 Describe what happened to the paper and the cloth in Step 3. Explain why this occurred.

a) the blue gradually disappeared.

b) water reacted with carbon dioxide to form a weak acid

4 What are chemicals called that change color to show the presence of an acid or a base? Describe the pH scale. Tell how it is used.

a) indicators

b) a system that measures acids and bases

c) environmental monitoring, medical testing, swimming pool testing, etc.

5 Public swimming pools try to maintain pH levels around 7.5. A pH test yields a result of 6.2. Based on what you've learned, what problem does this pool have, and how might it be corrected?

the water is too acid (acidic), so a small amount of a base must be added to neutralize it

(teacher note: The ideal pool water is slightly base, but that's a needless complication for this answer.)

What Happened

Review the section with students. Emphasize bold-face words that identify key concepts and introduce new vocabulary.

Thymolphthalein is a special chemical called an indicator. Indicators change color when acid or base levels change. Thymolphthalein is blue in a base, but clear in an acid. In Step 2, you added sodium hydroxide (a base), making a very blue solution. But when you painted this on the paper and blew on it gently, it began to disappear! This is because the water began to react with carbon dioxide in your breath to form a weak acid. Even though the chemical change was small, the indicator helped you discover it. In Step 4, the acetic acid neutralized the base, removing the color.

Acids and bases are measured with a system called a "pH scale." A reading of exactly 7 is neutral (neither acid nor base). Readings below 7 indicate an acid. Readings above 7 indicate a base. The pH scale is used in many ways, from environmental monitoring, to medical testing, to swimming pool tests — even checking a field's pH balance to produce better crops.

What We Learned

Answers will vary. Suggested responses are shown at left.

Conclusion

Read this section aloud to the class to summarize the concepts learned in this activity.

Food for Thought

Read the Scripture aloud to the class. Talk about how good deeds and kindness flow from a heart full of love. Discuss ways we can reach out to others during the summer break.

Journal

If time permits, have a general class discussion about notes and drawings various students added to their journal pages. Discuss correct and incorrect predictions, and remind students that this "trial and error" process is part of the scientific process.

CONCLUSION

Indicators are chemicals that change colors to indicate an acid or a base. Indicators are measured on a pH scale. A reading of exactly 7 indicates neutral. Readings below 7 indicate an acid. Readings above 7 indicate a base.

FOOD FOR THOUGHT

Matthew 7:15-20 Indicators are a great tool for determining what something really is. A clear liquid might be cool, refreshing water — or it might be a burning acid! An indicator can keep us from harm by helping us tell them apart.

This Scripture describes an indicator you can use for people. Jesus said a person is known by their "fruit." Thorn bushes don't produce grapes, and thistles don't bear figs! Delicious fruit comes only from the right fruit tree, just as kind deeds only come from the right kind of heart (see Galatians 5:22, 23). It's only when our hearts belong to God that we can produce the right kind of spiritual fruit.

JOURNAL   My Science Notes

Extended Teaching

1. Repeat the activity, only this time put the solution in the refrigerator overnight. Have students compare the results to the original activity. How are they similar? How are they different?

2. Invite a professional gardener to visit your classroom. Ask him/her to show how pH soil testing works and describe methods used to neutralize soil acidity. Have students write a paragraph about one thing they learn.

3. Visit a local pharmacist. Ask him/her to explain different kinds of antacids and how they work. Have students write a paragraph about one thing they learn.

4. Have students test the pH of common materials (drinking water, milk, orange juice, rain water, etc.) using universal pH paper. Challenge each team to create a poster depicting the results.

5. Using the Internet, have students research parts of the US subject to acid rain. Find out what effects (if any) acid rain has on these enviroments. Challenge each team to contribute materials for a classroom bulletin board.

ASSESSMENT

PEANUT POWER

True/False (Circle T for true, F for false.)

T F **1.** Peanuts are seeds.

T F **2.** To "dissect" something means to put it back together.

T F **3.** A large portion of every seed is food for the embryo as it begins growth.

T F **4.** Many plants use seeds to reproduce.

T F **5.** Roots always grow toward sunlight in a process called phototropism.

Multiple Choice (Fill in the circle beside the best answer.)

6. The purpose of the peanut's shell is to . . .
- ○ **a.** supply food for the growing plant.
- ○ **b.** protect the seed before it starts to grow.
- ○ **c.** soak up rainfall so the seed will rot.
- ○ **d.** improve the appearance of the seed.

7. Every seed contains . . .
- ○ **a.** a food supply and a fully-grown plant.
- ○ **b.** materials for germination like sunlight and water.
- ○ **c.** an embryo and initial food supply.
- ○ **d.** a hollow core of empty air.

8. Scientists call the "baby plant" portion of a seed the . . .
- ○ **a.** endosperm
- ○ **b.** food supply
- ○ **c.** embryo
- ○ **d.** seed coat

9. The process of a seed sprouting and beginning to grow is called . . .
- ○ **a.** endosperm
- ○ **b.** embryo
- ○ **c.** food supply
- ○ **d.** germination

10. After germination, a plant's leaves grow toward light. This process is called . . .
- ○ **a.** phototropism
- ○ **b.** geotropism
- ○ **c.** germination
- ○ **d.** photoperiodicity

LESSON 2

SCATTERING SEEDS

True/False (Circle T for true, F for false.)

T   F   **1.** The farther seeds are scattered, the less chance they have to survive.

T   F   **2.** Plants produce an abundance of seeds to increase the chances that some will survive.

T   F   **3.** A cocklebur is a good example of seeds that are scattered primarily by wind.

T   F   **4.** Some seeds have tiny hooks which help them hitch rides on passing animals.

T   F   **5.** Taste helps fruit-bearing plants increase the chances of their seeds being scattered.

Multiple Choice (Fill in the circle beside the best answer.)

6. A cocklebur seed is very similar to which part of Velcro®?
- ○ **a.** the hook portion
- ○ **b.** the loop portion
- ○ **c.** both the hook and loop portions
- ○ **d.** neither the hook nor loop portion

7. A piece of cloth is very similar to which part of Velcro®?
- ○ **a.** the hook portion
- ○ **b.** the loop portion
- ○ **c.** both the hook and loop portions
- ○ **d.** neither the hook nor loop portion

8. It's important for a plant's seeds to be scattered because . . .
- ○ **a.** scattering ensures that fewer seeds will grow.
- ○ **b.** it's easier for birds and animals to find the seeds.
- ○ **c.** not enough water or nutrients are available in a small area.
- ○ **d.** young plants survive better the closer they are to the parent plant.

9. Which of the following is not a method plants use to scatter seeds.
- ○ **a.** wind
- ○ **b.** water
- ○ **c.** animals
- ○ **d.** other plants

10. George de Mestral invented Velcro® after observing . . .
- ○ **a.** birds carrying berries away from a bush.
- ○ **b.** animals attaching themselves to seeds with tiny hooks.
- ○ **c.** how seeds become attached to animals.
- ○ **d.** the "Hitchhiking Plants" special on the Discovery channel.

LEACHING LEAVES

True/False (Circle T for true, F for false.)

T   F   **1.** Because of a chemical called chlorophyll, most plants look green.

T   F   **2.** Green plants can use oxygen and water to make carbon dioxide.

T   F   **3.** In this activity, the heavier pigments were found at the top of the filter strip.

T   F   **4.** Photosynthesis produces oxygen and food for living things.

T   F   **5.** Humans and animals need plants in order to survive.

Multiple Choice (Fill in the circle beside the best answer.)

6. The chemicals which give all living things their colors are called . . .
- ○ **a.** polishes
- ○ **b.** chlorophyll
- ○ **c.** pigments
- ○ **d.** tints

7. The process plants use to make food for themselves is called . . .
- ○ **a.** germination
- ○ **b.** chlorophyll
- ○ **c.** photosynthesis
- ○ **d.** growth

8. In this activity, the leaf pieces were . . .
- ○ **a.** a much darker color after soaking.
- ○ **b.** the same color before and after soaking.
- ○ **c.** a much lighter color after soaking.
- ○ **d.** many different colors after soaking.

9. Why did the filter strip show color variations, but not the leaf?
- ○ **a.** The colors were in the fingernail polish remover.
- ○ **b.** The colors were in the filter strip.
- ○ **c.** The chlorophyll in the leaf covered the other colors, making them look green.
- ○ **d.** The strip separated the dissolved pigments so they could be seen.

10. In this activity, the fingernail polish remover _____ the _____ in the leaves.
- ○ **a.** destroyed, pigments
- ○ **b.** dissolved, water
- ○ **c.** destroyed, water
- ○ **d.** dissolved, pigments

True/False (Circle T for true, F for false.)

T   F   **1.** Decomposition is never a helpful process.

T   F   **2.** Plants use sunlight to store energy.

T   F   **3.** The bag with no yeast decomposed faster than the bag with yeast.

T   F   **4.** Microbes that cause decomposition are everywhere.

T   F   **5.** Washing your hands protects you from some negative effects of microbes.

Multiple Choice (Fill in the circle beside the best answer.)

6. Scientists call the material produced by living things . . .
- ○ **a.** organic
- ○ **b.** inorganic
- ○ **c.** inert
- ○ **d.** inanimate

7. The decompostion process is vital because it allows plants to recycle . . .
- ○ **a.** salts
- ○ **b.** yeasts
- ○ **c.** nutrients
- ○ **d.** bacteria

8. Scientists refer to microscopic forms of life as . . .
- ○ **a.** yeasts
- ○ **b.** organisms
- ○ **c.** insects
- ○ **d.** microbes

9. The primary process by which plants are able to recycle nutrients is called . . .
- ○ **a.** destruction
- ○ **b.** decomposition
- ○ **c.** micro-management
- ○ **d.** nutrition

10. How did the banana slices in the two bags compare?
- ○ **a.** The rate of decomposition was identical for both bags.
- ○ **b.** The banana slices in the bag with the yeast decomposed slower.
- ○ **c.** The banana slices in the bag with the yeast decomposed faster.
- ○ **d.** The banana slices in the bag with no yeast decomposed faster.

True/False (Circle T for true, F for false.)

T   F   **1.** Preservatives make materials decompose more rapidly.

T   F   **2.** Refrigeration is a form of food preservation.

T   F   **3.** Putting salt on a food makes it decompose more rapidly.

T   F   **4.** In the long run, preserving food makes all food cost more.

T   F   **5.** Salt preserves food by slowing the growth of microbes.

Multiple Choice (Fill in the circle beside the best answer.)

6. A more scientific term for spoilage or rotting is . . .

   ○ **a.** preservation
   ○ **b.** salting
   ○ **c.** preservatives
   ○ **d.** decomposition

7. What affect do preservatives have on the rate of decomposition?

   ○ **a.** Preservatives increase the decomposition rate.
   ○ **b.** Preservatives decrease the decomposition rate.
   ○ **c.** Preservatives have no affect on the decomposition rate.
   ○ **d.** Preservative is simply another term for decomposition.

8. What might happen if there were no way to preserve food?

   ○ **a.** Food would spoil slowly and food costs would rise.
   ○ **b.** Food would spoil slowly and food costs would fall.
   ○ **c.** Food would spoil quickly and food costs would rise.
   ○ **d.** Food would spoil quickly and food costs would fall.

9. What might happen if dead things stopped decomposing?

   ○ **a.** The nutrients plants need to make food would soon be unavailable.
   ○ **b.** The nutrients plants need to make food would be easily available.
   ○ **c.** No decomposition would mean much more food for animals.
   ○ **d.** There would be no noticeable change in the food cycle.

10. Which of the following is not a kind of microbe?

   ○ **a.** yeast
   ○ **b.** mice
   ○ **c.** fungi
   ○ **d.** bacteria

True/False (Circle T for true, F for false.)

T   F   **1.** Living things can be arranged into groups based on characteristics.

T   F   **2.** Latvian is the language scientists use to name all living things.

T   F   **3.** Scientific names are usually similar to the creatures' common names.

T   F   **4.** Latin is a "dead" language (new words and meanings can't be added).

T   F   **5.** In this activity, some teams ended up with different groupings of beans.

Multiple Choice (Fill in the circle beside the best answer.)

6. Sorting living things into groups based on their characteristics is called . . .
- ○ **a.** decomposition
- ○ **b.** classification
- ○ **c.** taxation
- ○ **d.** dissolution

7. A scientific term which means the same thing as classification is . . .
- ○ **a.** dissolution
- ○ **b.** groupism
- ○ **c.** decomposition
- ○ **d.** taxonomy

8. In this activity, why did different teams end up with different groups of beans?
- ○ **a.** Each team used the same "yes/no" questions to sort the beans.
- ○ **b.** Each team used different "yes/no" questions to sort the beans.
- ○ **c.** Each team used the same "yes" questions, but different "no" questions.
- ○ **d.** Each team used different "yes" questions, but the same "no" questions.

9. What might have happened if each team used identical questions to sort the beans?
- ○ **a.** The final bean groups would be identical.
- ○ **b.** The final bean groups would be very different.
- ○ **c.** The teams would be unable to sort the beans.
- ○ **d.** There would only be two groups of beans.

10. Why can't scientists just use English to name living things?
- ○ **a.** Many people around the world don't like English.
- ○ **b.** English is a "dead" language (new words and meanings can't be added).
- ○ **c.** New meanings and new words are added to English every year.
- ○ **d.** English doesn't have enough words for scientific research.

True/False (Circle T for true, F for false.)

T F **1.** Camouflage makes it easier to see living things in their natural surroundings.

T F **2.** Creatures with colors and shapes similar to their environment are harder to see.

T F **3.** Failure to capture enough prey means that a predator would likely starve.

T F **4.** When prey animals are easy to see, they are more likely to survive.

T F **5.** Prey are animals that kill and eat other animals.

Multiple Choice (Fill in the circle beside the best answer.)

6. When a prey animal does not blend with its surroundings, it's easier for a predator to . . .
- **a.** run away
- **b.** see
- **c.** hide
- **d.** ignore

7. Why is it difficult to find green toothpicks in a patch of green grass?
- **a.** They are smaller than other toothpicks.
- **b.** They are brighter than other toothpicks.
- **c.** They blend in with the color of the grass.
- **d.** They contrast with the color of the grass.

8. How would this activity change if the "territory" used was red clay dirt?
- **a.** All the toothpicks would be harder to find.
- **b.** Green toothpicks would be harder to find.
- **c.** Red toothpicks would be harder to find.
- **d.** Red toothpicks would be easier to find.

9. How does being camouflaged affect prey?
- **a.** It increases their chance of being seen.
- **b.** It decreases their chance of being seen.
- **c.** It increases their chance of catching other animals.
- **d.** Camouflage does not affect prey.

10. When prey have good camouflage, what affect does this have on predators?
- **a.** It makes it harder for predators to find prey.
- **b.** It makes it easier for predators to find prey.
- **c.** It increases predators chances of being eaten.
- **d.** It decreases predators chances of being eaten.

True/False (Circle T for true, F for false.)

T F **1.** Your eyes and brain work together to help you see.

T F **2.** Right-handed people are always left eye dominant.

T F **3.** Left-handed people are always left eye dominant.

T F **4.** Eye dominance can only be determined by an opthomologist.

T F **5.** Almost everyone has one eye that is dominant.

Multiple Choice (Fill in the circle beside the best answer.)

6. The human brain has two halves. Each half is called a . . .
- ○ **a.** halvisphere
- ○ **b.** quartersphere
- ○ **c.** hemisphere
- ○ **d.** hemoglobin

7. The left side of your brain receives signals from . . .
- ○ **a.** your right eye.
- ○ **b.** your left eye.
- ○ **c.** both eyes.
- ○ **d.** neither eye.

8. An injury to the right side of the brain might create vision problems . . .
- ○ **a.** in the right eye.
- ○ **b.** in the left eye.
- ○ **c.** in both eyes, alternating back and forth.
- ○ **d.** Brain injuries don't affect vision.

9. A person with a dominant right eye would . . .
- ○ **a.** always be right-handed.
- ○ **b.** never be right-handed.
- ○ **c.** probably be right-handed.
- ○ **d.** always be left-handed.

10. Most (but not all) right-handed people . . .
- ○ **a.** are left eye dominant.
- ○ **b.** are right eye dominant.
- ○ **c.** don't have a dominant eye.
- ○ **d.** demonstrate dual dominance.

True/False (Circle T for true, F for false.)

T　F　**1.** A camera and a human eye have no similarities.

T　F　**2.** A lens helps control where light goes and what it does.

T　F　**3.** Glasses and contacts are special lenses which help people see.

T　F　**4.** When a lens focuses light, it can create an image.

T　F　**5.** Unlike a camera, the human eye does not need light to function.

Multiple Choice (Fill in the circle beside the best answer.)

6. The purpose of a lens is to _____ available light into an image.
- ○ **a.** spread
- ○ **b.** focus
- ○ **c.** deflect
- ○ **d.** absorb

7. All of the following use a lens except . . .
- ○ **a.** glasses
- ○ **b.** binoculars
- ○ **c.** microscopes
- ○ **d.** mirrors

8. Where is the image stored inside a disposable camera?
- ○ **a.** in the lens
- ○ **b.** in the shutter
- ○ **c.** on the film
- ○ **d.** on the mirror

9. Where is the image focused inside your eye?
- ○ **a.** on the lens
- ○ **b.** on the lid
- ○ **c.** on the retina
- ○ **d.** on the iris

10. A lens can help control what aspect of an image?
- ○ **a.** its position
- ○ **b.** its size
- ○ **c.** its clearness
- ○ **d.** all of the above

POUR PROBABILITY

True/False (Circle T for true, F for false.)

T   F   **1.** Every kind of atom remains the same element forever.

T   F   **2.** All atoms constantly release potentially dangerous energy.

T   F   **3.** A radioactive element's "half-life" relates to how half its atoms act when heated.

T   F   **4.** Unless an element is radioactive, its nucleus is very stable.

T   F   **5.** The "half life" of different radioactive elements can vary enormously.

Multiple Choice (Fill in the circle beside the best answer.)

6. The center of an atom is called the . . .
- ○ **a.** nucleus
- ○ **b.** neutron
- ○ **c.** proton
- ○ **d.** electron

7. Scientists refer to the odds of something happening as a . . .
- ○ **a.** possibility
- ○ **b.** probability
- ○ **c.** potential
- ○ **d.** prevention

8. The "half life" of a radioactive element is . . .
- ○ **a.** the time is takes for most of the atoms to break down.
- ○ **b.** the time it takes for half of the atoms to recharge.
- ○ **c.** the time it takes for half of the atoms to break down.
- ○ **d.** the time it takes for most of the atoms to recharge.

9. Radioactive elements eventually break down into more . . .
- ○ **a.** mutated forms.
- ○ **b.** unstable forms.
- ○ **c.** stable forms.
- ○ **d.** radioactive forms.

10. In the simulation, the fraction of disks that came up white each time was about . . .
- ○ **a.** 1/4
- ○ **b.** 1/2
- ○ **c.** 1/8
- ○ **d.** 2/8

WELDED WATER

True/False (Circle T for true, F for false.)

T F **1.** Water is made up of particles called molecules.

T F **2.** When molecules are held together by mutual attraction, it is called adhesion.

T F **3.** Cohesion causes molecules to repel each other.

T F **4.** Some insects can "walk on water" because of cohesion.

T F **5.** Surface tension is when cohesion forms a kind of skin on top of water.

Multiple Choice (Fill in the circle beside the best answer.)

6. Scientists call the ability of water molecules to attract each other . . .
- ○ **a.** adhesion
- ○ **b.** cohesion
- ○ **c.** cooperation
- ○ **d.** welding

7. Water molecules mutually attracted at the top of a glass of water create . . .
- ○ **a.** cooperative bonding.
- ○ **b.** surface tension.
- ○ **c.** tensile stress.
- ○ **d.** molecular glue.

8. Which of the following is a good analogy of cohesion?
- ○ **a.** tiny magnets attracting each other
- ○ **b.** tiny magnets repelling each other
- ○ **c.** two pieces of tape stuck together
- ○ **d.** two boards fastened with screws

9. A "belly flop" into a swimming pool hurts because . . .
- ○ **a.** a smaller portion of your body repels the water.
- ○ **b.** a larger portion of your body attracts the water.
- ○ **c.** a smaller portion of your body must break the surface tension.
- ○ **d.** a larger portion of your body must break the surface tension.

10. Two closely falling streams of water often merge into one because . . .
- ○ **a.** the streams are too thin to fall separately.
- ○ **b.** adhesion creates an attachment between the molecules of the two streams.
- ○ **c.** cohesion creates an attachment between the molecules of the two streams.
- ○ **d.** the friction from the fall creates heat that "welds" the streams together.

BALLOON BURST! LESSON 12

True/False (Circle T for true, F for false.)

T   F   **1.** All materials react to stress in the same way.

T   F   **2.** Air pushed into a balloon creates a kind of stress.

T   F   **3.** Some materials can handle a lot of stress.

T   F   **4.** It is impossible to modify materials to handle more stress.

T   F   **5.** An inflated latex balloon is an example of a stressed material.

Multiple Choice (Fill in the circle beside the best answer.)

6. Adding a piece of adhesive tape to an inflated balloon should . . .
- ◯ **a.** increase the stress of the area covered.
- ◯ **b.** decrease the ability of the area covered to handle stress.
- ◯ **c.** increase the ability of the area covered to handle stress.
- ◯ **d.** have no affect on the balloon's ability to handle stress.

7. Pushing a pin into the bottom of a balloon demonstrates . . .
- ◯ **a.** a balloon may not pop if a pin is inserted slowly.
- ◯ **b.** a balloon may not pop if a pin is inserted rapidly.
- ◯ **c.** a balloon may not pop if punctured in an area of high stress.
- ◯ **d.** a balloon may not pop if punctured in an area of low stress.

8. Blowing more air into a balloon . . .
- ◯ **a.** increases the stress on its surface.
- ◯ **b.** decreases the stress on its surface.
- ◯ **c.** causes the surface to contract.
- ◯ **d.** has no affect on stress.

9. Making a plastic milk jug thicker would most likely . . .
- ◯ **a.** allow it to hold more milk.
- ◯ **b.** allow it to handle stress better.
- ◯ **c.** allow it to crack and break.
- ◯ **d.** make it lighter and easier to carry.

10. Which of the following describes the relationship of materials to stress.
- ◯ **a.** Some materials can handle a lot of stress.
- ◯ **b.** Some materials can be modified to handle more stress.
- ◯ **c.** Sometimes stress areas can be bypassed altogether.
- ◯ **d.** all of the above

True/False (Circle T for true, F for false.)

T F **1.** Gravity affects some objects, but not others.

T F **2.** Inertia keeps an object in place until an opposing force comes into play.

T F **3.** Scientists know ways to turn off the force of gravity.

T F **4.** The pull of gravity decreases as objects go faster.

T F **5.** Gravity is a force.

Multiple Choice (Fill in the circle beside the best answer.)

6. When you hold a clothespin motionless above the floor . . .
- ○ **a.** your upward pull is less than gravity's downward pull.
- ○ **b.** your upward pull is greater than gravity's downward pull.
- ○ **c.** your upward pull is equal to (but opposite) gravity's downward pull.
- ○ **d.** none of the above

7. What forces are involved in holding an object motionless above the floor?
- ○ **a.** gravity and inertia
- ○ **b.** gravity and compression
- ○ **c.** compression and inertia
- ○ **d.** compression and adhesion

8. In this activity, gravity . . .
- ○ **a.** pulled more on the bottom clothespin.
- ○ **b.** pulled more on the top clothespin.
- ○ **c.** pulled on both clothespins equally.
- ○ **d.** did not affect the clothespins.

9. Before you released the top clothespin, the rubberband . . .
- ○ **a.** applied force in only one direction.
- ○ **b.** applied more force to the top clothespin.
- ○ **c.** applied more force to the bottom clothespin.
- ○ **d.** applied equal force to both clothespins.

10. What force caused the rubber band to stretch?
- ○ **a.** air
- ○ **b.** gravity
- ○ **c.** inertia
- ○ **d.** latex

True/False (Circle T for true, F for false.)

T F **1.** Any moving object has momentum.

T F **2.** The faster an object moves, the more momentum it has.

T F **3.** Momentum is based on a combination of size and speed.

T F **4.** Small objects can have greater momentum than large objects.

T F **5.** Momentum can be transferred from one object to another.

Multiple Choice (Fill in the circle beside the best answer.)

6. Momentum is a combination of . . .
- ◯ **a.** time and temperature.
- ◯ **b.** size and space.
- ◯ **c.** size and speed.
- ◯ **d.** speed and space.

7. When one object hits another, what can be transferred?
- ◯ **a.** inertia
- ◯ **b.** momentum
- ◯ **c.** friction
- ◯ **d.** sound

8. Two identical objects moving the same speed would probably have . . .
- ◯ **a.** identical momentum.
- ◯ **b.** transferred momentum.
- ◯ **c.** different momentum.
- ◯ **d.** no momentum.

9. Two different objects moving at the same speed would probably have . . .
- ◯ **a.** identical momentum.
- ◯ **b.** transferred momentum.
- ◯ **c.** different momentum.
- ◯ **d.** no momentum.

10. Two identical objects moving at different speeds would probably have . . .
- ◯ **a.** identical momentum.
- ◯ **b.** transferred momentum.
- ◯ **c.** different momentum.
- ◯ **d.** no momentum.

True/False (Circle T for true, F for false.)

T F **1.** Scientists call a twisting force "torque".

T F **2.** An object spins easier if torque is balanced.

T F **3.** To balance torque, you must find the object's center of gravity.

T F **4.** The center of gravity for any object is always its exact center.

T F **5.** Center of gravity is dependent upon shape and mass.

Multiple Choice (Fill in the circle beside the best answer.)

6. Adding weight to one side of an object will . . .
- ◯ **a.** change its center of gravity.
- ◯ **b.** change its direction of torque.
- ◯ **c.** make the balance point impossible to find.
- ◯ **d.** have no affect on torque.

7. Torque is . . .
- ◯ **a.** created by a cork.
- ◯ **b.** similar to inertia.
- ◯ **c.** a twisting force.
- ◯ **d.** the center of gravity.

8. A baseball bat's center of gravity is . . .
- ◯ **a.** closer to the handle of the bat.
- ◯ **b.** closer to the heavy end of the bat.
- ◯ **c.** in the exact center of the bat.
- ◯ **d.** impossible to determine.

9. When a spinning object is balanced . . .
- ◯ **a.** there is more torque on one side than the other.
- ◯ **b.** there is less torque on one side than the other.
- ◯ **c.** there is no torque involved.
- ◯ **d.** equal torque exists on both sides.

10. You can usually balance a teeter-totter by . . .
- ◯ **a.** moving the weight on both ends toward the center.
- ◯ **b.** moving the weight on the heavy end toward the center.
- ◯ **c.** moving the weight on the light end toward the center.
- ◯ **d.** replacing the fulcrum.

BUOYANT BOAT

True/False (Circle T for true, F for false.)

T F **1.** All matter on Earth is constantly being pulled downward by gravity.

T F **2.** Gravity and buoyancy are opposing forces.

T F **3.** A boat's shape allows it to displace water.

T F **4.** If a boat weighs more than the water displaced, the boat floats.

T F **5.** Heavy materials like steel are never buoyant.

Multiple Choice (Fill in the circle beside the best answer.)

6. The shape of a boat helps it . . .
- ○ **a.** distort water.
- ○ **b.** deflect water.
- ○ **c.** defend water.
- ○ **d.** displace water.

7. For a boat to float well, the water displaced must be . . .
- ○ **a.** lighter than the boat and its contents.
- ○ **b.** heavier than the boat and its contents.
- ○ **c.** exactly the same as the boat and its contents.
- ○ **d.** unrelated to the boat and its contents.

8. If gravity is greater than buoyancy . . .
- ○ **a.** the object will sink.
- ○ **b.** the object will float.
- ○ **c.** the object will fly.
- ○ **d.** none of the above

9. A leaking boat sinks because the incoming water . . .
- ○ **a.** adds weight.
- ○ **b.** adds gravity.
- ○ **c.** causes rapid swelling.
- ○ **d.** releases floatation fluids.

10. If buoyancy is only slightly greater than gravity . . .
- ○ **a.** the boat sinks.
- ○ **b.** the boat floats high in the water.
- ○ **c.** the boat barely floats.
- ○ **d.** Buoyancy and gravity are always equal.

LESSON 17
FINGERTRAP FORCE

True/False (Circle T for true, F for false.)

T F **1.** A fingertrap is a device that transfers force.

T F **2.** Pulling away causes a fingertrap to twist and compress.

T F **3.** Pushing in causes a fingertrap to relax and release.

T F **4.** It is easier to work with a force than to work against it.

T F **5.** Forces can be created, but not transferred.

Multiple Choice (Fill in the circle beside the best answer.)

6. The fingertrap transferred force . . .
- ◯ **a.** by twisting and compressing.
- ◯ **b.** by expanding and releasing.
- ◯ **c.** by contrasting and comparing.
- ◯ **d.** all of the above

7. Hitting a ball with a bat is an example of . . .
- ◯ **a.** destroying a force.
- ◯ **b.** transferring a force.
- ◯ **c.** destroying compression.
- ◯ **d.** forcing a transfer.

8. Pushing a fingertrap inward makes the fibers . . .
- ◯ **a.** contract, thus increasing compression.
- ◯ **b.** relax, thus increasing compression.
- ◯ **c.** contract, thus decreasing compression.
- ◯ **d.** relax, thus decreasing compression.

9. The tightening fingertrap is most similar to which force?
- ◯ **a.** gravity
- ◯ **b.** buoyancy
- ◯ **c.** torque
- ◯ **d.** momentum

10. Which of the following is not an example of transferring force?
- ◯ **a.** a stone sitting in a field
- ◯ **b.** a girl throwing a softball
- ◯ **c.** a boy shooting baskets
- ◯ **d.** two children playing catch

True/False (Circle T for true, F for false.)

T   F   **1.** A block and tackle is a simple machine.

T   F   **2.** A block and tackle can lift very heavy objects using minimal force.

T   F   **3.** Machines can be used to greatly increase force.

T   F   **4.** Machines can be used to change the direction of force.

T   F   **5.** Machines work well because they eliminate friction.

Multiple Choice (Fill in the circle beside the best answer.)

6. How many wheel/axle combinations are used in a typical block & tackle?
- ○ **a.** one
- ○ **b.** two
- ○ **c.** three
- ○ **d.** none

7. A machine made from two or more simple machines is called . . .
- ○ **a.** a transferrable machine.
- ○ **b.** a complicated machine.
- ○ **c.** a multiplying machine.
- ○ **d.** a compound machine.

8. Machines are commonly used to . . .
- ○ **a.** change the direction of a force.
- ○ **b.** destroy a force completely.
- ○ **c.** eliminate all effects of a force.
- ○ **d.** none of the above

9. Which of the following is an example of a machine to increase force?
- ○ **a.** a helium balloon
- ○ **b.** a rope
- ○ **c.** a car jack
- ○ **d.** none of the above

10. Machines are helpful when we need to . . .
- ○ **a.** divide forces.
- ○ **b.** multiply forces.
- ○ **c.** destroy forces.
- ○ **d.** none of the above

True/False (Circle T for true, F for false.)

T   F   **1.** The "ocean of air" surrounding Earth is called the stratosphere.

T   F   **2.** Scientists refer to balanced pressure as equilibrium.

T   F   **3.** Earth's atmosphere is constantly pushing on everything.

T   F   **4.** A large difference in air pressure has little affect on most things.

T   F   **5.** Normally, air pressure is about equal inside and outside your body.

Multiple Choice (Fill in the circle beside the best answer.)

6. When pressure is the same on both sides of a barrier, it is called . . .
- ○ **a.** equality.
- ○ **b.** environment.
- ○ **c.** equilibrium.
- ○ **d.** entrophy.

7. If water flows out of a jug and air can flow in freely . . .
- ○ **a.** the air pressure in the jug goes up.
- ○ **b.** the air pressure in the jug goes down.
- ○ **c.** the air pressure in the jug will equalize.
- ○ **d.** none of the above

8. If water flows out of a jug, but no air can get back in . . .
- ○ **a.** the air pressure in the jug goes up.
- ○ **b.** the air pressure in the jug goes down.
- ○ **c.** the air pressure in the jug will equalize.
- ○ **d.** none of the above

9. Air pressure . . .
- ○ **a.** can be equally balanced on both sides of a barrier.
- ○ **b.** can be different on either side of a barrier.
- ○ **c.** neither of the above
- ○ **d.** both of the above

10. Forcing air into a sealed container would probably . . .
- ○ **a.** cause the air pressure to go up.
- ○ **b.** cause the air pressure to go down.
- ○ **c.** cause the air pressure to equalize.
- ○ **d.** result in equilibrium.

True/False (Circle T for true, F for false.)

T F **1.** Air pressure is the force of the air constantly pushing all around us.

T F **2.** Since Earth's atmosphere is huge, air pressure normally changes slowly.

T F **3.** Removing air from a sealed container causes air pressure to rise.

T F **4.** Light objects are not affected by air pressure changes.

T F **5.** Large or sudden air pressure changes can result in violent weather.

Multiple Choice (Fill in the circle beside the best answer.)

6. A sealed container of air is a miniature model of . . .

○ **a.** compression

○ **b.** expansion

○ **c.** the atmosphere

○ **d.** a marshmallow

7. Reducing the volume of a sealed container of air causes the air to . . .

○ **a.** compress, increasing air pressure.

○ **b.** expand, increasing air pressure.

○ **c.** compress, decreasing air pressure.

○ **d.** expand, decreasing air pressure.

8. Increasing the volume of a sealed container of air causes the air to . . .

○ **a.** compress, increasing air pressure.

○ **b.** expand, increasing air pressure.

○ **c.** compress, decreasing air pressure.

○ **d.** expand, decreasing air pressure.

9. A sealed container of air helps us see changes in air pressure because . . .

○ **a.** the "atmosphere" inside is much smaller.

○ **b.** it allows us to change pressure quickly.

○ **c.** neither of the above

○ **d.** both of the above

10. A marshmallow works well for this activity because . . .

○ **a.** it is brightly-colored.

○ **b.** it contains a low percentage of air.

○ **c.** it contains a high percentage of air.

○ **d.** it contains a high percentage of sugar.

True/False (Circle T for true, F for false.)

T   F   **1.** To measure wind speed, meteorologists use an anemometer.

T   F   **2.** An anemometer can change the direction of the force coming toward it.

T   F   **3.** Straight wind is an example of rotary motion.

T   F   **4.** The spinning cups of an anemometer create linear motion.

T   F   **5.** Air is not matter and it has no force.

Multiple Choice (Fill in the circle beside the best answer.)

6. Meteorologists measure _____ _____ to help with accurate forecasts.
- ○ **a.** electric polarity
- ○ **b.** wind speed
- ○ **c.** Nielsen ratings
- ○ **d.** room temperature

7. Scientists refer to movement in a straight line as . . .
- ○ **a.** rotated motion.
- ○ **b.** rotary motion.
- ○ **c.** linear motion.
- ○ **d.** line movement.

8. Rotary motion creates . . .
- ○ **a.** torque
- ○ **b.** gravity
- ○ **c.** buoyancy
- ○ **d.** matter

9. A spinning device must be balanced because . . .
- ○ **a.** balance increases linear motion.
- ○ **b.** balance minimizes spin.
- ○ **c.** balance increases wobble.
- ○ **d.** balance minimizes wobble.

10. The purpose of an anemometer is to . . .
- ○ **a.** measure air pressure.
- ○ **b.** measure wind speed.
- ○ **c.** measure humidity.
- ○ **d.** all of the above

True/False (Circle T for true, F for false.)

T   F   **1.** All rocks sink, the Porous Pumice activity proves this.

T   F   **2.** An object more dense than water will float.

T   F   **3.** The whipping cream you used "whipped" because of the air you added.

T   F   **4.** Pumice contains a lot of air trapped inside.

T   F   **5.** Magma is solid rock made from melted rock.

Multiple Choice (Fill in the circle beside the best answer.)

6. One similarity between whipped cream and pumice is that . . .
- ◯ **a.** both are dense and solid.
- ◯ **b.** both are full of air.
- ◯ **c.** both are hard and flat.
- ◯ **d.** both contain sugar compounds.

7. Magma is the scientific term for . . .
- ◯ **a.** sedimentary rock.
- ◯ **b.** melted rock.
- ◯ **c.** bubbles of trapped air.
- ◯ **d.** volcanic gas.

8. Releasing the pressure on the gas trapped in magma creates . . .
- ◯ **a.** sedimentary rock.
- ◯ **b.** melted rock.
- ◯ **c.** bubbles of trapped air.
- ◯ **d.** volcanic gas.

9. Which best decribes the condition of rocks deep underground?
- ◯ **a.** low pressure and low temperature
- ◯ **b.** low pressure and high temperature
- ◯ **c.** high pressure and low temperature
- ◯ **d.** high pressure and high temperature

10. Scientists refer to material made from melted rock as . . .
- ◯ **a.** igneous
- ◯ **b.** metamorphic
- ◯ **c.** indigent
- ◯ **d.** sedimentary

True/False (Circle T for true, F for false.)

T   F   **1.** Over time, polluted rain can dissolve limestone.

T   F   **2.** Erosion is a process the breaks things down over time.

T   F   **3.** Air pollution can react with water in the atmosphere to produce acid rain.

T   F   **4.** Acid rain causes drops of hydrochloric acid to fall from the sky.

T   F   **5.** Acid rain can create serious problems in the environment.

Multiple Choice (Fill in the circle beside the best answer.)

6. Pouring hydrochloric acid on limestone produces . . .
- ○ **a.** acid rain.
- ○ **b.** carbon dioxide gas.
- ○ **c.** oxygen and water.
- ○ **d.** calcium and lime.

7. Air pollution can react with water in the atmosphere to produce . . .
- ○ **a.** oxygen.
- ○ **b.** carbon dioxide.
- ○ **c.** hydrochloric acid.
- ○ **d.** acid rain.

8. An example of erosion is . . .
- ○ **a.** a ditch cut by rain.
- ○ **b.** a statue rusting.
- ○ **c.** a dune getting smaller.
- ○ **d.** all of the above.

9. Chemical erosion results in . . .
- ○ **a.** physical changes only.
- ○ **b.** chemical changes.
- ○ **c.** biological changes.
- ○ **d.** none of the above

10. The chemical name for limestone is . . .
- ○ **a.** calcium carbonate.
- ○ **b.** hydrochloric acid.
- ○ **c.** calcified lime.
- ○ **d.** carbon dioxide.

True/False (Circle T for true, F for false.)

T F **1.** Water can be filtered by its movement underground.

T F **2.** Any kind of filter can remove harmful bacteria from water.

T F **3.** Water filtered through soil, sand, and rocks always gets muddier.

T F **4.** Any clear, cold spring produces water that is safe to drink.

T F **5.** Earth's water cycle helps filter impurities from water.

Multiple Choice (Fill in the circle beside the best answer.)

6. Water on the top of the ground is called . . .
- ◯ **a.** ground water.
- ◯ **b.** filtered water.
- ◯ **c.** surface water.
- ◯ **d.** none of the above

7. Water underground is called . . .
- ◯ **a.** ground water.
- ◯ **b.** filtered water.
- ◯ **c.** surface water.
- ◯ **d.** none of the above

8. Which of the following is a totally pure form of water?
- ◯ **a.** ground water
- ◯ **b.** surface water
- ◯ **c.** rain water
- ◯ **d.** none of the above

9. Substances that make water unsafe to drink are called . . .
- ◯ **a.** purities
- ◯ **b.** filters
- ◯ **c.** funnels
- ◯ **d.** pollutants

10. Almost any kind of filter can make water . . .
- ◯ **a.** pure
- ◯ **b.** cloudy
- ◯ **c.** clearer
- ◯ **d.** chemical

True/False (Circle T for true, F for false.)

T F **1.** A glacier is a mountain of ice that never moves.

T F **2.** Glaciers are formed by tremendous weight compressing snow into ice.

T F **3.** Most glaciers begin on wind-swept mountain peaks with little snowfall.

T F **4.** Glaciers grow or shrink depending on global climate.

T F **5.** Some glaciers are so heavy they push Earth's crust down several feet.

Multiple Choice (Fill in the circle beside the best answer.)

6. The enormous force that creates glaciers comes from . . .
- ○ **a.** mountains
- ○ **b.** valleys
- ○ **c.** gravity
- ○ **d.** rain

7. The downward pressure of a glacier's weight causes it to . . .
- ○ **a.** lock solidly into place.
- ○ **b.** move slowly downhill.
- ○ **c.** revolve on its axis.
- ○ **d.** melt rapidly.

8. As snow piles grow higher and heavier . . .
- ○ **a.** bottom layers melt quickly and flow away.
- ○ **b.** top layers melt quickly and flow away.
- ○ **c.** bottom layers begin to compress into ice.
- ○ **d.** top layers begin to compress into ice.

9. The weight of a glacier can . . .
- ○ **a.** cause the Earth's crust to sink.
- ○ **b.** cause it to begin to move downhill.
- ○ **c.** vary depending on global climate.
- ○ **d.** all of the above

10. Glaciers . . .
- ○ **a.** can be over one mile thick.
- ○ **b.** existed only during the "ice age."
- ○ **c.** get larger and larger every year.
- ○ **d.** none of the above

True/False (Circle T for true, F for false.)

T   F   **1.** Scientists use images or models to better understand things.

T   F   **2.** The first telescope was invented by Galileo.

T   F   **3.** Early astronomers thought Saturn's rings were made of sunlight.

T   F   **4.** The atmosphere of Saturn is toxic to life as we know it.

T   F   **5.** The rings of Saturn are made up of pieces of rock and frozen debris.

Multiple Choice (Fill in the circle beside the best answer.)

6. Galileo contributed to our understanding of Saturn by . . .
   ○   **a.** inventing the telescope.
   ○   **b.** inventing the CD.
   ○   **c.** modifying early telescopes to make them stronger.
   ○   **d.** determining that the atmosphere of Saturn is toxic.

7. Saturn is different from Earth because . . .
   ○   **a.** it has rings.
   ○   **b.** it has a toxic atmosphere.
   ○   **c.** it has constant violent winds.
   ○   **d.** all of the above

8. The rings of Saturn . . .
   ○   **a.** are made of pieces of rock and frozen debris.
   ○   **b.** reflect the light of the sun.
   ○   **c.** can be seen through powerful telescopes.
   ○   **d.** all of the above

9. Astronauts walking on Saturn would see . . .
   ○   **a.** beautiful rings high in the sky.
   ○   **b.** a peaceful, but barren landscape.
   ○   **c.** swirling clouds of toxic gas.
   ○   **d.** nothing. They could not survive on Saturn.

10. Scientists believe winds on Saturn . . .
   ○   **a.** are light and gentle.
   ○   **b.** can exceed 1,000 miles per hour.
   ○   **c.** are constant at 100 miles per hour.
   ○   **d.** do not exist since Saturn has no air.

NAME _____ DATE _____

True/False (Circle T for true, F for false.)

T   F   1. An apple can be a model for understanding Earth's layers.

T   F   2. The outer layer of the Earth is called the core.

T   F   3. The center of the Earth is called the crust.

T   F   4. The layer between the core and crust is called the mantle.

T   F   5. Earth's crust is solid and unchangeable.

Multiple Choice (Fill in the circle beside the best answer.)

6. Scientists believe Earth's core is . . .
- ○ **a.** made mostly of rocks, soil, and sand.
- ○ **b.** in a state between liquid and solid.
- ○ **c.** made mostly of molten iron.
- ○ **d.** none of the above

7. Scientists believe Earth's mantle is . . .
- ○ **a.** made mostly of rocks, soil, and sand.
- ○ **b.** in a state between liquid and solid.
- ○ **c.** made mostly of molten iron.
- ○ **d.** none of the above

8. Scientists believe Earth's crust is . . .
- ○ **a.** made mostly of rocks, soil, and sand.
- ○ **b.** in a state between liquid and solid.
- ○ **c.** made mostly of molten iron.
- ○ **d.** none of the above

9. The layer of Earth most subject to erosion is the . . .
- ○ **a.** core
- ○ **b.** mantle
- ○ **c.** crust
- ○ **d.** none of the above

10. The thickest layer of Earth is the . . .
- ○ **a.** core
- ○ **b.** mantle
- ○ **c.** crust
- ○ **d.** none of the above

Copyright ©2003 The Concerned Group, Inc.

True/False (Circle T for true, F for false.)

T F **1.** Light is a form of energy that travels in waves.

T F **2.** Waves come in different lengths.

T F **3.** All wavelengths look the same to human eyes.

T F **4.** A prism is a device that bends (refracts) sound.

T F **5.** Rainbows are colorful because raindrops act like prisms.

Multiple Choice (Fill in the circle beside the best answer.)

6. Roy G. Biv is . . .
- ○ **a.** the man who invented prisms.
- ○ **b.** the man who discovered how rainbows work.
- ○ **c.** an acronym for the colors in a rainbow.
- ○ **d.** an acronym for types of energy that travel in waves.

7. Which of the following does not travel in waves?
- ○ **a.** heat
- ○ **b.** prism
- ○ **c.** sound
- ○ **d.** light

8. Scientists refer to bending light as . . .
- ○ **a.** reflection
- ○ **b.** separation
- ○ **c.** reduction
- ○ **d.** refraction

9. Human eyes see different wavelengths of light as . . .
- ○ **a.** sounds
- ○ **b.** colors
- ○ **c.** lights
- ○ **d.** none of the above

10. A drop of water can act like a . . .
- ○ **a.** mirror
- ○ **b.** wave
- ○ **c.** prism
- ○ **d.** sound

PAPER MICROSCOPE

True/False (Circle T for true, F for false.)

T   F   **1.** Many scientific devices use lenses.

T   F   **2.** A lens is a curved piece of glass that bends light.

T   F   **3.** The first lenses were invented in the 1800s.

T   F   **4.** Light can be focused by moving a lens back and forth.

T   F   **5.** Focusing an image makes it harder to see.

Multiple Choice (Fill in the circle beside the best answer.)

6. Which of the following does not use a lens?
- ○ **a.** microscope
- ○ **b.** binoculars
- ○ **c.** telephone
- ○ **d.** eye glasses

7. Improving the image seen through a lens is called . . .
- ○ **a.** measuring
- ○ **b.** bending
- ○ **c.** imaging
- ○ **d.** focusing

8. Lenses are commonly made from . . .
- ○ **a.** glass
- ○ **b.** plastic
- ○ **c.** both of the above
- ○ **d.** neither of the above

9. Another word for "refract" is . . .
- ○ **a.** bend
- ○ **b.** twist
- ○ **c.** reflect
- ○ **d.** bounce

10. The latin word "lenses" comes from . . .
- ○ **a.** focusing
- ○ **b.** lentils
- ○ **c.** refraction
- ○ **d.** grapes

True/False (Circle T for true, F for false.)

T   F   **1.** Sound is a form of energy that travels in waves.

T   F   **2.** Rapid back-and-forth movements are called wavelengths.

T   F   **3.** Musical instruments do not require energy to create sound.

T   F   **4.** Changing the length of a sound wave changes the sound you hear.

T   F   **5.** Changing how fast a wave vibrates changes the sound you hear.

Multiple Choice (Fill in the circle beside the best answer.)

6. Which of the following does not involve waves?

○   **a.** gravity
○   **b.** heat
○   **c.** light
○   **d.** sound

7. When you listen to a CD player, what vibrates to create the sound you hear?

○   **a.** the electricity
○   **b.** the radio station
○   **c.** the speakers
○   **d.** the CD

8. How is a rubber band similar to a violin?

○   **a.** both are made from a form of latex
○   **b.** both can produce sound through vibration
○   **c.** neither requires energy to produce sound
○   **d.** A rubber band and a violin have no similarities.

9. Which combination best describes how sound is produced?

○   **a.** sound, vibration, energy
○   **b.** energy, sound, vibration
○   **c.** vibration, sound, energy
○   **d.** energy, vibration, sound

10. Which of the following is needed for humans to speak?

○   **a.** air
○   **b.** vibration
○   **c.** vocal chords
○   **d.** all of the above

True/False (Circle T for true, F for false.)

T   F   **1.** Magnets are surrounded by an invisible energy field.

T   F   **2.** It is impossible to observe the effects of a magnetic field.

T   F   **3.** The influence of magnetic fields is multi-dimensional.

T   F   **4.** How magnets are oriented to each other affects their behavior.

T   F   **5.** Similar poles pull together or attract each other.

Multiple Choice (Fill in the circle beside the best answer.)

6. Every magnet has . . .
- ○ **a.** two poles, one north and one south.
- ○ **b.** two poles, one east and one west.
- ○ **c.** only a "north" pole.
- ○ **d.** only a "south" pole.

7. Placing the similar poles of two magnets together causes . . .
- ○ **a.** the magnets to attract each other.
- ○ **b.** the magnets to repel each other.
- ○ **c.** the magnets to explode violently.
- ○ **d.** nothing at all.

8. Placing the opposite poles of two magnets together causes . . .
- ○ **a.** the magnets to attract each other.
- ○ **b.** the magnets to repel each other.
- ○ **c.** the magnets to explode violently.
- ○ **d.** nothing at all.

9. The behavior of iron filings can help us see . . .
- ○ **a.** the small "n" on the North Pole of a magnet.
- ○ **b.** the small "s" on the South Pole of a magnet.
- ○ **c.** the effects of a magnetic field.
- ○ **d.** none of the above

10. Multi-dimensional magnetic fields affect things . . .
- ○ **a.** above and below.
- ○ **b.** in front and in back.
- ○ **c.** on either side.
- ○ **d.** all of the above

STUDENT STATIC

True/False (Circle T for true, F for false.)

T F **1.** There are two basic types of electricity: current and static.

T F **2.** Current electricity is based on moving electrons.

T F **3.** Static electricity is based on non-moving protons.

T F **4.** Electrons have a positive charge.

T F **5.** Electrons can be transferred from one object to another.

Multiple Choice (Fill in the circle beside the best answer.)

6. The electricity that powers household appliances is . . .

○ **a.** current electricity.
○ **b.** static electricity.
○ **c.** transfer electricity.
○ **d.** none of the above

7. Walking across a fluffy carpet wearing wool socks creates . . .

○ **a.** current electricity.
○ **b.** static electricity.
○ **c.** transfer electricity.
○ **d.** none of the above

8. Rubbing a balloon against your hair captures . . .

○ **a.** positively-charged electrons.
○ **b.** negatively-charged electrons.
○ **c.** positively-charged protons.
○ **d.** negatively-charged protons.

9. Electrons can be _____ from one object to another.

○ **a.** charged
○ **b.** destroyed
○ **c.** transferred
○ **d.** changed

10. Current and static electricity are similar because . . .

○ **a.** both are totally safe.
○ **b.** neither can move from place to place.
○ **c.** both are positively charged.
○ **d.** both are based on electrons.

True/False (Circle T for true, F for false.)

T   F   **1.** Removing heat from a solution is an example of chemical change.

T   F   **2.** Liquids become solids when their molecules slow down and stick together.

T   F   **3.** Adding salt to water makes the water easier to freeze.

T   F   **4.** The temperature where a liquid becomes a solid is its freezing point.

T   F   **5.** Physical change means a material is the same substance but a different form.

Multiple Choice (Fill in the circle beside the best answer.)

6. Thermodynamics is the study of . . .
- **a.** relationships between heat and other energy forms.
- **b.** how various chemicals react to each other.
- **c.** relationships between ice and salt.
- **d.** all of the above

7. In order for something to freeze, its molecules must . . .
- **a.** speed up and stick together.
- **b.** speed up and repel each other.
- **c.** slow down and stick together.
- **d.** slow down and repel each other.

8. Scientists call the temperature at which a liquid becomes a solid its . . .
- **a.** boiling point.
- **b.** transfer point.
- **c.** freezing point.
- **d.** melting point.

9. Scientists call the temperature at which a solid becomes a liquid its . . .
- **a.** boiling point.
- **b.** transfer point.
- **c.** freezing point.
- **d.** melting point.

10. Which of the following is not a physical change?
- **a.** burning
- **b.** boiling
- **c.** freezing
- **d.** melting

True/False (Circle T for true, F for false.)

T **F** **1.** Chemical changes always result in a different substance.

T **F** **2.** The oxidation process always makes an object very cold.

T **F** **3.** Chemical changes can release energy.

T **F** **4.** Burning is a form of rapid oxidation.

T **F** **5.** The air we breathe reacts chemically with some materials.

Multiple Choice (Fill in the circle beside the best answer.)

6. In addition to rusting, another form of oxidation is . . .
- ○ **a.** mold
- ○ **b.** rotting
- ○ **c.** burning
- ○ **d.** none of the above

7. When iron combines with oxygen the result is . . .
- ○ **a.** freezing
- ○ **b.** physical change
- ○ **c.** burning
- ○ **d.** oxidation

8. Rust is also known as . . .
- ○ **a.** iron oxide
- ○ **b.** iron pyrite
- ○ **c.** oxidary
- ○ **d.** none of the above

9. A chemical change always . . .
- ○ **a.** results in oxidation.
- ○ **b.** results in a different substance.
- ○ **c.** changes the form, but not the substance.
- ○ **d.** changes the substance, but not the form.

10. What is the relationship between burning and rusting?
- ○ **a.** Rusting is a chemical change; burning is a physical change.
- ○ **b.** Burning is a chemical change; rusting is a physical change.
- ○ **c.** Both are oxidation, but burning is a much faster form.
- ○ **d.** There is no relationship between burning and rusting.

True/False (Circle T for true, F for false.)

T   F   **1.** All chemical change takes place at the same pace.

T   F   **2.** Steel wool has an extremely low iron content.

T   F   **3.** The common name for iron corrosion is rust.

T   F   **4.** Some chemicals can accelerate corrosion.

T   F   **5.** A coating of bleach and acetic acid can protect against rust.

Multiple Choice (Fill in the circle beside the best answer.)

6. A common way to protect metal from corrosion is . . .
- ○ **a.** galvanizing
- ○ **b.** painting
- ○ **c.** plating
- ○ **d.** all of the above

7. Water causes iron to rust more quickly because . . .
- ○ **a.** its highly acid pH chemically corrodes the metal.
- ○ **b.** it keeps the metal in constant contact with oxygen.
- ○ **c.** it keeps the metal in constant contact with bleach.
- ○ **d.** none of the above

8. Another term for the corrosion of iron is . . .
- ○ **a.** rusting
- ○ **b.** bleaching
- ○ **c.** galvanizing
- ○ **d.** alloying

9. Rusting is . . .
- ○ **a.** a combination of oxygen and acetic acid.
- ○ **b.** a combination of oxygen and bleach.
- ○ **c.** a chemical change.
- ○ **d.** a physical change.

10. A piece of steel wool sitting on a clean, dry shelf . . .
- ○ **a.** will rust very rapidly.
- ○ **b.** will rust very slowly.
- ○ **c.** will not rust at all.
- ○ **d.** must be exposed to water to rust.

True/False (Circle T for true, F for false.)

T F **1.** Chemical indicators change color when acid or base levels change.

T F **2.** Acids and bases are measured with a system called a pH scale.

T F **3.** A solution with a reading of 2 on the pH scale would be a base.

T F **4.** A solution with a reading of 8 on the pH scale would be an acid.

T F **5.** A solution with a reading of 7 on the pH scale would be neutral.

Multiple Choice (Fill in the circle beside the best answer.)

6. A chemical indicator would be helpful if you were . . .
- ○ **a.** testing the water in a swimming pool.
- ○ **b.** conducting environmental monitoring.
- ○ **c.** doing certain kinds of medical testing.
- ○ **d.** all of the above

7. The thymolphthalein in this activity was used as . . .
- ○ **a.** a pH scale.
- ○ **b.** an indicator.
- ○ **c.** a base.
- ○ **d.** an acid.

8. Water can form a weak acid when it reacts with . . .
- ○ **a.** thymolphthalein.
- ○ **b.** oxygen.
- ○ **c.** carbon dioxoide.
- ○ **d.** none of the above

9. A solution with a pH reading below 7 would be . . .
- ○ **a.** an acid.
- ○ **b.** a base.
- ○ **c.** neutral.
- ○ **d.** an indicator.

10. A solution with a pH reading above 7 would be . . .
- ○ **a.** an acid.
- ○ **b.** a base.
- ○ **c.** neutral.
- ○ **d.** an indicator.